Look to the

WILDERNESS

Look to the
WILDERNESS

by

W. DOUGLAS BURDEN

WITH PHOTOGRAPHS

An Atlantic Monthly Press Book

LITTLE, BROWN AND COMPANY • BOSTON
TORONTO

The lines at the beginning of each chapter are from *This Is the American Earth* by Ansel Adams and Nancy Newhall and are reprinted by permission of Sierra Club and Nancy Newhall. Copyright, 1960, by the Sierra Club.

Chapter 1 first appeared in *The Living Wilderness*, Chapters 4 and 6 in the *Atlantic Monthly*, and Chapter 5 in *Sports Illustrated*.

ATLANTIC–LITTLE, BROWN BOOKS
ARE PUBLISHED BY
LITTLE, BROWN AND COMPANY
IN ASSOCIATION WITH
THE ATLANTIC MONTHLY PRESS

Published simultaneously in Canada
by Little, Brown & Company (Canada) Limited

PRINTED IN THE UNITED STATES OF AMERICA

To those many lovers of the wilderness who, in spite of enormous odds, are making a real fight for its preservation

*The truly gifted soul lives
in an attitude of courtesy to
the universe.*

JUSTICE CURTIS BOK

Introduction

I FIRST MET DOUGLAS BURDEN in Peking. He had just come down from the bandit-infested mountains of the Sino-Mongolian frontier where he had been hunting the world's greatest bighorn sheep. We became friends immediately — the kind of friends who are irresistibly drawn together by similar dominating interests. Both of us had the same passionate love of nature, thirst for adventure, and the insatiable desire to see what lay beyond the horizon's rim in the little-known places of the earth.

My second meeting with him in Peking was dramatic and typical of his adventure-loving spirit. It was in 1926. Douglas and his wife were en route to the Dutch East Indies to study and collect specimens of the almost mythical "dragon lizards" of Komodo Island. They were to visit me in Peking before going south.

But suddenly North China had erupted in flame. Two powerful war lords snarled at each other between Peking and Tientsin. Peking was completely isolated. The Manchurian army lay across the motor road, no trains were running and our only communication with the outside world was by wireless telegraph. Piles of sandbags barricaded the huge gates in the age-old Tatar walls. The streets were deserted, shops closed and an air of impending calamity hung like a black cloud over the city. If the Manchurian troops forced the gates, Peking would certainly be looted and many people killed.

Notices were sent to all foreign residents by their respective legations instructing them where to assemble in the event of extreme danger. Green lights and guns were the designated signals.

The Burdens had reached Tientsin by sea and I telegraphed them to remain there until the situation clarified. Characteristically, waiting didn't suit Douglas. At the club he discovered an American, long a resident of China, who because of a very sick wife in Peking was attempting to get through the besieging army in spite of the danger. The Burdens joined him.

Fortunately for them, on the road they picked up a Manchu general whose car had broken down. He was on his way to negotiate a settlement between the war lords, and was the only man for whom the gates would be opened.

That evening I had gone to the East Gate near my house to see what was what. Just as the police in charge of the gates had reiterated that they were under strict orders not to open them, they suddenly added, "But please draw your car to one side for a moment because a very important general is about to arrive." And, just as I backed my car out of the way, the gates swung open and, amid the acclamations of the multitude, in came Douglas. It was a triumphal entry, if there ever was one, and seemed miraculous. The Burdens were safe, but it had been an adventurous trip. The road was mined in a dozen places and the human heads hanging from posts and trees were grim evidence that this was not a phony war.

But for Douglas Burden it was the kind of experience that made life worth living. He was a born naturalist and explorer and the spirit of adventure was in his blood. He found his happiness in seeking out the wildest and most inaccessible corners of the earth.

During the days of his youth, like all explorers, he was completely indifferent to what the city dweller considers to be the essentials of comfort. No bed was ever as desirable as a sleeping bag beside a campfire. He loved the night wind on his face and to look up at the stars. Then, he felt closer to the wild creatures of the forest than to man. I know, because it meant the same to me.

Many times when I was bone-tired, cold or miserably wet, I have asked myself why I was punishing my body to collect one particular animal. It was, I have admitted wearily, because I am a primitive at heart. So is Douglas Burden.

Douglas contracted amebic dysentery in Nicaragua during his early travels. For eighteen years he battled the devastating disease. But in spite of the handicap of indifferent health, he could never deny the lure of the wilderness. He journeyed to many lands and fortunately kept records of his wanderings. These form the basis of this book. In my opinion it ranks with the best of its kind. The author's sensitive appreciation of nature, his beauty of expression and vivid descriptions, will awake nostalgic memories and give a very special happiness to all lovers of the Lone Trail.

ROY CHAPMAN ANDREWS

Carmel Valley, California
May 22, 1959

Acknowledgments

MY FIRST DEBT is to my father and mother, who introduced me to the wilderness at the age of nine and whose love of the north woods led me into so many glorious adventures.

My second debt is to the Indian Archie Miller, who, though small in stature, strode through my childhood like a giant among men. Next comes Henry Lucas, who taught me to travel mountain-men style. And then Defosse, the great white hunter of Indo-China, whose observations were as accurate as his shooting and whose love for his jungle home was contagious; and Na-mon-gin, the Mongolian bandit whose patience was the greatest I have ever seen; and Rahima Loon, one of the foremost travelers of Central Asia, whose diffident ways and steadfast persistence brought the rewards we were after; and Juan, that fabulous Indian of the rain forest with whom I spent but a few days.

Then come my friends of the trail.

Sonny Whitney, the very best of travel companions over a great stretch of years; and

Laurie Foster, who, no matter what happened, made every trip a success; and

Willie Chanler, whose ebullient enthusiasm, dauntless spirit, and craving to go and see were a constant source of enjoyment and stimulation; and

Mason Sears, everlastingly good fun and good-humored, whose sensitive appreciation of native peoples everywhere led to his appointment as the United States representative on the Trusteeship Council of the United Nations; and

Jack Emery, always generous in heart and strong in adversity; and

Sheffield Cowles, whose enthusiasm and delightful humor added so much to every expedition; and

Shiela and Blake Lawrence, my endlessly rewarding sister and brother-in-law, both lovers of the wilderness; and my old friend, the late

Roy Chapman Andrews, whose great career of exploration helped so much to stimulate my early travels.

Then come all those kind spirits who helped me with this book: My friend

Ted Weeks, the brilliant editor of the *Atlantic*, who initiated the idea and whose encouragement and editing skill brought it to fruition; and

Sig Olson, whose nature writings (*The Singing Wilderness* and *Listening Point*) are the best I have ever read and who has given so tremendously of his time and of his keen sense of what is fitting in any given situation; and painstaking

Jean Packard, so endlessly generous and who helped me so much in getting down to the bare bone of my meaning; and

Lib Schley, always searching for mystical overtones; and

Mary Thurber, with a quick eye for overwriting or anything superfluous; and

Electra and the late Watson Webb, and Ethel Derby and Francie and Whitney Tower, all so encouraging; and

[xii]

ACKNOWLEDGMENTS

C. M. Bogert and Harold Anthony at the American Museum of Natural History, who made a scrupulous search for error; and

Mrs. Roberta Richardson, my secretary, patient beyond belief, who has typed many drafts of this manuscript and never for one moment expressed exhaustion at the constant changes; and last but by no means least, my wife

Betsy, whose constructive criticism was always most helpful.

To all of these I owe deep gratitude.

* * * * * *

And finally, special acknowledgment is due to Nancy Newhall for permission to use underneath my chapter headings quotations from her incredibly beautiful *This Is the American Earth*, a master-piece of prose poetry.

Foreword

AS THE TITLE SUGGESTS, these stories are about the wilderness — wilderness in different parts of the world: the north woods, the jungle, the Himalayas, Mongolia, Komodo and many other places. The central theme of each story is always the same. Primarily, each one seeks to capture the feeling of some particular wild place and to suggest the happiness I knew there and the deep peace and fulfillment that wilderness adventures can give.

There are moments when the meaning of wilderness runs deep in the blood. It is never possible to grasp it or even to explain it to those who don't feel it, for it is altogether too elusive, too unreachable. It can only be suggested, and if it is suggested well enough, those with sympathetic vibrations will understand. It is for them that this book is written.

W. D. B.

Contents

List of Illustrations

PART ONE

1

A Night to Remember

"You shall know the night . . .
You shall see earth sink in darkness and the universe appear.
No roof shall shut you from the presence of the moon."

I HAVE OFTEN wondered what there is about the wild places of our world that gives some people such a strong feeling of elation. What is the quality of wilderness that stretches the spirit and the mind?

Sometimes it is the sense of danger; sometimes it is in the achievement and conquest, the difficulties overcome or shared; sometimes it is discovery, perhaps a new meaning revealed and an ever-increasing awareness of the orderliness of the whole; or a new sensation, a new feeling of wind on the face, a new sensuous pleasure never experienced before.

But beyond all these there lies for me a fascination that runs infinitely deeper. It is the sense of mystery that dwells in the remote unreachable heart of any true wilderness. Sometimes this sense of mystery is felt as a yearning to reach out beyond ourselves, a strange inner aching to identify ourselves with the all-pervading magnificence of nature. And yet, though it can strike us with compelling force, there is no way of knowing in advance what may suddenly bring it into being.

It might be a vision of jungle hills with the early morning mists playing over them and the green disk of the sun just breaking through; or the blueness of night on a calm sea when the balmy air is suffused with the soft smells of an unseen tropical island. Sometimes it is the sight of beckoning peaks marching away into a cloud-tattered sky; or the crashing of great green combers on a barrier reef.

Or it might be something as simple as the strong scent of warm pine needles as a bark canoe touches an unknown shore; or the trembling ripples of reflected sunlight on a paper birch set deep in a dark evergreen embankment; or even the magic of the moon on a black New England swamp when the white wisps of mist are twirling the surface.

And yet again, it might be brought into sharp focus by a sound.

This story is about two of the most wonderful sounds of our northern wilderness. One winter's night when barely fifteen, I listened to them so intently that the enchantment of those sounds and the sense of mystery they invoked still stand out over a chasm of time with the sharpness of a dream from which one has just emerged.

It was early January and deep frost had taken a solid grip on the Canadian north. I was with Archie Miller, the great Indian hunter, then in his prime and already a legendary character in the forests of Quebec. The snow was deep, and for a long time we shoveled with our snowshoes to get to the ground. Then, for over an hour, the axes rang with the bite of sharp steel on green birch, and after that we lit a fire that curled and snapped and sparkled and gave us a momentary sense of well-being before the outer cold of 35 degrees below zero crept down our backs and seized every part of our bodies not facing the flame.

Archie Miller —
fabulous hunter of the northern forest.

In the dry cold air the fire consumed itself so fast we kept adding great logs. The tea boiled and we had a snack of fried venison. Time passed slowly, but I was happy despite the discomfort for the sheer delight of being in the company of the quiet man on the other side of the flame. He had taught me all I knew about the woods. We had been alone together many times before, and the days spent with him had been the very best of my childhood years. Archie Miller was a hawk-eyed man with the ears and eyes of the wilderness itself. He was completely a part of the forest he loved. He belonged to it.

By 9 P.M. we had already been stoking the fire for four hours. Then, with but one blanket apiece, we stretched out on some balsam boughs, hugged the warmth as close as we dared, and tried to get some sleep. Though my back was close to the fire, I had to force myself to lie still. After a long effort, I heard Archie move. He came over to me and, ever so gently and quietly, he stretched his blanket over mine and tucked it in. That was just like him — goodhearted and kindly man that he was.

I did not stir or take any notice of his gesture for to have done so would have caused him embarrassment. Instead, I continued to lie there, frigid as an icicle, pretending. The blankets were almost useless. Two were little better than one. While the fire burned on one side, the cold seared right through on the other. I endured it as long as I could. Then, at midnight, I got up. The full moon had long since risen over the hardwood ridge beyond Otter Pond, and the whole world was a velvety stillness of purple and white. Not a breath of air was moving — nothing but the indescribable magic of a northern night in the heart of winter. I glanced at Archie. He was simply sitting there looking into the fire. Neither of us spoke.

It was then we heard it. A long, loud, resonant and compelling call filled every shadow with foreboding. The heart of every small animal that moves must have missed a beat when that dread call spread through the forest. And many small furry bodies must have settled, terror-stricken, into immobility.

For sheer, fearless savagery and death-dealing power, no bird that flies — not even the bald eagle — can compare to the great horned owl. He is the silent killer of the night — the incarnation of sudden destruction. No lover of the wilderness can hear the call of this great bird without some deep responsive stirrings.

We listened for a distant answer. There was none. The owl called again — a deep, full-throated, magnificent challenge, ending in a savage catlike squall. I whispered to Archie, "See if you can get him to come closer." Archie could call every animal in the north woods, including deer and even wolves. He smiled his wonderful smile, chuckled to himself for a moment, then put his head back and perfectly imitated the great owl but in a somewhat higher register. Immediately came the answer. Archie called once more. Then we waited. A moment later the great bird arrived, silent as a shadow, directly over our camp. He came to rest on a high pine limb, folded his wings, rolled his head and turned his enormous eyes down upon us. Their brilliant yellow was reflected in the light of the fire.

I had hoped that Archie could bring him closer, but I never imagined the great bird would settle right over us. I watched his glaring tigerish eyes, the tufted horns on either side of his head. I could see the powerful ripping beak, the strong feathered legs, and the clutch of his rapacious talons. For a full minute the great horned owl examined us. Then suddenly a nearby tree was shattered by the frost. It snapped with the sharpness of a bullwhip, and the owl opened his wings and coasted away, ghostlike, into the moon-drenched forest.

It was good that sleep was impossible, for the gleaming black-and-whiteness of the night beckoned us to be on the move. "Let's get some trout," I said.

Always full of the sense of fun, Archie made no reply to my comment. I could see from the responsive smile on his face and the sparkle of merriment in his dark eyes as he glanced at me that the idea pleased him. That he would take his time I knew from of old, particularly when haste interfered with the sacred rite of preparing his pipe, so I simply watched and waited.

The plug of tobacco held edgewise in the fingers of his left hand he now shaved methodically with his razor-sharp hunting knife and rolled the fluffy shavings between both palms, then filled his pipe and tamped the tobacco down with a leathery forefinger. Then he reached for a small stick, lit the end in the fire, held it over his pipe and sucked. Curling down into the bowl, the brightening flame softened Archie's deep-lined features, adding a certain bold magnificence to his arresting personality.

Short, stocky, and powerfully made, Archie Miller always carried an immense sense of reserve strength. Here was a man who could take a full five hundred pounds over a portage and yet do still more if he had to. Here was a man with such an unerring sense of direction and such owl-like vision he preferred in summer to travel in the cool of the night and sleep by day. Here was a man who could always get game when nobody else could. Here was a man who, even when alone, was truly happy in his wilderness home.

Now he slowly turned and warmed his back at the fire and, with hands outstretched behind him toward the blaze, flexed his short, long-striding legs and looked off into the forest, listening. He was always listening. He did not say a word but his actions were eloquent, and every unhurried move was the personification of grace. Three more logs he cast upon the flames, then with a deft twist he imprisoned his finely moccasined feet in the smoke-tanned thongs of his snowshoes. His ax — he never moved without it — he passed through the belt at his back. His buckskin mitts, which

[7]

he rarely wore, he now drew on. Then we headed through the deep gloom of cedar and spruce and out into the ghostly white purity of open sparkling snow. A billion diamond facets spread over the surface of the lake reflected in their diminutive rays the silver of the full moon that now stood directly overhead.

Our snowshoes bit softly into the cushioning snow. The straining rawhide squeaked like resin at each stride. A few hundred yards from shore, we stopped where we could hear well from every side and there stood for a moment to listen to the silence. We listened hard and we listened so long that finally the night was filled with a ringing that seemed to descend from the stars.

On the far shore, a giant white pine rose against the starry sky. Because of some defect, it had escaped the ax and so, like a towering sentinel, it now dominated this small area of our ever-dwindling wilderness. I knew the tree well, for when quite young and paddling back to camp one night in a bark canoe I had heard a lynx scream from its branches.

Then we advanced fast through a world of silver light over the open lake. Archie led the way and at a spot selected by him we stopped. One twist of each foot and he was out of his snowshoes and his ice chisel was at work, making a wonderful crunch as the blows sank deep. It took but a few minutes to cut a round hole through a foot of black ice, and then the dark water gushed into the ice-filled hole. Archie used a snowshoe to scoop out the loose ice, and I dropped in my hook — baited with frozen bacon. No patience was necessary. The overpopulated trout, imprisoned beneath the ice, could hardly wait. They struck hard and fast. As soon as a beautiful glistening speckled form was yanked from his watery home and deposited in 35 degrees below zero of snowy frost, the cold seared so fast into his heatless body that after a few increasingly torpid wriggles, he was frozen stiff.

For a long time we stood silently by this dark hole in the ice.

Vapor hung in the air at each breath, and Archie's walrus mustache was coated with rime. Then all of a sudden it came pulsating through the night — the most eerie and arresting and blood-curdling sound of the North American continent, the hunting call of timber wolves on the trail. It was faint at first, at the very edge of hearing. Archie and I looked at each other in that first moment of excitement. Then the big grays burst over the hardwood ridge above our lake and came leaping in giant loose-limbed strides down the long slope toward the marsh below us. The deep stillness of our world was shattered as these savage shadows swept through the forest, old voices and young voices — low and high but pure in tone, all blending with each other. I was captivated by the sheer volume and musical beauty of it. Its ringing clarion quality filled our valley to the brim.

They thrust themselves into our blue-white silence, and though we could not see them I knew that the lead wolf was following, jump for jump, in the tracks of the deer, the other wolves saving their strength by following directly in those of the leader.

Their howling breathed the very essence of a primordial world. It spoke of the great heritage we have so rapidly destroyed. And it spoke also of timeless things — of the importance of wild predators and the struggle for existence through whose basic law life has forged ever upward.

Archie, true Indian that he was, listened with utter concentration. His pipe was glowing now from hard drawing, and he was wreathed in smoke. His Luger was at his belt, and I knew that if the wolves made a kill, Archie Miller, intent upon securing their meat, would slide away to become, in his turn, a silent shadow stalking the wolves in their first mad flush of victory. But they did not kill — not within earshot. It must have been a mighty buck that they followed, for we heard them a long time, their voices growing ever dimmer as they forced him down a narrow valley

[9]

— the buck hoping for open rapids, the wider-ranging wolves no doubt knowing there were none.

And then there was silence again.

I felt as if in another world and could hardly bear to move. Archie looked at me hard with jaws clenched tight on his pipe. "We go now," he said.

Then with a quick movement he picked up our frozen fish, and, with snowshoes complaining rhythmically, we traveled as fast as we could go, out of the magic spell — out of the singing night — and back to our balsam boughs, a birch-log fire, and a feast of new-caught trout.

2

Early Days in the Quebec Woods

"You shall enter the living shelter of the forest.
You shall walk where only the wind has walked before."

EVEN AS a child I was never quite content to be guided, to
follow in the footsteps of another man. No doubt it was this
eagerness to be independent that led to my learning how to find
my way alone in the woods.

Until this skill is acquired, a man must always rely on someone
else. And this is not good, for only when alone does one get the
full sense and feel of the forest. Only when alone does it have its
full impact upon you.

Mine was a learning acquired in a roundabout way. In fact, it
came through the acquisition of a birch-bark canoe I had seen on
the banks of the Ottawa River at Stonecliffe, Ontario. I was only
fifteen and it was a pure case of love on sight.

So often with envy in my eyes I had seen the great woodsman
Archie Miller fare forth in a bark canoe so small we called it "the
peanut shell." Though it barely supported Archie and his dog, one
felt with that canoe he could travel clear to the Barren Lands.

My canoe was lying there all alone, turned over on the rocky shoreline. It, too, was peanut size and wonderfully made. My craving for it became intense. Nobody was around. I picked it up, set it in the river, and shoved off. There was magic in that small bark canoe. Light as a feather, it responded to the least touch of the paddle, and when leaning back against a thwart with knees spread wide against the yielding cedar ribs, I felt perfect control over an instrument so delicate it seemed almost alive.

The canoe belonged to an Indian and, with my father's help, I purchased it for about eighteen dollars. From old Mike Simone, the Ojibway storyteller, I obtained two handmade hardwood paddles that were a dream of lightness and pliant strength. When tied to the thwarts and with a tumpline carefully set between the blades, it was possible to portage the canoe anywhere and that, too, gave a sense of mastery. Aside from my dog, that little bark canoe was the most important possession of my childhood. Together with Archie Miller, it inspired the urge to find my way where there were no trails.

Archie told me that finding one's way is largely a matter of practice, so from our home camp I would paddle across the lake and hit the wild shoreline at any odd spot. Leaving the canoe at the water's edge in the blueberry brush, I would walk off into the woods, paddle in hand. The idea was to notice the course so carefully that I could retrace my steps exactly and hit the canoe right on the nose without resort to a compass. Whenever I missed the canoe, there was no telling whether I was to the right of it or the left, and the subsequent floundering made me feel very foolish.

At first I never dared to go far, but as confidence grew, the distance increased and it became easier to remember the contours of the land, an old shiko, a dense patch of spruce, a certain fallen tree or glacial boulder. Finally I could travel for several miles and retrace my steps with no trouble at all.

I remember well the evening I made my first portaging trip

The home of moose and bear and wolves and lynx — the forest of Quebec.

alone in the forests of Quebec. I was headed for an old swamp the
beavers had recently dammed. The swamp was only a mile and a
half from home camp, but when there I felt as remote as if at the
ends of the earth. My little canoe balanced well and there was
something quite satisfying about its rhythmic creaking and the
resilient feel of the thwart and the strain of the taut tumpline.
There was something pleasant, too, about the sense of adventure,
but best of all was the arrival — that first step out of the forest
into the open where you pause and let the stern of the canoe drop
so you can see out from under and scan the shoreline; then the
careful advance through the swamp grass to the water's edge; seeing the track of a moose in the mud; stepping out on an old log
that slants into the water; then rolling the canoe off your shoulders and setting it down into the water with concentrated care.

I remember, too, untying the paddles and picking one up, being
very careful not to strike the canoe, enjoying the feel of lightness
after the weight had been removed, then simply standing there for
a long time, looking and listening. Everywhere the dead trees
were reflected in the water. A small animal left a wake far down
the marsh. Otherwise nothing but the silence of the forest and a
single whitethroat whistling. I leaned over and grasped a gunwale
in each hand, stepped gently into the middle of the canoe, gave a
little shove and settled myself into a kneeling position. For a long
time I hoped to hear some big animal move. But there was nothing — nothing but the whitethroat, whose plaintive haunting
notes, repeated time and again over the dismal swamp, still ring in
my ears.

Perhaps there was something at the far end. I started to paddle
with the rhythmic Indian motion that is strong and satisfying.
There is a triple action to each stroke: first the forward swing of
the dripping blade, barely skirting the surface; then the soft bite
into the mirror-blackness and the gentle click of the stem as it

sweeps back to make contact with the gunwale; finally, the twist of the blade and the forward push of upper arm and shoulder and back that gives the canoe a powerful forward thrust, raising the bow and simultaneously straightening course, followed immediately by the gentle slosh as the bow settles again.

With each stroke there is also that wonderful tinkle of water against the sides where the roughness of the bark and the black gum seams sewn with willow root cause a friction, so that there is an alternate tinkle and slosh, tinkle and slosh, as you glide over the smooth surface. As I approached the far end, not knowing what I might see, paddling became silent, the thin blade feathering forward without a sound and constantly turning in the fingers. But again, there was nothing — nothing but the sudden loud squawking of a flock of black ducks deep in the grass.

I cupped my hand over my mouth, held my nose between thumb and forefinger, and produced my best imitation of a black duck call. It was futile. The only answer was a great blue heron that rose lazily out of the grass and with legs outstretched flapped his slow and weary way across the marsh.

Then ahead, I saw another beaver dam. How large was the flooded area above? I had to see.

The beavers had excavated a narrow channel in the muck so they could swim directly to the base of this second dam. I rammed the canoe up this channel until the bow abutted the foot of the dam. It was six feet high and everywhere there were signs of beaver cuttings. On the narrow top, the mud was fresh and my moccasins sank into it to form new rivulets of escaping water that cascaded into the compact mass of interwoven branches.

Because of a steepened topography, the area flooded was small in comparison with the broad expanse I had just left, but a hundred yards beyond was still another dam, and curiosity beckoned again.

I made my way to shore and started to work around the flooded area. I had not gone more than thirty yards when my attention was arrested by the vociferous scolding of a couple of red squirrels deep in the woods on the far side. Immediately I stood still. A moment later a pair of blue jays started screaming their most raucous cries. Surely something had attracted the attention of both squirrels and jays.

I heard a breaking of big branches. Unquestionably a heavy body was moving through the forest, and it was moving fast in my direction. Something was about to happen, and I was suddenly terribly excited.

At my belt was an army issue .45 Colt automatic. Though I could not hit a barn door with it, I felt considerable security in the mere possession of a powerful firearm. In order to be prepared, I now drew it from its holster and pulled back the breech, allowing the first cartridge to slide from the magazine into the chamber.

The crashings in the forest grew louder. They were quite different from anything I had ever heard before. What could it be? Automatically, my mind ruled out the possibility of moose. Certainly not a deer, even if running for its life. And no wolf pack was ever born that would make so much noise. Judging purely from the sound, it could have been made by men on the full run — and yet that, too, was an obvious impossibility.

When you are alone in the forest and the silence is broken by some big unseen animal moving down upon you, expectation and excitement stream into your blood so fast that your heart suddenly pounds — and here was something very big moving with the noise and speed of an express train.

With growing alarm, I waited until suddenly a large bear followed by two fully grown cubs charged out of the forest at a full gallop and hit the beaver dam that I had just been on. Three great shaggy black creatures raced across the dam, splashing as they went. They were two thirds of the way across before I had recovered enough to take action. Then, grasping the Colt firmly in both hands — Archie Miller style — I fired at the mother bear. Immediately she dropped down the far side of the beaver dam out of sight. I fired at the first cub, who vanished in like manner, as did the second cub at the third shot. For one fleeting moment I had sweet visions of having shot three bear with three shots. Then I heard them again crashing off through the forest. They had left as hastily as they arrived. What had they been fleeing in the first place? The speed of their arrival certainly indicated flight, and yet what could have caused it? And what would the story have been had I been standing on the dam when they burst out upon it?

I worked my way back and made a careful inspection for any blood signs, but there were none. Every shot had been a clean miss. Yet even so, I felt elated. It was my first encounter with bear when alone and I would have a story to tell on reaching camp. Paddling back across the marsh, my mind worked over every detail of what I had heard and seen. For future reference there was much to be learned, and as I portaged my canoe back to camp I had a deep sense of satisfaction. For me, still very much of a greenhorn in the woods, that first portaging trip had been a day of days.

This urge to find my way alone led to another incident — the most frightening of my childhood years in the woods. And for those who do not know wilderness, it should be said that there is a great difference between woods that are tame and woods that are wild. Tame woods are woods with no wolves in them. They may have bear and bobcat and deer and even moose and coyotes, but they *feel* tame. The presence of wolves, on the other hand, injects a spirit into the forest that pervades the very shadows and brings a different kind of watchfulness into your eye and a different kind of hearing to your ears and a very different kind of prickliness to your skin if you are alone when darkness settles down.

It happened on an early autumn evening. I was about sixteen at the time. The Indian Mike Simone and I were making camp at Low Dam beyond the head of Bear Lake.

Low Dam — so called because of the enormous area of water backed up by a small dam during the first lumbering operations over a hundred years ago — is a tremendous marsh with two giant branches.

Where there had once been a dense stand of tamarack there are now bare poles and deep wallowing mudholes and several acres of gaseous swamp — good only for ducks and long-legged, loose-jointed moose who can thrust their heads under water for a full minute to emerge with a streaming mouthful of succulent growth.

Mike was busy at camp and I had paddled out to see what I could see. Low Dam was a true swamp wilderness, and one rarely set out upon it without seeing game.

On this particular evening I took the left fork in the direction of High Dam. There was a slight ripple and the late evening sunlight shimmered in reflected golden waves like a million "Tinker Bells" on the bare tree trunks. Though paddling very carefully, I saw nothing — but on reaching the upper end of the flooded area, I remembered that Archie had once told me of a long slim pond only a mile or so due north.

The evening was still and pleasant, and my mind began toying with the idea of finding that pond. I now knew how to find my way back, and the worst that could happen would be failure to locate the pond.

The more I thought about it, the more intriguing the idea became, and I pushed my canoe among the fallen tamarack and as far into the mud as I could thrust it. Leaving the canoe, I teetered along on logs half submerged in the muck and gradually, with the help of my paddle, worked back toward firmer ground until I stood at last at the edge of the forest.

There was a well-used moose trail leading directly north, and this I followed out of the low country and up into higher ground that gradually converged into a pass between low ridges.

The country was getting rougher with more slash until finally I reached one of those sections where a williwaw had smashed the forest with sledge-hammer blows. Few trees were left standing, and what was once deep woods was now a pile of jackstraws with raspberry bushes growing between the fallen logs.

I circumvented the impassable area and then saw light between the trees and a moment later some reflections. Filled with curiosity and excitement, I worked down to the shore and stood looking out onto a long narrow unnamed body of water that was so out of the way of all human passage it seemed to be possessed of solitude. A haunting melancholy brooded over the valley. It lay as in a different world on the other side of silence. For a while, I simply stood transfixed by a strange feeling of contentment.

Very quietly I climbed a nearby rock, sat down, and just looked and listened until I, too, became filled with the inner spirit of those still and lonesome waters and the forests around them.

Well up the pond the smoothness of the surface was broken by a V that struck out from the right-hand shore. Then I saw a large black head. A beaver swam up the middle of the pond, rolled over and quietly disappeared. On the left shore, less than two hundred yards away, was a sharp-edged cliff that dropped with an abrupt overhang into the dark water. The cliff was surmounted with a tight stand of stunted black spruce, and on the near edge was such a beautiful glacier-smoothed slab of rock sloping toward the pond it seemed just the place for a wolf to step out.

Dusk was now gathering fast, and though absorbed by the total wildness of the scene I began to think about returning to Low

Dam. But the place had a deep fascination for me and I could hardly tear myself away.

It was then I heard the faint but unmistakable grunt of a bull moose. It came out of the distance from the far end of the pond, and the deep challenge, repeated again and again, held me in utter absorption. So I just waited and listened. And I waited too long, for on my return trip there happened something that had often tormented my dreams — the sudden knowledge of wolves coming close when I was alone.

It was the only time in all my wanderings in the north woods that it ever happened to me — and late that evening, when so deeply moved by the lonesomeness of the unnamed pond, their arrival took a real grip on my mind.

There was still enough light so that over the open pond you could see clearly, but in the forest all outlines were now very dim and blurred. I had traveled about one third of the way to Low Dam when back at the pond, directly behind me, a chorus of wailing cries shattered the quiet of the autumn evening. It lasted only for a moment — a short staccato burst of primeval sound — and then there was silence. My heart jumped and I stood stock-still. Wolves will howl when they first strike the scent of man but they do not ordinarily howl when following his track. They just like to come close in the dark out of curiosity. I concluded immediately that they had hit my trail and were now on it.

No matter how much one may know that wolves will not attack, their near presence when the light has failed has a most disturbing effect.

Like the buck that stands listening until that last dreadful moment, so I stood rooted to the spot until sudden terror forced the strength into my limbs and I bolted toward Low Dam.

I kept hoping to hear them again way back, but there was not a sound. As the light fades, your eyes no longer watch the ground.

They seek a higher level for a better sense of direction. I had reached for the ax at my belt, so I now had the ax in one hand and the paddle in the other. With legs stretched to the utmost, I fairly skimmed the ground. When a fallen tree was in the way, I either jumped over it or up on it. There was no attempt to move quietly. Where there was underbrush, I crashed through, holding up the paddle to protect my eyes. My whole object was speed, and fear gave my feet wings. It was all I could do to prevent myself from breaking into a run. But to run would magnify fear as well as the chance of losing my way and falling down. I *must* not lose my way and I *must* not fall down.

There was still no sound from the wolves, and their silence was sinister. The mental picture of these savage creatures in the darkness behind me was like the ghosts of a haunted house to a child. I thought I heard them breaking through the brush — behind at first and then on either side. I can't say now whether this was imagination or reality. It is difficult fully to recapture periods of fear. In any event, I sensed their presence so deeply they might just as well have been there. To this day, I am sure they were there, very close. Fortunately, the route was all downhill and easy to follow.

At last the longed-for glimmer of light between the trees appeared. I can scarcely remember reaching Low Dam and plowing out through the muck to my canoe. But I vividly recall the wonderful feeling of safety regained when I was out upon the water.

Then for the first time since I had heard the howling, I remained motionless and listened. The forest was silent and hostile. Not since I was nine years old had its heart seemed so black with menace. Up the marsh I could hear a moose wallowing in the water. Then there was an exciting whistling of wings. A sudden commotion filled the air as a flock of black ducks banked hard this way and that and settled with a hush near my canoe. Only after they had landed did they see me and leap from the water again, leaving many small ripples to reflect the last of the light in the sky.

The stars were tumbling out, and very gradually the soothing peace of the night began to quiet an overagitated mind. Chill air drifted down upon the marsh and already little curtains and wisps of mist were playing over the warm surface. I paddled slowly back to camp, pulled the canoe well up and turned it over, and followed the trail to the campsite. The warm glow of our fire lit up the nearby stunted spruce. I sat down on a log, looked into the flame and held my hands toward it. Here was warmth and comfort — a magic circle of security against the outer darkness and mystery of the great Canadian forest.

"You been gone long time," Mike said. "What you see?"

"I didn't see anything," I said, "nothing but some ducks. But I heard things. Did you hear anything?"

"Yes, me hear wolves," he said, "just once very short."

"Yes," I said, "I did too."

Mike had some pickerel ready for the frying pan. As he squatted there cooking he said, "I mind the time when me and Archie was at San Joachim . . ." So began one of his endlessly enchanting stories that never ended until I had eaten supper and fallen asleep in my blankets while gazing into the ever-changing embers of the campfire.

3

This Was Adventure

"Seeking somewhere, in some last far place, our birthright: the wild majesty, beauty, freedom through which for a million years Man grew . . ."

JACK AND I were two very youthful greenhorns in the savage wilderness of Montague Island, Alaska. Montague is a precipitous narrow backbone of rock thrusting out of the blue Pacific like the neural spines of a prehistoric monster. Roughly fifty miles long and from three to ten wide, it guards the southern limits of glacier-bordered Prince William Sound. Salmon run up its short steep rivers and ptarmigan thunder across its abrupt peaks.

Our arrival in late July, 1919, on this magnificent uninhabited island was the fulfillment of a childhood ambition. Many years before, I had happened upon Charles Sheldon's book *The Wilderness of the North West Pacific Coast Islands*. In that book was a chapter called "Hunting the Big Bear." There were pictures of Montague and the bear that lived there, and from that day on I had a longing to reach its desolate shores.

Now the dream had come true. A few hours earlier, we had been dropped in Channing Bay by a Japanese fishing boat. We rowed ashore where the bleached rib bones of a whale arched out of the sand. Then we pitched a tiny tent on a rocky promontory, fought clouds of mosquitoes, and headed into the hills. Even in the long summer daylight of these northern latitudes, 5 P.M. was an unusual hour to begin a day's hunt, but our spirits were high and dominated decision.

Leaving the shore of the bay, we entered a beautiful stand of broadly spaced Sitka spruce. Beyond was a slope of slippery slanting grass that scaled steeply upwards. At the top of this pitch a beautiful valley opened before us, its flanking ridges converging to the island's great divide. A lone eagle floated high above it. Ahead in our path lay a deep precipitous ravine that slanted down the mountainside. We could clamber in and out only by grasping every shrub and root. Climbing was rough, yet in the glowing afternoon of a northern summer there was joy in fighting our way up.

In front of us stood the last of the timber—a small copse of mountain hemlock. As we entered the subdued light of these stately evergreens, there was a sense of foreboding and danger. It was a wild and somber place. Here, suddenly, we found ourselves in the private abode of the great bear. You could smell their recent presence, a rank and subtle odor permeating everything. Toothmarks were upon all the big trees, their claws had ripped and torn the brown earth, and we expected momentarily to encounter one of these formidable creatures. The Alaskan brown bear is the largest land carnivore on earth. On Kodiak Island and the Alaskan Peninsula they reach a weight of fourteen hundred pounds, and while stories of their attacks on man are exaggerated there is no more doubt about their courage when cornered or surprised than about their ability to press home a charge with unbelievable swiftness. On Montague, the brown bear was lord of creation. The island was theirs. I slipped a cartridge into the chamber; Jack did likewise. Then, with rifles ready, we scouted very slowly through

[24]

the grove. A yawning chasm flanked the western edge from which emerged the roar of waters from the melting snow. The bear had left. Perhaps we would meet one coming home, for a large trail led through a heavy growth of brambles toward the open hills.

For untold centuries, these great bear passing to and fro had stepped in exactly the same spots and their shuffling padded feet had left deep pigeon-toed imprints in the hard sod. These imprints we now followed out of the grove, past the brambles, and through the last of the scrubby dwarf spruce. Immediately ahead the ground dropped abruptly away. Before reaching a spot where we could look over into the depression, we suddenly heard what sounded just like a bear coming full speed up the bank. Gravel and stones were giving away and we could hear deep grunts suggesting extreme anger at our intrusion. In fact, there was not the slightest doubt in my mind that at the next second an infuriated brown bear would charge into view. But at that moment, my eye caught a movement far up the mountainside. One huge boulder that must have weighed many tons was crashing down the steep slope out of the mist. It came hurtling in enormous leaps, causing great splashes of snow and smashing everything in its path as it thundered through the alders and devil's-club and ended up with a deep crunching impact in the bottom of the main ravine. A big sound far away had seemed like a much smaller sound near to. So vividly had our imaginations pictured a charging bear that Jack and I both felt quite shaken.

After that we worked our way through the devil's-club and up onto the steep open grassy slopes where the going was so slippery we repeatedly fell.

Then we *really* saw a bear. He looked very light-colored crossing a big patch of snow below the divide. We watched him until he shambled out of view. It made us feel small to see the long, steeply rising slopes and the fading light and the big tawny bear.

[25]

A marmot whistled a shrill squeak and dove into his hole. Clouds were moving across the sky, carrying the threat of rain. We pushed on, not speaking a word but unconsciously vying with each other's climbing speed. Finally we stood at the head of the valley. It was a forbidding spot—a great rounded gorge where a glacier once nestled. At the back of the amphitheater black ramparts pinnacled up to unseen cloud-covered summits. Driving sheets of rain suddenly came down on us in sharp gusts. It was cold and we were soon soaked to the skin.

We worked on up. The rain stopped as suddenly as it had come. Then the clouds lifted and, as they did, we moved up onto a rounded ridge, the very summit of Montague, and stood gazing down the farther slopes to the broad Pacific whose great waves seemed no bigger than tiny ripples. To the northeast, as far as eye could see, the heaving backbone of Montague stretched away. To the northwest, dimly in the distance loomed the dark and hulking mountains of the Kenai.

It was as though we stood on the roof of the world. On every side we looked down into magnificent wild valleys that fell away beneath our feet. The slope to the Pacific was far steeper than the one we had just climbed. The roar of cascading waters rose on the wind, then faded away, and we were left standing amid the silent summits with the darkness slowly descending.

After the long climb we felt weak and hungry, so we sat down and devoured a whole package of hard seedy raisins.

While we were eating, two eagles appeared below us. With banked wings they turned in tight spirals. A thermal current was carrying them upward so fast that before our raisins had been consumed they had gained several thousand feet and were already well above us. Comparing the ease of their ascent with ours made us seem dismally earth-tied.

There was no telling which way the bear had gone, so we parted company to explore the divide in opposite directions. We would meet at the same spot.

The wind was coming up again and it was getting colder. One does not have to travel far when working the crest of a range to uncover new valleys to the eye. I had not gone a quarter of a mile before I saw another bear directly below me. He was very busy digging out a marmot and did not see me as I worked down to him. His coat was shaggy and I could see at once that the pelage was no good. Nearby was a round boulder, irresistibly placed. I gave it a shove and watched with intense interest as it hurtled past the bear, missing him by inches. He glanced up as it rocketed by, then went right on with his digging. Another boulder was at hand so I tried again with the same result. He paid no attention. I scrambled sideways to a third boulder. This time, in its erratic bouncing course, it crashed against a rock very close to him and flew into pieces. He hopped over, took a sniff, and immediately reared, looked for one brief moment in my direction, then dropped to all fours and plunged down the mountain with express-train speed. He had scented the touch of my hand.

It was a fine example of a bear's great fear of man. I watched him with my field glasses. When he struck the alders, he smashed through them as though they were reeds of grass — never slowing his speed. On the far side of the valley he climbed hard and fast. Only when he reached the summit did he pause and swing his great head for a long look back and down. Then slowly he turned and disappeared into the safety of another valley.

For some reason I was beginning to feel dizzy and vaguely distressed. It was about ten o'clock. I was cold and suddenly weak. Heavily I climbed back up to the divide and continued along it. Then came a warning throbbing in the temples and sickness all through. I sat down to rest and, as I did so, two ptarmigan — until then unseen — exploded from under my feet and catapulted downward into space, their wings set as they banked this way and that and finally dove over an outlying spur and sank out of sight toward the darkening Pacific.

As I started back to meet Jack, the headache became acute. Could this be mountain sickness? I staggered back to our meeting place. Thank God, Jack was already there. I said, "I'm sick and I've got to get back to camp as quickly as I can." With that, we took off down the mountain. It didn't seem to matter which way I went. There was no question of selecting a good course. It was only important to get down to the safety and comfort of camp.

Suddenly nausea struck and I was violently ill. Directly below was a deep ravine. I fell into it, not caring what happened, clutching at any handhold to ease the sheer descent. I was repeatedly sick.

The tough-skinned raisins were responsible. However, after a while, I felt better.

By now the world of Montague was in deep twilight. All the outlines were dim but the skyline was still clearly defined despite the glowering clouds sweeping above. It was close to midnight and I was still floundering recklessly forward, only wishing to get down as fast as possible and not caring where I went or how, when Jack's voice stopped me.

"You're lost," he shouted. "I've never seen this goddam valley before. You're sick and don't know what you're doing. I'm not going to follow you another foot."

The words frightened me. It was so sudden. "Look," I said, "see that big boulder? Remember on the way up we were on the other side of it? We're coming down only a few hundred yards from where we went up. And look at the skyline — that sharp hogback and the saddle in the hills."

He shook his head. "I tell you we're lost. I've never been in this valley before."

"Look, Jack," I said, "camp, blankets, food, are right down there and that's where I'm going as fast as I can." I started down and never looked back.

After a while I became aware that he was following. My direction was right and by the time I reached camp all signs of illness had disappeared. I knew that Jack could not help but resent my being right and I felt a most uncomfortable tension while waiting for him to appear. On the beach below the promontory, near the protruding rib bones of the big whale we had noticed on landing, were his enormous vertebrae, half buried in the sand. It suddenly occurred to me that one of them would make a wonderful seat to cook from. I felt like being active to ease the constraint between us caused by our misunderstanding. So I jumped down to the beach and tugged and wrestled to loosen the vertebra from its sandy grip. It gave way and I hoisted it clear of the sand — a full eighty pounds of bleached bone. The ribs had parted leaving only short spurs, but the dorsal spine was a long, well-curved scimitar. I struggled up the steep bank with my prize and on reaching the campsite leaned well over and finally dropped it. That was my big mistake — dropping it those last few inches — for it landed on uneven ground and the big dorsal spine whipped up and struck me a terrific blow on the skull, laying bare the bone and knocking me unconscious. When Jack arrived, he found me out cold. The incident somehow formed a perfect apology though hardly according to plan. When I came to, Jack helped me into the tent. Having exchanged one headache for another, I felt very weak again. The mosquitoes were swarming and I asked Jack for my Yukon head net, a wire mask like a narrow-mesh fencing helmet. It has a canvas collar that fits over the head and down the neck and under the shirt. The wire is so stiff that even when one is lying down no portion of it touches the face. It affords complete protection.

Jack was wonderful. He took the best of care of me. First he

brought me the mask and examined the wound. He said it would
have to have a lot of stitches. I told him I was sorry for being so
stupid. Jack started a fire and did some cooking. The buzzing of
thousands of mosquitoes filled the tent, but as far as I was con-
cerned, it was a thoroughly frustrated buzzing as I was snug inside my head net. Our tent was pitched in a well-used bear trail,
coming up from the beach on one side, crossing the promontory,
and going down on the other side. I began to wonder how many
bear might want to make the crossing during the remainder of the
night, and while thinking these thoughts I fell asleep.

Early the next morning when I woke up I still had quite a headache but the bleeding had stopped. I heard someone calling. Jack
was not in the tent. I looked out. There he was on the beach, waving a balloon-silk parka. Then he fired a rifle. Far across the bay
was a fishing boat at the salmon traps. At last Jack came up and
said he would take me to the copper mine on Latouche Island
where there was a doctor who could sew my scalp. I didn't say
anything but I felt mighty bad to have spoiled our Montague
trip. The Japanese boat captain said we were lucky, there would
not be another boat for many days.

Jack and I had come through a difficult experience that, but for
his generosity, could easily have had unpleasant consequences.
Nothing more was ever said about it, but we had both learned a
good lesson — we had been awakened to one of the dangers of
wilderness travel, the possibility of separation.

The trip to Latouche was grim. As usual, we were at the mercy
of a single gas engine that behaved badly. Moreover, it was rough.
I lay in a heaving hammock directly above the engine and the
stench of gas fumes and dead fish was nauseating.

Late though it was when we reached Latouche, the local doctor
promptly sewed up my scalp. The following morning I felt fine
again and was ready to go.

Our next destination was the small town of Seward at the head of Resurrection Bay on the Kenai Peninsula. Seward was over eighty miles away — most of it over the open Pacific Ocean.

No boat was due at Latouche for ten days — too long a time to wait. Fortunately, there was an old fishing dory on the beach. It had an engine in it and it was for sale — $175. So there, we thought, was our answer. We would push off in the morning and make the run to Seward. It all looked very simple.

We examined our Coast and Geodetic Survey chart of the area. Once we left Latouche, there was no hope of protection until we rounded the promontory into Resurrection Bay — nothing but jagged cliffs plunging into the sea, a deadly and menacing coastline where huge Pacific swells smash against the towering rock walls only to be thrown back to encounter new ones just arriving and creating a heaving wilderness of threatening water.

It was all very casual. I knew nothing about the sea and placed complete trust in the judgment of Jack, who was a down-East sailor. The manager of the Latouche copper mine obviously thought we were mad but we happily ignored his words of caution. The dory was reasonably tight and it was a short matter to load up with gasoline and a few supplies.

The little Ford engine started well and we cruised out over beautiful inland waters surrounded by mountainous islands. Once clear of Latouche Passage, we felt like Captain Cook himself braving the unknown. Anybody could rightly have said, "There go a couple of crazy idiots." But we were blissfully unaware of just how crazy we were. A big blue whale lazed along in the quiet water, his great tail flukes standing high in the air as he sounded.

Then we ran out into the open sea. The day was gray and threatening but there was no wind, and we rode the big slick swells in fine style. Our speed we estimated at six miles and so calculated ten hours to round the headland into Resurrection Bay

[31]

— ten glorious hours whose outcome hung on a rusty old Ford engine and the dispensation of the weather. Once past Danger Island, we were truly in the open sea.

For some time everything went well. Then we came close to a great hulk awash, a dead whale — an island of gray blubber that floated massive and formless. I did not recognize the species but the deep longitudinal markings suggested a blue whale. One wondered how such a colossus could have been stricken.

Then a thought hit me: the killer whales — could it have been they? I had read about them and knew the killer was the most formidable predator on this planet. Certainly no creature that swims begins to equal the killer whale in ferocity and strength. He can be more rightfully compared with the king of tyrant dinosaurs, *Tyrannosaurus rex*, that dominated his age on land eighty million years ago.

Tyrannosaurus was probably the most terrible engine of destruction the world has ever seen, but while Tyrannosaurus had a minute brain, the killer whale is a remarkably intelligent animal. They often hunt in packs with teamlike precision. As soon as a killer is sighted Eskimos head for shore, for they know that he is to be feared above all animals.

The killer whale is from twenty to thirty-five feet in length. His entire form, compact like a lethal torpedo, breathes speed and power. He is vicious and sinister and smart. His great dorsal fin cuts the water six feet above his back, flaunting his banner like the telltale periscope of a prowling submarine.

In the Arctic and Antarctic killer whales skirt the ice and sometimes rise vertically with heads six to eight feet above the surface, looking for prey. And when they find it they strike the floes with their great backs and smash them to pieces in order to dump seal or penguin or any living creature into the water. Killers have been seen throwing enormous bull sea lions fifteen feet into the air —

playing with them like a cat with a mouse. Like the wolf and the tiger, the killer lives by attack and his capacity is almost incredible. In the stomach of one killer seventeen porpoises and sixteen seals were reported.

I was ignorant of much of this that August day when we cruised past the big dead whale, but I did know of the incredible voracity of this powerful animal. When a few minutes later enormous dorsals cut the water directly ahead, they struck me with sudden fear. Never before had I set eyes on a killer, but it was impossible not to recognize those scimitar-like dorsal fins.

Suddenly I understood the big dead whale. The killers had killed him and eaten out his lips and tongue. When first sighted, the orcas were not more than four hundred yards away. I was sitting up in the bow at the time. It would have been easy to alter course and avoid getting anywhere near them.

I shouted to attract Jack's attention and pointed to them the next time they broached. He looked and nodded and kept on course.

The whales scarcely seemed to be moving, so we gradually overtook them. At a distance of two hundred yards they looked more menacing than ever and, by the size of the dorsals, I felt sure they were all three bulls.

The nearer we got, the more frightened I became. Maybe Jack did not know what they were. Maybe he thought the sound of our engine would scare them away. I cupped my hands and shouted across the wind, "Look out — those are killer whales!"

Once again Jack nodded happily and kept on course. We were gaining on them fast. It was almost as though they were curious about us and awaiting our arrival. Jack seemed to be aiming directly at them expecting, no doubt, to put them to rout. When all three surfaced less than thirty yards ahead of us and then sank silently from view, I held my breath in fear. If killers could break up ice pans two feet thick, what could they do to a flimsy dory!

One flick of the tail and our boat would be in pieces and we in 40-degree water with them.

It was one of those moments when your mind comes to a dead stop. You simply hold on to yourself tight and the seconds are timeless. We came directly over where they had been. As we did so, a big ugly head broke the surface less than a yard to the left of our dory, so close I could have reached out and touched it. A small black pig-eye suddenly looked straight at me as the killer canted his head to one side. The lips parted and I could see a big row of blunt teeth. Warm vapor gushed from his great lungs with a giant panting sigh and he sucked in a torrent of air. Then the white curved markings on his side came into view. Finally, as his head arched downward and disappeared into his element, the great dorsal fin cut the surface and rose so high it seemed to stand above me. It made a curious zipping sound. He was followed immediately by the other two, who duplicated his movements. Then the waters closed.

They were obviously without fear of us or our boat. They investigated — they saw us — they let us alone — and, though attacks on even very small boats may be extremely rare, at that particular moment I felt sure we had only the dead whale to thank for their unrapacious behavior, for no doubt their bellies were full.

We never saw them again though we scanned the ocean ceaselessly.

Very soon our dory began to pound on the freshening seas and the spray burst across us. Though the engine was boxed in, I was vaguely worried, but I lacked the sense to unpack the tent and spread it over the box for additional protection.

Now suddenly the precariousness of our situation struck home. We looked at the black Kenai cliffs that plummet from such great heights into the sea. We looked to the south at the increasing array of whitecaps sweeping toward us from the open Pacific. We looked ahead and thought we could just discern the spearhead of dark rock that formed the entrance to the giant fiord known as Resurrection Bay.

We were crossing the Gulf of Alaska; Blying Sound lay ahead. It was true wilderness — the wilderness of an icy northern sea abutting the stark bleakness of cold gray cliffs, not a blade of green anywhere, not a speck of sand, not a discernible yard of protected water. It was all cold gray, but after the close meeting with the killers the excitement of adventure was in our blood.

The dark descended with an increasing wind. Scud swept in from the open Pacific. The pounding grew and the salt spray drove in ever-increasing sheets across our port beam. We could no longer see the headland of Resurrection Bay. A pocket compass was our only guide. It gyrated hopelessly with the increasing movement of our dory. The engine continued to purr pleasantly, but how completely our lives depended upon it became ever more obvious, for should it die the onshore wind and seas would soon have us upon those monstrous cliffs.

We were wet and cold and hungry for we had been at sea in an open boat for over ten hours. Then in the dimness ahead loomed Barwell Island, the spear of rock that marked the entrance. The great haven of Resurrection Bay lay before us. In a few minutes we rounded the wave-torn headland and gazed upon the calm waters of Eldorado Narrows and as we did so — at that very moment — our faithful little engine suddenly began to sputter. It choked and heaved and then, almost immediately, with a series of convulsive kicks, it died. By purest chance the engine had barely succeeded in bringing us into calm waters. The gods had certainly smiled upon us. Skill had had nothing to do with our reaching safety, good luck alone was responsible.

Resurrection Bay is a typical U-shaped fiord carved out of the raw rock by stupendous glacial power and later drowned as the vast continental ice sheets melted away and restored their captured water to the oceans. The southeast wall of the bay is a giant ridge of rock spearing like an arrow into the Pacific. It towered three thousand feet above us. About half a mile away, indented in those sheer cliff walls, we marked a little cove of shingle beach. It offered a landing, so, side by side, we started to row our cumbersome craft toward shore.

It was then that I turned to Jack and said, "Look, there's something I must know. Why in God's name didn't you alter course when those killers were dead ahead?"

"Oh," he said, "they were just whales. I knew they wouldn't bother us."

"But they weren't just whales. They were *killer* whales," I replied. "Didn't you hear me when I shouted to you?"

"Yes," he said, "I heard you but I knew they wouldn't bother us."

I was tempted to say "A hell of a lot you know about it" but I restrained myself. Furthermore, he may just have been right, for investigation yields no record of a killer ever having smashed an engine-powered boat and devoured the occupants; though if that ever happened, there would be no one left to tell the tale.*

We had no food, a dead engine, and were still some seventeen miles from Seward, which could be reached only by water. However, there was something exciting about landing on this wild cavity of beach cut out of the great cliff walls. For a while we just stood there, surveying our new home and wondering what to do next. As we were turning the problem over, the sky, which had so long been threatening, chose this moment to let loose a deluge.

---

* In 1957 off San Diego, California, a female killer and young approached the stern of a large tuna boat. Someone aboard shot at the young one, whereupon the mother hurled herself right up on the deck of the boat where, after creating havoc, she was finally subdued with concentrated rifle fire.

The wiring of our engine had undoubtedly short-circuited from the soaking it had received and this meant that our only chance of reaching Seward under power was to dry it out. This in turn necessitated pitching the tent and building a fire in front of it. But to obtain firewood and poles for the tent, we had to scale the slippery rock cliffs directly above our strip of beach. Then, while standing in a precarious position, we chopped down some tough and gnarled old trees and watched them hurtle down to the campsite. It is never easy to start a fire in a downpour but a poncho carefully held gave protection until it was well under way.

We dragged the battery and all the wiring out of the boat and into the tent. But our theory turned out to be defective in that no good fire was possible in such heavy rain. All we succeeded in doing was to fill the tent with smoke. Finally we had to give the whole thing up and try to get some rest.

Our last sandwich had long since been eaten but we were so tired that even hunger, soaking wet clothes, and a bed of stones could not keep us awake.

The next morning held a rude surprise. Though still wet through and cold and aching in every muscle, these complaints were nothing when compared to the sickening spectacle of our dory. It was completely stranded. The tide, we knew, was full but it did not even reach the rudder of our boat. So there we were with a one-ton waterlogged craft high and dry on a rocky beach of rubble. What had happened? The Pacific Coast tide tables gave us the answer. We had landed at the highest tide of the month.

At first we attempted to wedge the dory down with our tent poles — an effort that failed completely. Obviously rollers would have to be placed under it, but since no rollers would roll on such coarse rubble it was necessary to set some long logs up and down the beach for the rollers to roll on. That meant wedging the dory up high enough to place the rollers underneath.

It took the better part of the day to scale the cliffs and chop down the few accessible trees that still clung to their bare walls, and we worked most of the night to block the dory up and place our rollers underneath. Prying the dory down the beach was then a relatively simple matter. It was a great satisfaction when we reached the spot where we had calculated the next high tide would float it.

Then we gave up and got some sleep. By nine o'clock in the morning the tide was lapping against the propeller and by ten our dory was afloat.

One colossal effort remained. We had to get to Seward, seventeen miles away at the head of the fiord. We had not sighted a single boat since we left Latouche, and there was little possibility of help, so we would have to row it — and a long row it would be with the propeller dragging against us the whole way.

We might have waited for the tide to turn but we felt that by keeping close to shore we would reduce its effects to a minimum. We took our time and started at about twelve-thirty. Rowing that big sluggish dory against a current was like trying to pull an elephant through the water. Amid the towering peaks and the vastness of the fiord, our progress was barely discernible, and I began to wonder if our energy would ever last long enough. We could not have been making half a mile an hour. However, by three-thirty the current slackened and we began to get ahead in good shape. Then, a little later, with the current in our favor, we moved out across the fiord to the western shore. When darkness came down, the mountains on either side loomed so high I felt as if at the bottom of a tremendous crevasse. The lights of Seward beckoned, but they seemed to remain endlessly far away.

Rough times are part and parcel of wilderness travel and I have often noticed that the tougher the time the more valuable the experience. The pain of it soon goes but the memory of success remains. With Seward in sight, victory seemed certain and our hearts were high. I remember passing Tonsina Point. The tide was running out again and the set against us was particularly strong. Jack, as an old oarsman, wanted to give her ten but I just didn't have what it takes.

I remember, too, hearing wolves howling. These turned out later to have been a pack of Malemutes running wild; they sound almost exactly like wolves. Finally, at 3:30 A.M., fifteen hours after starting, we tied up at the Seward dock and walked up the main street. The whole town seemed to be asleep. Then we saw a light: one restaurant was open. It went under some such name as Diamond Dick's Café. It was the hangout of the "old-timers" and even at that hour some of them were still there. When we entered, everybody stopped talking and looked at us. Finally, someone spoke up and asked us where we had come from.

It was hard to answer in much detail for the incredible smell of bacon and eggs and coffee completely captured our attention. After the bleakness of night in the fiord, the restaurant seemed bright and cozy and warm, and our weary bodies began to relax. There was a fulfilling sense of having reached our destination in spite of adversity. As we started to tell of our adventures, the atmosphere, too, was immediately friendly. For a long time it was a case of talking and eating and eating and talking, and the combination of the food and the friendly atmosphere and the pleasant sense of accomplishment fairly made us glow. I can remember to this day some of the faces we saw that night. There was August Tobin, a husky Swede. He had been north of the Arctic Circle for twenty-seven years. This was his first trip "south." He had been a gold prospector on the famous Koyukuk River — the greatest gold river in the Western world. Another man was Tom Donahue. He was said to be dog crazy, for he spent his life feeding a large pack of Malemutes which he would neither use nor sell.

His last job in the United States had been as a steelworker on the Queensboro Bridge in New York.

In spite of our exhaustion, we stayed and listened for a long time to the fascinating comments of these hardy adventurous men. And it was time well spent for we soon learned that survival in the north depends on infinite care and attention to detail. These old-timers would never have lived so long had they played their luck as we had.

Years later, in reading a book called *Arctic Village* by Robert Marshall, I learned that in testing population intelligence quotients by far the best results he ever obtained were in a small village north of the Arctic Circle inhabited one third by Eskimos, one third by Indians, and one third by whites. Marshall's explanation of this fact was that the north does not permit survival of the unfit. And the unfit are, above all, the unintelligent.

Evidently it was for us a case of learning the hard way. An important lesson had hit home on Montague. Now a still more important lesson had been learned on our brief trip from Latouche to Seward.

But to get back for a moment to Diamond Dick's Café. Jack had always had a hankering to go prospecting and that evening he met a prospector with whom he later went off into the hills. It was there, too, that I met that wonderful tough little hunter, Henry Lucas, who conducted me into the glorious mountains and moose flats of the Kenai. Good fortune was smiling on us again for we were each able to pursue our separate bents. Jack and I parted company for a few weeks, and when we met again before heading home, it was a very welcome and happy reunion for we had so much to tell each other. And I am sure, if Jack ever reads these lines, he will still remember with infinite pleasure the smell of bacon and eggs in that cozy little restaurant in Seward and the heart-warming welcome in that early August morning of 1919.

4

Siwashing on the Kenai

"To the primal wonders no road can ever lead; they are not so won.
To know them you shall leave road and roof behind;
   you shall go light and spare."

TRAILING a wounded bear through heavy alders on a steep Alaskan mountainside is not the most restful way of spending a summer evening, nor is it the best way of making preparations for a stormy night.

Henry Lucas, my Alaskan guide, and I had been tracking him for several hours before darkness forced us to give up. Then we struggled upward out of the engulfing tangle and into the open hills. Already the clouds were down upon us. Once in the open, the wind was so strong we had to lean against it. In the dim light, it took a long time to find the scrubby mountain hemlocks we were looking for. They were not more than four feet high, stiff and unyielding from battling the mountain gales, but they provided enough wood for a campsite.

A mountainside usually varies only in degrees of steepness, but there was one spot between two hemlocks where the slope was sharply reduced. We tied a six-by-four strip of canvas between these two scrub trees, sloped it back and set some rocks on it to hold it down. Then with a sharp stone we dug a little trench on the upper side to carry off the water. After that we started a fire.

"Siwashing" is the only way to travel in the hills, but I began to realize that it automatically involves a contest in toughness.

"Siwash" is an Alaskan term meaning Indian and "siwashing" is to camp the way the Indians do — with nothing but rifle, fry pan, tea pail, salt, tea, and a little sourdough. Siwashing releases you from the necessity of returning to any fixed campsite. You are free to go where you please — to move as the spirit moves you. You need only drop down far enough from the summits to find wood for a campfire. Then in the morning you climb again and spend the day on top of the world. And of course, you have to live off the country.

But every night the contest begins anew, for the tougher you are the less fire you need. And as the protecting warmth dwindles with the dying embers and the chill enters your bones, you lie there pretending to be asleep and hoping the other man will rouse up to put on more wood.

Henry told me that when he was siwashing with the great guide Andy Simons, he became tired of keeping fire for him. So finally one night he got up very quietly and walked off over the dark mountainside for a quarter of a mile and built himself a new fire. He was just getting himself cozily fixed before a fine bright flame when Andy moved in and lay down without saying a word. After that, Henry admitted defeat just as I already had.

There was a wild roaring that filled the air. It came down to us from the summits. The wind struck in blasts and scattered the embers from the fire. It was cold, for the wind came directly off the great Kenai snow fields that stretched for a vast area along the divide.

Smoke and ashes whirled into our eyes. Henry cooked a bannock in the fry pan, a mess of sourdough with grease, water, and salt added to taste. He could not see what he was doing and it came out thoroughly charred — but we ate it anyway, with our eyes closed against the smoke.

Now the rain came down in sheets. We had no blankets and no extra clothing. Henry said, "Maybe fire go out." He reached out to collect all the wood we had gathered and set it around on top of us under the canvas. It did not do much good because the canvas was so old it leaked. Henry said, "Siwashing no good tonight."

I replied, "No, no good."

"Too bad," he said, "we lose bear."

"Yes," I said, "I've been thinking about him. Do you think he will recover?"

"I don't know," replied Henry. "Bear plenty tough — him headed straight down for glacier. Maybe try to cross."

The canvas snapped in the gusts. Henry put more wood on the fire. Occasionally it flared up in spite of the rain and I could see Henry's lean, dark, sensitive face with quick-moving eyes looking into it. No matter what happened, Henry never complained. A good man, I thought.

By lying feet to head, there was just room for both of us under the canvas. For a long time I lay there, trying not to roll downhill. Then I took a stick of wood and wedged it in against me on the low side. For a while I slept. Then the storm lashed us with still greater fury. Our canvas strip formed an eddy that sucked the smoke in on top of us. Feeling suddenly choked, I jumped up and ran out into the rain to get some fresh air in my lungs. Henry came out too, even he could not stand it. Then, with hunting knife in hand, I dove back under the canvas and slit a hole in it near the bottom and stuck my head out into the rain. No, I thought, "Siwashing no good tonight."

Toward dawn the wind abated and I pulled my head in. Water

had been trickling down my neck all night and I was soaked and cold, tired and stiff. I looked at Henry. He was curled up in a ball and there, tucked under one ear for a pillow, was our dingy little sack of salt. He was sleeping.

Breakfast was another charred bannock, and tea in a tin cup that burned the lips and was too hot to hold. We were still submerged in a blanket of driving cloud. Directly below us was Skilak Lake, totally invisible. To the southwest was Skilak Glacier and the great snow fields of the Harding Range, along which we hoped to find bear and the beautiful Alaskan white sheep (*Ovis dalli*).

It had taken us nearly a week to reach our present position. From Kenai Lake above the town of Seward we had had to run some eighteen miles of rapids to Skilak — a wild ride down foaming canyons, past whirlpools of black water. In two and a half hours we had been hurled out upon the heaving gray of Skilak Lake. A bad wind beat down upon us from the glacier gorge. It came at us out of a wind funnel and threatened to swamp our little boat. So we made for shore where we spent the night in a deserted Indian hut. Known locally as a "bribery," it was built of poles and bark and shaped like two lean-tos facing each other with a smoke hole between. We found it warm and comfortable. After that, we rowed for many miles across the lumpy glacial waters of Skilak Lake. Then we worked up into the lower hills where we had been hunting hard without success. Now we were headed for the high country.

Misery makes one move. Even after hot tea, we were still congealed and needed to warm up with exercise. Besides, there is always hope of better things elsewhere. So in spite of rain and wind, we struck camp and headed off into a wet bank of cloud. We each carried a small pack with tumpline, a climbing stick, and I had a telescope and my Mannlicher held by a strap across the chest. The wall of gray-white mist made us feel blind. Our altitude was about

Wiry, tough Henry Lucas
above Skilak Glacier.

three thousand feet and we decided to move higher in hopes of a break in the weather. About ten o'clock there was a sudden rift in the clouds and we saw a patch of blue. Nearby ridges began to unfold as the clouds dispersed. The brief views were unbelievably intriguing. A hole would form in the clouds; we would look down and see a bear half a mile away in the valley — a sudden magnificent spectacle — and a moment later, the cloud-blindness would be upon us again.

Gradually, however, there were more and more apertures of captivating beauty. After three hours, we came into a great basin — a rugged sheer-walled cirque — where we saw nine rams feeding at the base of the wall; four more were just below the top of the mountain, five more lying down at the very summit, surveying the entire range. My telescope soon showed that the five on the top were old veterans. It was just the place where fine old rams should be, dominating the scene. One ram in particular had an outstanding head. With his wide, sweeping, full-turn horns, he epitomized the dignity and grace of his kind.

They were a long way off and we were travel-worn and hungry, but those superb creatures demanded a supreme effort. To reach them we had to drop down into the bottom of a chasm before tackling the main wall. The descent was easy via a steep snow-filled gully. Henry took a run and a jump and glissaded in a squatting position down the steep slope with his climbing stick thrust under one arm into the snow to control his speed. I followed. At the base we cupped our hats and drank some snow water. It tasted flat. When we were about halfway up, a severe snowstorm came over the summit and burst upon us with sudden fury. It was right in our faces and so thick we could not see twenty feet. The flakes were enormous and in ten minutes there was an inch of snow and Henry and I were both as white as the mountainside, for the snow was wet and clung to our clothing. However, the sudden cold freshened us and the snow muffled the sound we made on the rock slides, so we gained the top under cover of its all-concealing blanket and with intense excitement began scouting for our rams.

It is an eerie and ghostly feeling, creeping about in a blinding snowstorm on top of a mountain looking for game. You gaze out in all directions into a misty vault of wind-driven snow. Even the rocks beneath your feet are a deadly, shadowless, even white. You could easily step over a precipice. The sky seems to be above you and below and on all sides. After about ten minutes of fumbling in the storm, we nearly stepped upon a pair of rock ptarmigan that relied to the last second on their concealing coloration. They rose like thunderbirds and immediately dove into the white void at our right. I wondered in such blindness how they could make a safe landing. With zero ceiling what instinct would allow them to reach ground again unharmed? I wondered also if the rams had heard the warning sound.

Soon afterwards we saw fresh tracks of our rams. They had been disturbed either by the ptarmigan or by an eddy of scent or by some intuitive awareness of danger. It would have been useless to follow them; nothing to do but wait until the storm cleared. Meanwhile, we ate some bannock left over from breakfast. Though leaden and soggy and tasteless, it was at least a filler. By the time we had finished, the clouds were dispersing. Immediately we rose and circled a nearby peak only to look back and see our rams trot right by where we had just had lunch. Though too far for a shot, they loomed larger than ever.

As soon as they disappeared we took after them. Then for a few minutes a blanket of cloud obliterated everything. When it passed, the rams had completely gone, but with its passing, the whole sky cleared while openings formed below as through the eye of a telescope. To one side we could suddenly look down on

Skilak Glacier, seven miles away. It lay like a great sprawling monster wedging a path for itself between the hills. On the other side, through Rocky Pass, Skilak Lake yawned into view. It was a sheet of quivering light. Then valleys opened under our feet with long green slopes below the snow line, and here and there small blue lakes appeared — beautiful glacial tarns, nestling in the rugged hills.

At last the sun came out in full force and, since the tracks showed that the sheep had taken off at full speed, we found a cozy spot sheltered from the wind and stretched out for a good rest. It was an utterly glorious location. Here we were, just Henry and I, together in a great wilderness. We had seen Bill Kaiser at his fox ranch on the edge of Skilak Lake, but aside from Bill there was not another human being in this vast area of mountains. No hunter had even reached Tustumena Lake that year. To be so alone on these wild summits amid such solitude gave us a wonderful feeling of independence.

In front of us stretched an endless panorama of snow and ice. It was the great ice field rolling up to the horizon in a gigantic arc like the curvature of the earth. Here and there nunataks pierced its virgin sheet with their black spearlike heads. It was a wintry scene, clear and cold, and the wind off the ice seemed to sweep to the very marrow of our bones.

Henry was like an Indian. When traveling he did not speak, but I sensed that the spirit and beauty of the mountains touched him too. It was good to share these feelings and I suddenly realized that was why Henry was here, why he preferred to lead the primitive life of a trapper. It was because he truly loved the wilderness.

After a while, we changed our socks and aired our feet. Since we had not taken off our shoe-pacs all night, it was restful to be rid of them for a while. Then the crusty remains of the much-abused bannock reappeared from the bottom of Henry's pack and we munched on it again. It was so beaten that after sampling it Henry said briefly, "Better get some meat." With that, we started out again to look for a ram, but we kept going too long and darkness descended. While in the open hills, it was not too difficult to travel at night for it was never really pitch-black, but once down among the alders and the long grass looking for a spot to camp, we were in plenty of trouble. We had come into a mighty hollow with the dark mountains frowning down on us from every side. We stumbled and fell and waded an icy stream and at intervals Henry, the silent one, roared angry threats at any brown bear that might be concealed in the willow scrub. An unfortunate porcupine fell victim to Henry's stick. Finally, in the thick blackness of the alders, we set up our canvas and cooked "porky" for supper. We skinned him and roasted the meat on sticks over the embers: a porcupine is reasonably tasty if he has not been feeding too much on spruce. This one went quite well.

In the middle of the night I woke up with a start. Something was wrong. I felt nervous and apprehensive and reached for my rifle, listening intently. The fire was almost out, nothing but the dimmest embers remained, and though the alders hemmed us in on every side a congealing wind crept in off the ice. I had taken off my shoe-pacs and was using them as a pillow. Suddenly some instinctive fright made me rise up in stocking feet. As I did so, rifle in hand, there was a fearful "woof" a few feet away and a bear catapulted off through the alders. My heart pounded. The bear's violent crashings aroused Henry but didn't bother him. He said that bears came into camp quite often when the fire went down. I had no idea whether it was a brown or a black, but whatever he was he was evidently more startled than I. We could hear him smashing through the underbrush for a long way. After that, we built up the fire and chatted for a while, enjoying the recent momentary danger. Then we stretched out again in the glowing warmth and went to sleep.

We had now arrived in the very heart of the hunting country. The time had come to go after the sheep in earnest. Besides, our sourdough was gone and meat was essential. At dawn we started off again. A few hours later we sighted a large band of ewes and lambs with some young rams. Against the dark brown and greens of the valley bottoms their whiteness stood out in bold relief. Henry examined the sheep through the telescope. As he closed it with a series of sharp clicks he said, "We get one." They were headed for a nearby pass. The wind was in our favor so it was a simple matter to post ourselves in their path behind a large boulder.

While waiting, we heard the guttural rasping call of a raven. It was good to hear him and I enjoyed it, for he is a lonely wayfarer, a dweller of the waste spaces of the world. Winter and summer he adheres to his solitary haunts. Where humans move in, the raven moves out. As usual, he was without company, sending his bleak and dismal cry down the valley. It was a cry of solitude, and it imparted to us a strong sense of his own incredible loneliness.

The roaring of the upper air that had been almost continuous now ceased, and a consuming silence filled the entire world around us. After many days of siwashing alone with Henry, I felt the need of other company and the call of the raven together with the sudden startling absence of sound left a pang of emptiness.

But there was little time for such thoughts — the beautiful band of sheep had arrived in range. I selected a fat young ram and shot him through the neck. That night we roasted strips of mutton on hot slabs of rock; the meat with salt added never tasted so good. The weather turned momentarily warmer, and with thick soft sheepskins to stretch out upon, we feasted and slept and slept and feasted and renewed our strength.

In the middle of the night the cold crept in again off the ice sheet. It began to snow, but the flakes melted as soon as they hit the ground. Next morning I saw for the first time an animal that is rarely encountered face to face. He was moving towards us with an ungainly gallop. It was a wolverine — the much-dreaded carcajou — a creature of immense strength and cunning and with such savagery and fighting ability he has been known to stand off a pack of wolves. Though relatively small, rarely weighing more than forty pounds, he is, above all animals, the one most hated by Indians and trappers. The wolverine belongs to the weasel family. He is a fine tree climber and a relentless destroyer, and God pity anything he takes the trail of. Deer, reindeer, and even moose succumb to his attacks. We sat on a rock and watched him come, a bobbing rascal in blackish-brown. As a trapper, Henry wanted me to shoot him; but I refused, for I felt that this was the most fascinating and little-known of all our wonderful predators.* His hunchback gait was awkward and ungainly, lopsided yet tireless. He advanced through all types of terrain without change of pace and with a sense of power that seemed indestructible. His course brought him directly to us and he did not notice our immobile figures until he was ten feet away. Obviously startled, he rose up on his hind legs with paws outstretched and swayed from side to side like a bear undecided whether to charge. Then he tried to make off at top speed and watch us over his shoulder at the same time, running headlong into everything in his path.

For several days thereafter we saw nothing but bear — I counted thirty-five. The ripe blueberries had brought them into the open. Two of them I shot for their fine glossy early fall hides, but bear were not our primary concern. It was the sheep we wanted, and Henry was getting worried. We would look down

* Since the male wolverine occupies a very large hunting area and fights to the death any other male that intrudes on his domain, wolverines are always scarce and in order to avoid extinction need all the protection that man can give.

into some new valley yawning under our feet only to find it empty
or with a few ewes and lambs. Then Henry would say, "Where
sheep go? What happen? Must be someplace." We would travel on
again, deeper and deeper into the hills. Finally Henry decided the
big rams must be in the roughest country beyond Iceberg Lake,
and there we decided to go.

After several hard days combing the many tributary valleys of
Benjamin Creek, we arrived. It was very cold and we spent an uncomfortable night with but a few hours' sleep. Then we climbed
to the lower edge of the crags and followed a sheep trail for about
four miles. Without the trail, walking would have been difficult, for
we were in extremely rough country. As it was, a fall on my left
knee produced such weakness I could not move for half an hour.
The incident made me realize what a tough predicament we would
be in should anything serious happen to either of us.

Once out from under the crags, we climbed a steep gorge. A
stream catapulted over a precipice and near the base of the spray-
ing falls I noticed some moss. It was emerald-green with a soft
fluffy surface that caught the spray in crystal drops. The mist and
spray from the falls settled upon the moss, adding to the drops so
that they changed shapes and rolled about its surface like glittering
quicksilver, seeming to be alive. They looked so much more satisfying than snow water that I lay down and drank. Nearby, and as a
contrast to this soft green, was a bed of scarlet leaves growing
neat upon a rock. In the bright sunlight their brilliance was startling.

On reaching the summit of the range, all fatigue was drained
from us by the sheer exhilaration of the view. It filled the heart
and mind with the magnificence of our world. At our feet lay the
great ice field rising pure white until in the distance the blue sky
joined the snow in a clear-cut line. Sailing out upon this expanse,
two black fortresses of rock rose up like control towers from a

battleship. They were bedded over in the bow with banks of wind-swept snow and their flanks were mantled with dashes of spray.

Vast as it was, this gleaming sheet of snow was but a fractional remnant of the great Wisconsin Ice Age. The mountains we had been hunting had only recently emerged from a deep blanket of ice that had molded most of their contours into smooth and rounded forms with U-shaped valleys and vast stretches of polished striated rock. The indelible imprint of titanic forces marked everything we saw, and the sense of time stretching in both directions made me realize that but one character is universal and everlasting and that is change — endless change — from one form to another, from one condition to another. These mountains which had so recently been buried under the ice sheet, a hostile, frozen land, were now the home of sheep and bear and wolverine, of caribou and moose and fox; a complex community of living creatures. We stood at the knife edge of two worlds, the world of lifeless glacial ice and the throbbing warm-blooded world of mammals.

Turning to the north, I saw a great chain of mountains rising, peak upon peak, into the distance. Farther to the north lay the Benjamin Valley, a pleasant green in the warm sunshine. To the northwest, the great volcanoes of the Alaska Range rose shining into the sun. They stretched endlessly westward into the great Aleutian chain. I looked across another lower range and down into Tustumena Lake, a bed of silver in the dark green moose flats. Directly below us was Iceberg Lake whence we had recently come, and the Kelley Glacier with cataracts of melting waters foaming from its mouth. For a moment their roaring filled the air. It rose and died and rose again on the wind. An eagle floated lazily over the basin. Nearby was a glacial cirque — a vertical gorge of rent and ice-battered rock. This was a glorious spot and I could not help wondering how long it would remain so. Much of the appeal

The Great Kenai ice field.
The numerous bands of sheep were
sighted from the peak at the extreme right.

of this wild land lay in its lonely remoteness. Here were no gasoline fumes or tin cans. No sign as yet of that great killer of the
wilderness, the paved highway.* For wilderness and highways are
an utterly incompatible combination. Where a highway exists,
wilderness is no more.

Henry had become increasingly disturbed for we had not yet
located any large numbers of sheep. However, the slopes facing
the ice sheet were still to be explored, and this we now proceeded
to do as the afternoon shadows gathered. Beneath us the mountainside plunged steeply down and tucked its feet under the glacier.
Glancing over a sharp ledge, we looked down on bands of white
sheep everywhere. They numbered ten to fifty in each band.
Some had gouged out resting places in the talus and lay peacefully
viewing the ice field in the evening sun while others grazed slowly
along, working their way up from lower levels. After many days
of hard work, Henry and I had stumbled on a true hunter's paradise. In this far corner of the mountains the finest rams had secreted
themselves. But as usual, the biggest heads seemed to be in the most
inaccessible spots. One mistake on our part, and all the sheep on
that whole mountainside would be gone. With so many pairs of
far-seeing eyes on the constant alert, the greatest care was necessary to avoid detection. We decided to play it safe. Using a deep
draw in which to remain completely invisible, we dropped down
fifteen hundred feet to find a place to siwash in the alders. If necessary, we would go without a fire and even without supper.
Once in the alders, it was possible to survey the whole mountainside while remaining unseen. From their protection, we looked up
into a great amphitheater, and everywhere sprinkled over it were
white dots. At the foot of some steep ledges were the biggest

* Today the Sterling Highway passes just north of Skilak Lake and swings south-
westward along the edge of Cook Inlet, rendering this whole country easily accessible.

rams. We fastened the telescope on them. They were dream heads that we could only gaze at with hopeless longing. No other wild creature equals the noble appearance of a fine old mountain ram. His arched neck, his battering full-turn horns, gnarled and wrinkled with the passing years, proclaim him a creature that is truly the product of his wild and rockbound home. His very bearing carries a sense of the greatness of the land he inhabits.

We saw many big heads but all of them either so well positioned or so surrounded by lesser sheep that an approach was impossible. As the sun went down, most of the sheep began to change positions, but no opportunity for a stalk arose.

Finally, just as it was getting dark, two fine rams appeared above an outlying spur of alders. Here was our only chance. Following a series of bear trails through the thick underbrush we started after them. For fifteen minutes we climbed laboriously on hands and knees, Henry leading the way, and he managed to gauge it just right for when we reached open ground, there were our rams about a hundred and sixty yards away.

I waited for a full two minutes until I had stopped panting. Then setting the hair-trigger, I fired at the nearest ram, which immediately crumpled up and rolled down the mountain toward us. His companion ran a considerable distance and paused. My hair-trigger went off just as I was drawing a bead and the shot was wild. However, the next time he stopped he too was knocked down.

Before climbing up to them, we looked around. In the dim light I could just see the sheep all over that mountainside on the move — all climbing, seeking escape from the death-dealing explosions that had shattered their peaceful home.

We made a hasty job of the skinning and slid back down through the alders. Though very cold, it was a happy siwash camp that night. There was hard work ahead, packing heads and pelts and bearskins over Rocky Pass and down to Skilak Lake, but our elation was great and we felt deeply relaxed and satisfied.

Our physical objectives had been obtained. We had gotten what we came for — sheep and bear — but more than that, I had learned what real travel is in a still untouched wilderness — real travel pioneer style, as the mountain men of our old West had known it. Night and day in the open through all kinds of weather had made us as tough as a couple of old bears, and we gloried in the feeling of it. Best of all, I had come to sense deeply the ever-changing moods of our great northern frontier, the Alaskan mountains. I had absorbed something of their magnificence and grandeur. A little of their beauty and strength would remain a part of me to the end of my days.

5

The Battle of the Giants

". . . to save wild beauty whole for future ages and keep unmarred the earth's great gestures for our spiritual use."

THE SIWASHING expedition had come to an end and Henry Lucas and I had made ourselves gloriously comfortable in Bill Kaiser's log cabin at the edge of Skilak Lake.

Bill — big, smiling, easygoing — seemed bursting with happiness to have company. He was talkative. On the other hand, I was hungry for reading material and was soon absorbed in some old *Saturday Evening Posts*. Since this was not to Bill's liking, he disappeared down a trap door and emerged with some potent rhubarb wine. As a result, we soon found ourselves engaged in an enthusiastic shooting competition. Naturally, we were all proud of our prowess and at the outset were quite evenly matched, but by the simple expedient of drinking one drink for their two I soon gained an advantage and finally won.

The shooting led to stories of the great bear and particularly of the giant Kenai moose we were about to pursue. The Kenai moose is the largest of his tribe, far larger than his Canadian cousin. His horns not infrequently weigh a hundred pounds and on rare occasions have a spread of six feet. A moose is a very easy animal to shoot, particularly during the rutting season when he seems to be devoid of fear. Thus the prospect of hunting them offered little challenge. However, when Bill began to bet that we could not get a six-foot head I promptly took him on and told Henry I would not pull the trigger on any animal with a spread of less than seventy-two inches. The situation had suddenly changed. Bill had put an entirely different complexion on our hunt, for we had now set a mark for ourselves that would be far from easy to fill.

For the remainder of the day we made preparations for a trip which we planned on a thoroughly luxurious level. In contrast to our mountain adventures, we would have the very best of wilderness homes, an Indian tepee and, in addition, ample food and bedding.

That night I sat up late reading and at dawn we were off again, rowing down a wave-tossed lake toward the great moose flats.

These so-called moose flats are a broad alluvial plain that slopes off gently northwestward from the base of the Kenai Mountains to Cook Inlet. Rivers from the melting snows meander across this incline which, with its potholes and ponds and swamps and eskers, glacial boulders and curving sand hills, bears all the characteristics of a true glacial morain. Except for Bill Kaiser's cabin, there was no human habitation in the vast stretch of land between Kenai Lake and the tiny Indian village of Kenai where the Kenai River empties into Cook Inlet.

At noon we landed on a sandy beach. The country had been burned over years before and presented a bleak and dismal aspect. However, the great burn brought into being a young and succulent growth of willow and quaking aspen that produced the largest moose in the world.

We had heavy loads to pack over the ten-mile portage to the Funny River, where we planned to camp. The trail was blazed with bleached moose horns which over the years had been hung on the dead trees to mark the way. Underfoot it was firm from long years of travel by man and beast.

Now that we had left the mountains, I was back in my woods clothes. For comfort in the bush, nothing is more important than proper footgear, and I had the very best — knee-high Eskimo sealskin boots and smoke-tanned moccasins lashed tight around the ankles. Over my underwear I wore flannel pajamas, the legs of which emerged under the trousers and hung loose and tattered over the skin boots so as to drain off the water from the wet grass on the outside. A sloppy sight, perhaps, but a perfect combination.

While we were packing in, a swollen-necked young bull disputed our passage, giving evidence the rut was on. He walked to within thirty feet of us, the hair on his spine standing on end. We yelled at him again and again and in abusive language ordered him out of there. We even threw stones, all to no avail. Finally we made a big detour and left him where he was.*

In the late afternoon, a white moose horn emerging from a pile of debris caught my eye. A brown bear had killed a big moose, as they often do during rutting when an old bull is sleeping against a tree. The bear had eaten his fill and then tried to cache the carcass. Sticks, stones, moss and grass had been scratched up and heaped over the remains — all but one horn.

It was a dismal place, this kill lair of the brown bear. As I thought of the tremendous strength and size of these giant moose, I tried to imagine how even a great bear could lay him low — what power to break a neck so swollen for battle! Henry told me he had once seen a brownie in pursuit, a thundering onslaught at a running moose. They had disappeared behind some spruce, so he did

* The behavior of this animal was quite different from that of the tame moose so often seen near Alaskan towns.

not see the kill, but when he arrived the bull was dead — his neck broken.

For a week Henry and I hunted hard. We had breakfast at day-break and started immediately afterwards, with a bit of the inevitable sourdough bannock to munch on at noon. Every day we saw moose that were too many to count, some with large heads, but each day we returned empty-handed, exhausted by the soft mus-keg and endless stretches of spruce that lay in littered confusion all over the land like piles of jackstraws. Nothing we saw even remotely approached horns with a six-foot spread.

The black flies were bad whenever the wind dropped and for these demons we were well prepared with Stockholm tar spiced with citronella. What a joy it was to smear on this revolting mess! It made Henry darker than a Cree and I was not far behind.

Henry was a man dedicated to his task. He spoke little; even under cross-questioning his answers were brief and to the point. Rarely did he permit himself an anecdote.

Only once do I remember a question of abstract curiosity. Our tepee was pitched in a thick sheltering grove of young spruce at the edge of Funny River. I had gone out to cut some more wood, for there is nothing more pleasant than a bright fire on a frosty autumn night. As I returned with an armful and saw the tepee glowing with warm flame, it seemed that no other shelter in the world makes such an inviting home on a cold wilderness night. It is nest and safety and comfort and warmth all combined. Outside is hostile darkness and perhaps storm and wind, rain or snow. In-side is peace and security — brightly lit and toasting, with an end-less draft of pure air that comes in the bottom and carries the smoke out the top but which, because of the inside flap, never touches the occupants.

I had dumped my load just inside the entrance and was seated on a raised bedding of logs and boughs while Henry cooked more

[60]

of his execrable bannocks. After he was through cooking, I added some wood to the flame, building the fire up Indian style so that we would have plenty of light while eating. In the ever-moving flames playing on his strong features, Henry's keen, mobile face was a study; sensitive but with repose and nobility, a face that somehow seemed to belong to this stupendous land. A tin plate was on my knees and I was spreading a thick layer of jam to soften some hard-fried bannock when Henry suddenly turned to me and said, "Douglas, what is fire?" I was surprised and flattered that he should have turned to me with a question that primitive man, forever struggling against darkness and cold, must have asked himself for countless eons. For a long time I gazed into the flames, not knowing how to answer. Finally I murmured, "Henry, fire is energy in the process of being released." This was a tough one, but I added, "Energy is latent in all things — even a piece of rock." I knew he would not understand the word "latent" but I went ahead anyway. "When you set fire to wood, the energy in that piece of wood is released in the form of heat and light." I didn't know what more to add. I felt inadequate to the occasion and failed completely to bridge the gap in our backgrounds. Henry lapsed into silence and disappointment. I wished somehow that I could have answered adequately a question that this lone trapper must have pondered many times.

The following day we were up and off as usual, striding over strewn jackstraws, sinking deep in the soggy lowland moss, and scouting endlessly from every high ridge with the telescope. We worked westward into lower country and at about two o'clock we suddenly saw our moose, his white horns looming large against the brown bracken on which he was lying. Two cows stood guard nearby. He was about three quarters of a mile away on an open ridge facing our way. There was no chance of getting any closer unseen, for between us was a broad expanse of swamp grass. Henry and I were stretched on our stomachs among the prone spruce poles. For a full five minutes Henry studied him through my thirty-power hunting scope. Then he said, "Maybe seventy-two inches — too far be sure." He had a measuring tape in his pocket and, still lying low, he marked out seventy-two inches on a dead spruce log with his hunting knife so as to fix the width in his mind.

We lay there from 2:30 to 4:15 and during all that time the great bull never moved. Henry looked at him through the scope. I looked at him, then Henry looked again. He was in love with my scope and hated to yield it to me even for a few minutes. Finally he said, "I think him seventy-two inches. We try get him." The sun came out for a while. The wind dropped and the black flies were at us. With the cows still standing guard, we could not move, but now that Henry had given his verdict we were filled with excitement.

At 4:15 we heard some grunting beyond the ridge. Evidently a challenge, for the bull got to his feet and strode away from us over the ridge. That was our chance.

As soon as he and his two cows were out of sight, we jumped up and sprinted across the intervening marshy ground. Long before we reached the ridge where he had been lying I was panting hard, but Henry gave me no respite. We pushed on to the top of the ridge, where we found ourselves confronted with a rare spectacle. The terrain before us was like a stadium closed in by ridges sloping down to the level ground in the center. The bronze-brackened ridges were covered here and there with stands of golden aspen shimmering in the late evening light. Moose were everywhere — young and old, cows and bulls, some alone, some in groups. We started to count them but soon gave up and concluded later there were at least three hundred in sight.

We looked for our big bull with his light-colored flat-lying horns, but he was nowhere to be seen. Then we noticed to our right, at the upper end of the amphitheater, another giant moose. He was standing alone with ears erect, looking out over the floor of the arena. Except for size and magnificence of appearance, he was totally different from the animal we were after; his horns were dark with enormous upturned palms and a forest of brow tines as big as a man's forearm.

He stood, motionless and alone, king of the herd. His very aspect carried such defiance we instinctively felt this was a young animal at the peak of his power. Then he grunted a deep-throated challenge again and again, all the time looking fixedly toward the open end of the low encircling hills at something we could not see. Finally came the answer and a moment later our white-horned giant strode magnificently into view and stood there, head high, accepting the challenge. Immediately Henry said, "Shoot! Shoot!" I was still panting from hard running and, though utterly galvanized by the entire situation, I fired and, happily, missed. The roar of the 9.5 mm. Mannlicher reverberated through the amphitheater but even against the silence the explosion had no more effect on that gathering than the buzz of a mosquito. Not one animal moved away, they did not so much as look in our direction.

Instead, they seemed to be watching the two giants on the floor of the arena as though knowing something important was about to take place. Again Henry said, "Shoot!" "No," I said, "let's watch." Henry could stand it no longer. "Come," he whispered, and started to move down the slope.

The two bulls were a hundred yards apart but they had marked each other as leaders and were slowly advancing for battle. Moose were on all sides as we sped down the slope. One cow was so close I could see the erect hair on her spine and thought she was certain to charge.

At the bottom of the slope was a log where we rested. We were now not more than fifty yards from the center of the arena. On

[63]

the far ridge and to the right were several dark congregations of animals and I noticed some of the younger bulls were taking advantage of the preoccupation of their seniors.

I had the feeling we had invaded the privacy of the most primitive and prehistoric of all the deer family — nothing was to be allowed to disturb it. We might as well have been on Mars, so little did our presence influence the behavior of this primeval gathering.

The two bulls were closing the gap between them. But there was no haste, no sudden rush. Their strides were slow and measured and dignified. Heads down, their necks were arched and bulging. They moved with great deliberation, sweeping their heavily pronged antlers ponderously from side to side with each forward step. I knew their eyes were bloodshot with angry fire.

These animals were no alien species. The attack was not to devour. Yet the will of each to destroy the other was deep in their blood. It was an urge as basic as sex itself — a part of the aggressive drive to dominate.

The two great bulls were now within a few yards of each other. Theirs had been a noble advance. Neither animal had in the slightest degree hastened the majestic rhythm of his forward march. Their great heads and enormously swollen necks were still swinging heavily when I became aware of an almost stifling stillness that fell abruptly on that wild assembly. It was like the final moment of quiet before the storm. I glanced at the surrounding hills. Not a single moose was moving. All stood stock-still, gazing down on the arena. We were witnessing something out of the dim and distant past — something not many civilized men would ever witness.

And then it happened: the resounding clash of antlers backed with nearly fifteen hundred pounds of taut sinew and bursting muscle. The mighty forward surge of two great beasts came to a dead stop. For seconds the contenders were so equal the battle seemed motionless — nothing but straining muscles thrusting forward against equal thrust. Forelegs were tucked under the belly, hindlegs braced far back.

At that moment I noticed for the first time the fighting advantage any moose has if his eyes and forehead are well protected with a fine array of brow tines. The younger bull had that protection. The older bull did not have it and soon blood was dripping from his head. For a moment he drew back slightly and then plunged forward again with all his might. The younger animal reeled backward a few paces and I could see how careful he was not to expose his flank to battering horns whose prongs could have driven into his lungs or pierced his intestines.

When moose fight it is often to the death and woe betide any animal that falls, for then the victor uses his sharp hoofs to cut his adversary to shreds. Now the bulls broke apart and as they did so the old one reared and slashed out with his foreleg, striking the young bull's chest.

It was a lightning play that I had seen once before when a spikehorn moose struck at a wolf. The old fellow drew blood but immediately the young bull closed again and there was a great straining back and forth; the soft earth became chewed and muddy as they circled and slashed, seeking some momentary advantage.

Yet in all the maneuvering and hard fighting, there was something about the old bull's behavior that was never completely convincing. Perhaps, I thought, he sensed his age and limitations. Perhaps he counted on his faithful cows to stand by him even in defeat, but whatever it was, I could not help feeling that here was a gladiator — fighting, defending, but without the determination to kill. Several times he broke off the engagement as if to say "enough is enough," and each time the younger bull came at him again harder than ever.

It is rare, I imagine, that animals so committed quit the field of battle. Yet sometimes an old veteran may decide to do just that. But how was it to be done? With horns thrusting against him, how could he escape? How turn aside without exposing his flank to impalement? But his was a beautiful maneuver, executed with consummate skill. The old bull broke loose the grip of horns, reared high like a stallion about to strike, and then with smooth, almost unbelievable agility, turned in the air and fell back to earth in full retreat, exposing only his rear end for a brief moment. The very instant he landed, he trotted off with head still high. Meantime, the victor stood his ground, not deigning to pursue. The hot breath was streaming from his nostrils. He called several times but no answer came. Among all the moose in that amphitheater there was no movement. I, too, felt immobilized. Now Henry came to his senses as if pulled out of a dream. "Come," he said. It was difficult to rise but when I did, I looked once more over that arena. The victor still stood like a statue even though some of the moose on the surrounding hills were beginning to move again. "Come," repeated Henry. We took off across the field of battle right under the nose of the victor. Ran as hard as we could go up the ridge and out of the stadium onto a broad open area of aspen and spruce. For more than half a mile we ran — when Henry suddenly stopped and pointed. There directly ahead, about a hundred and fifty yards away, was our bull. He was facing away from us, an impossible shot. The two cows, still with him, had seen us, for their ears were up and both had swung around toward us.

When you have been pursuing an animal for a long time and finally catch up with him in a situation where you are certain of a kill, the thought often comes over you to let him go and sometimes you do, for killing then seems wrong. But now, I had no qualms; I wanted that spread more than I had ever wanted anything before. The whole situation had built up to a final climax. The hunt had gotten into our blood. Henry had never secured a

Burden with seventy-two-inch moose head on the edge of Skilak Lake.

seventy-two-inch head. This might be his record as well as mine.

I was still panting hard when I dropped on one knee and moved the safety catch with my thumb. At that moment the old bull swung his head to see what the cows were looking at. In doing so, he exposed his vulnerable neck. I have missed many easy shots in my day. But though this one was far from easy and by all odds the most important shot of my early years, the bullet went home and the big bull fell and never moved again. When we reached him, he was dead. What a magnificent animal! For a moment I knew remorse at destroying a creature so fine. Yet the bull was past his prime, was on the decline, and I consoled myself with the thought that he probably had not had too long to live. Now he was down, his fine white horns shone against the bracken, and there was Henry dancing around him. He pulled the measuring tape from his pocket, fluttered it in the breeze, then jigged about as if daring himself to take the measurement.

Finally Henry sidled up to the wide-spread antlers, placed the end of the tape on the widest prong and asked me to hold it there. Then he ran it out across the total spread and held it for a while without daring to look. He had his thumb at the exact measurement and when at last he took courage and glanced at it, the reading was exactly seventy-two inches. With that my silent Henry burst into cheers and fairly jumped for joy.

We had won our bet and attained our goal and eventually these horns were duly recorded in *Records of Big Game*.

It was a tough trip home in the dark but by ten the next morning we were back with our bull. It was warm and the raw skin, meat, and horns attracted clouds of flies. But I was so proud of my animal I decided to portage the horns myself, no matter what they weighed or how bad the flies, and this I did with packboard and tumpline all the way to camp and then another ten miles to Skilak Lake.

Then came a trip down the foaming rapids to the little Indian village of Kenai. Shooting rapids is always exciting and this wild ride made a glorious end to our adventures. Henry and I had gotten along beautifully. Never had there been the slightest misunderstanding between us. He was a lone-wolf type and I had enough of those feelings myself to have a wonderful sense of kinship with him. Endless days of tough terrain, bad food, and often extreme physical exhaustion measure a man as few things do, and Henry had been grand. It was hard to imagine that we would not meet again.

I wanted to express my appreciation with something other than cash. As we clambered together down the loam cliff from Kenai village and mingled with the Indians boarding a launch for the run up Cook Inlet to Anchorage, I had a sudden inspiration. Digging into my packsack, I pulled out my beautiful telescope and said, "Henry, this is yours. I want you to have it. I will enjoy thinking of you using it." His answering smile was marvelous to see, and when he took the telescope I sensed a certain mistiness in his eyes that told me his heart was happy. He tried to speak, "Douglas . . ." and then he turned and walked away without another word. At the top of the bank he stopped. A moment later, the deep throbbing of a heavy-duty engine shattered the quiet and I was off in an unseaworthy launch overloaded with Indians, waving good-by to a wonderful guide by the name of Henry Lucas.*

* According to the late J. Watson Webb, Henry Lucas later became known as one of the two best guides in Alaska. While with Mr. Webb, Henry suffered a ruptured appendix in a camp and, though it was three days before he reached a hospital in Anchorage, he survived a desperate attack of peritonitis which would certainly have killed a lesser man.

Note: Oil has recently been struck on the moose flats of the Kenai. Another magnificent wilderness will thus succumb to the advance of civilization.

6

The Still Hunter

"What is the value of solitude?
— of peace, of light, of silence?"

IT WAS the 12th of November. The day was moderately
sunny with a slight breeze out of the south and the temperature about 36°. I started out with a strong sense of excitement and
a longing to melt into the forest and become a part of it. That
is the feeling a forest lover always has when going alone into the
woods. But any realization of it requires a transformation from
civilized conditioning that does not come easily. It takes plenty of
time to develop a sense of harmony with the wilderness. At first
my steps were awkward and hurried, my eyes didn't seem to focus
well on distant objects, and I felt very much the noisy and jarring
intruder I actually was.

For a while I sat on a log and listened to the wild shrieking of
the everlasting blue jay. Then a wandering band of twittering
chickadees came flitting all around in a most sociable way. Gradually the soothing feel of the Adirondack woods and all the familiar sounds and smells began to quiet an excess of enthusiasm so
that imperceptibly there was an increased awareness of every-

[69]

thing around me, and I felt at last that in spirit, at least, I was beginning to blend with my surroundings.

It was an area I had not visited since childhood — the marshy district northeast of Flatfish Pond in the heart of Whitney Park. The country was typical of the Adirondack Mountains — alternating spruce swamps and high ridges having a dominant northeast-southwest trend. In the ten thousand years after the icecap receded, the sandy soil developed a growth of truly magnificent white pine. Except along the lake shores, these monsters of the past have now been lumbered off, and forest regeneration consists mostly of spruce in the lowland and young beech on the hardwood ridges. Since beech buds are undesirable as deer food, it is natural, with such a large deer population, that this species should be selectively favored in young stands.

A really big buck was known to make his home in this section, so I kept my little .30-.30 Winchester in the crook of my left arm and constantly at the ready. However, hard crunchy snow made it impossible to travel quietly except on the slopes facing the sun where the snow had melted off, so I headed across the swamp in search of a more favorable exposure.

In the course of a large circle, only three does were disturbed, and all three heard me before I saw them, so difficult was it to travel silently. Finally at dusk, after three hours of slow motion through the woods, I found myself climbing the hardwood ridge toward the old telephone line to Craig's camp. It was then that things began to happen.

First of all, I caught a glimpse of a deer moving ahead of me. It was a buck. He had not seen me and was only slightly suspicious. I followed him with extreme care and found him hiding behind the roots of a big blowdown. Only his head was visible, projecting from behind the upturned roots. With my field glasses I counted the points — four on each side. I waited to see what he would do.

Evidently curiosity consumed him, for he soon strode out in full view less than fifty yards away. Since it was rapidly getting dark, I was anxious to have him move out of the way without alerting the whole forest, and this I accomplished by making some low whistling noises until he became sufficiently wary to ease quietly on up into the hardwood.

After he had gone, I circled on down an old lumber road toward the marshy bottom. I did not see a spikehorn that was standing in the road at the other side of a little rolling rise until, with a sharp whistle, he bounded off.

It was obvious, from these two encounters plus the innumerable signs, that I had come into a pocket of game and that deer were now very much on the move. Accordingly, I proceeded with great caution, stopping after every two steps to see what news the forest had to tell.

At this point, the surface of the old lumber road changed to sand. The sand had thawed and was so moist and soft as to make walking without a sound possible. I had just arrived noiselessly at a point in this sandy bottomland where four old lumber roads meet when I heard a twig snap in the spruce thicket toward Little Flatfish. Immediately I moved beyond a white boulder that stood in the middle of the road and crouched behind it. A moment later, an eight-point buck emerged from the spruce thicket and came right down the road toward me. I let him advance to within fifteen feet of me, when I made a loud "psst." He halted abruptly, a fine animal in superb condition, sleek and fat, his dark winter coat unmarred by any signs of fighting. Obviously, he could not make me out, still as I was, and although he reacted with a violent quiver all through his body each time I repeated the sound, I made it at least a half-dozen times at varying intervals before he finally decided to retire. This he did by forking up the very branch I had come down.

Here again there is a little rolling rise, and as he proudly walked from view with no sign of haste, I stood up from behind my rock to watch him. As I did so I saw, about a hundred yards away in the dwindling light, another larger buck advancing in my direction. As the two bucks neared each other the new arrival curled his neck down in a threatening manner as if he were about to charge, whereupon the eight-pointer left the road with a quick bound and disappeared into the heavy spruce thicket.

The big fellow continued to advance toward me. Again I sank down behind the rock and let him come up until he too was but a few feet away. Once again I made a loud "psst," and he too stopped with the same resulting noticeable quiver that flashed through his body. He was a magnificent ten-pointer with a very black muzzle and head. He kept reaching his nose out trying to sniff me, as if daring himself to advance farther. It must have been a full three minutes — and only after repeated "psst" noises on my part — before he slowly turned and, with that stiff-legged and rather embarrassed and caught-out look, quartered off up the same road the first buck had come down. His departure was no faster than his arrival.

November 13th. The big buck had been seen by George Cary in the esker country (a glacial formation of low sand hills). George said he was really big, a twelve-pointer surely. So Sonny Whitney with his usual generosity suggested that I have a go at him.

The day was still and mild with scarcely a sign of a breeze. I started early, and after I had gone for about half a mile down the old lumber road that leads into the heart of this country, it became increasingly and unpleasantly obvious that I was a target for all eyes. The lumber road was open and exposed, and no matter how carefully I advanced, I felt that I stood out like a sore thumb. Instead of being in the forest looking out, I seemed to be outside trying to look in. Therefore, to correct this situation, I picked the first good-looking deer runway and plunged into the woods to my left, moving at approximately right angles to my course until a good travel runway led off in the right direction.

The runway was overgrown with young saplings from two to three feet high, all cropped off at the top. These shoots were so stiff and snapped back so violently against my knee-high sealskin boots that in order to move quietly it was necessary to lean over and hold them off with my hand. As a result, progress for a while was very slow.

I had proceeded tediously in this way for about an eighth of a mile when the runway merged into another long-disused lumber road, which was covered with snow. A little farther on, another branch road came in at a sharp angle from the right. The character of the forest had now changed. On all sides it consisted of dense young spruce from twenty to thirty feet high. Through this tangle it would have been impossible to move quietly, so there was no choice but to stay in the road.

For a very long time I stood and listened, hoping to get some clue as to whether it would be advisable to take the right fork or the left. Finally, patience was rewarded. About a hundred yards away directly ahead in the thick spruce, a twig was broken by a large animal. Then another twig snapped a little farther to the right, and still another. I knew now I was close to a large herd of deer and that in all probability the big buck was with them. Luck was with me. The game had been located. It now remained to contrive a successful stalk. But my position was difficult. A lot of problems had to be overcome, and for the moment I could not determine how best to deal with them.

From the sounds I had heard it was my impression that the deer were quartering away from me. This meant that if I was ever to catch sight of them, I would have to move ahead myself.

I attempted an advance down the noisy snow-covered road. A

lot of grass was sticking up through the snow and I tried bending it over with my foot to see if this wouldn't muffle the inevitable crunch of each step. It helped, but not too much. When you are trying so hard to move silently and yet cannot fail to make a noise, it is exasperating. I had proceeded in this way a few steps at a time to a point just short of where the roads forked when suddenly two grouse that I had neither seen nor heard thundered off in the direction of the deer, their wings clicking against the brush as they dove through the heavy spruce cover. I damned those grouse, thinking to myself, "That does it — what chance have I now!"

In face of this adversity, my only hope was to wait it out. Fortunately, the temperature was so balmy it was possible to stand absolutely still in perfect comfort.

In such a situation time is hard to judge but my guess is that at least twenty minutes elapsed before the deer started to move again. When they did move, I stayed right where I was for quite a while, not wishing to run the risk of alerting them again too quickly. However, when the slight sounds of their movement indicated they were getting too far ahead, I was again forced to advance myself. I moved now by a special technique — a couple of quick tiptoe steps and then a long pause, followed by another couple of quick steps and another long pause. As I turned a corner into the right-hand fork, there, to my dismay, directly ahead was a red squirrel sitting on a stump eating nuts. He had been eating so quietly I had not heard him. At sight of me he promptly let loose a most vociferous scolding — thereby telling the forest a second time that an intruder had moved in. This was too much.

Straight ahead on the right-hand edge of the road was a very large white birch growing right up next to the thick spruce. Beyond this tree and to the left of it an open, heavily lumbered sand hill could be partly seen. If I stepped out around the birch, I would come into full view of any animal on that hillside; and although all the sounds of game had come from the heavy spruce thicket on my left, it was possible that one or more deer well ahead of the others might already have reached the open ground. So I leaned over as far as I could without actually taking a step and tried to look around the left-hand side of the tree. For a long time I examined the hillside carefully. There were many blowdowns with the great jagged circle of roots in the air; there were quite a few small young spruce; there was the usual low brown brush and patches of snow; but for the most part the hillside lay bare. Not a thing was to be seen. Finally, after the most intense scrutiny, I looked back at the ground and picked out two good spots for my next two steps. Then I took them as if walking on eggs, and looked up again.

And there HE was — about eighty yards away, well up on the hill and staring straight at me, head on. Unmistakably it was the big buck. The fine rack of horns offered convincing evidence he was a twelve-pointer. Somehow, his whole expression and the extreme concentration of his gaze telegraphed the information that I had not a moment to lose. No sooner had I seen him than I started to raise my rifle, but it was not yet halfway to my shoulder when he dug out of there like an explosion. In two jumps he was out of sight.

As soon as the big buck crashed away, the forest started to break loose on all sides. How many deer went out of that spruce thicket I don't know. There must have been seven or eight of them at least. In the midst of the noise, I ran ahead to where the thicket ended. I could now see well up to the left, and there was a spike-horn, still standing and evidently frightfully curious to know what the fuss was all about. Then I climbed up to where the big buck had stood, sat on a log, and looked back to appraise the wonderful view he had had of me when I stepped out from behind that birch tree. While I was sitting there contemplating my failure, the two grouse that had flushed from the spruce thicket emerged from the deer cover and walked along a log.

After a while, I started on the trail of the buck, wondering how far he had gone. His big jumps could be seen plainly, even on the hard ground. At the end of another quarter of a mile, where the high sand esker terminates and breaks down into a little valley, some particularly loud pecking on a tree attracted my attention and then I saw one of the great pileated woodpeckers, the famous "cock of the woods." Promptly on sight of me he started screeching and, with brilliant red crest erect, flew off hollering to the whole forest. At the same time, several blue jays started screaming, and in the midst of this din came the sudden heavy crashings of the big buck as he bolted away. Evidently he had stopped to see if he was being followed. It seemed that morning as if the whole forest were conspiring against me. Further pursuit was now hopeless, so I headed back for camp.

November 14th was the last day. It was warm, overcast, and absolutely still. Not the slightest rustle stirred the dry leaves on the beech trees. All traces of snow had disappeared and it was quiet underfoot. With no wind to carry scent, one direction was as good as another. However, the first thing to be learned was whether the deer were in the swamps or up on high ground. So I left the main lumber road and headed down an old skidway toward a big black spruce marsh. Some grass had grown up along the skidway, and since it was still wet at this early hour one could move in almost complete silence.

Nevertheless, it took about ten minutes to cover the first hundred yards. Fifty yards farther on near the bottom of the skidway and on either side was a steep bank about eight feet high. From behind the bank on the right came a very slight sound. It was made by a moving animal. I crouched down and waited. It was a long wait. Finally, a small doe stepped out behind the bank and looked straight at me without seeing me. Slowly she worked her way across the skidway till she disappeared behind the bank to the left.

After making certain she was not followed by a buck, I continued to move forward very slowly. Almost immediately a very small invisible twig in the grass broke under my weight. The sound seemed so slight it could not carry twenty yards. So I did not pause. At the next step, it happened again. Immediately the doe bounded from behind the bank and raced into the black spruce. She was so alarmed she did not stop to satisfy her curiosity. At three hundred yards she reappeared, still leaping away. How was it that so slight a sound had caused such fear? It was as if wolves were about.

Investigation proved the swamp to be empty, so I sought higher land. For several hours I saw nothing.

Toward midmorning I was beginning to tire of caution. A small travel runway led up a slope. Near the top a spruce blow-down crossed the runway. It was too high to swing a leg over without scraping the bark. However, since it was not yet possible to see down the far side of the ridge, I forced myself to be careful. Setting the rifle to one side and using both hands to hoist each leg in turn clear of the rough bark, it was possible to cross the obstacle without a sound. Then I stood stock-still and listened. My care was rewarded. Almost immediately a slight snap cut through the stillness.

It came from behind the big circle of roots that rose up directly in front of me. A tree had fallen away from where I was standing, and the woven mesh of roots had peeled all the soil from the underlying rock. On this smooth surface one could take three or four quick steps to the edge of the barrier and look around it. This I did, moving to the right edge. There was nothing in sight — and for good reason, because a moment later a fine-looking, very black-coated buck stepped around the left edge. Had I moved to the left rather than to the right, I would have met him face to face within three feet. Even so, he was not more than twelve feet away when he came to a stop and stared for a full minute at my frozen figure. He was a six-pointer and, judging from his breathing, he was traveling hard in search of a doe. I could not shoot him and very soon he trudged on in a businesslike manner, totally unaware he had been so close to man.

Now for a long time the woods seemed empty of game. It was the middle of a warm November day and the deer were probably lying up. So, by way of diversion, I decided to cross over into another valley where I had never been before. The intervening ridge turned out to be quite a marvelous spot — fine, open hardwood; sheer big cliffs of smooth rock carved by the ice; and here and there small clumps of spruce providing ideal hiding spots for deer. I remembered how very cautious Archie Miller used to be when advancing toward an evergreen thicket in the midst of hardwood; so with greatest care I now worked slowly upward. I saw no game on the way but I was aware again and again of a slight movement out of the corner of my eye. Sometimes it turned out to be a bird hopping to another branch, but more often it was the flitting of little white wood moths that seemed to fill the forest on this warm day. Flights of chickadees, some juncos, many woodpeckers, and of course the ever-entertaining blue jay passed by as I worked my slow way up to the top.

A well-used runway descended into the valley beyond. This new valley was of a different character — dark and somber, and the floor of it was covered with spruce. A feeling of strangeness, almost of hostility, was in the air. The valley was filled with silence. It put me on edge, and the noise I made moving in was a jarring note in the midday peace and stillness. And where the remaining unlumbered hardwood giants still stood, magnificent in their slow decay, with wind-blown fragmented tops wide-spaced over the carpeted floor, they spoke of time — not in weeks and years but in centuries. For these same giants, now so withered and rough and noble with age and still fighting out the remaining years of their existence, had once looked down on stalking wolf and mountain lion, on moose and painted Iroquois.

Part way across the bottom of the valley, I rested by a black and sluggish stream that sifted slowly by between soft banks of deep moss. My thoughts became increasingly disturbed and apprehensive. I remembered that only a year before there had been a certain long wet night alone in the hardwood with no supper, huddling a smoldering flame. I began to wonder if I would get lost. And then there was another thought which said: "There is something good about being alone at night with nothing in a great forest. A little circle of warm firelight surrounded by a barrier of black cold wilderness accents deeply your own puny size and vulnerability. The silence moves in close and there comes a deep relaxing sense of kinship with an infinitude of remote ancestors who huddled thus around fires generation after generation through the lengthy dawn of man."

Gradually the mood changed. Tension vanished and I sat in suspended animation — daydreaming in the perfect loneliness while, drop by drop, time slid gently by like the slow and even current of the stream.

The decision to move does not come abruptly. You think about it vaguely, wondering if you are starting too early or too late, and a lot of the time you don't think about it at all. Then suddenly you find yourself on your feet as though some outer force had taken the matter in hand. I looked through the barrel of my rifle, checked the ammunition, and tightened my belt. The time for action had arrived.

My skin boots sank deep into the soft, silent moss. The swamp spruce stood so close and thick that even on the runway twigs were broken by shoulders and hips too big to worm through.

This was not good and repeatedly I stood still for a long time, hoping for some news from the forest. Finally it came, ever so faintly, just one single very slight blat from the steep ridge that rose on the far side of the swamp. Nevertheless it was unmistakable: the signal of a buck calling to a doe.

I moved slowly and carefully off at right angles up the marsh, trying all the time to maintain an exact sense of the location of that single blat. The forest was stillness itself. The closer I got to the critical area, the slower my steps became. It was very exciting, creeping up. Then, with unexpected suddenness, there they were. I came upon them so close it was hard to believe we had not heard each other. They were just below me behind some fallen trees. The doe showed herself first. She was very calm but the buck seemed agitated. He was nervous, on his toes, ready to flee. He was a six-pointer. They seemed a happy family. It was fun to watch them but difficult to move without precipitating an alarm. Since one never knows what may be ahead, it is always best, whenever possible, to leave game undisturbed; so I retired as cautiously as I had come.

Once again for a long time the woods seemed to be dead — not a movement, not a sound. As I stood, wondering what next to do, the thought of the big buck filled my mind. The esker country where he lived was now not far away. If I traveled hard, I could get there in time for one final hunt. The very thought made my legs fly. By four o'clock I arrived and was working very carefully up a rather open ridge. It was magnificent deer country. The time of day was ideal and there was plenty of fresh sign. I advanced very slowly, holding every piece of brush to one side and studying each step so as to reduce sound to an absolute minimum, yet not forgetting to look long and carefully between steps at all the terrain.

Suddenly I saw a small doe about sixty yards away. Though still lying down and facing me, she had not seen me. This presented a difficult problem. How could the doe be made to move without alerting the forest? I advanced one step, thereby revealing my head. Instantly she got to her feet and stared at me. I did not move again and finally, after a few nervous flicks of the tail, she daintily moved off. When she disappeared, I resumed my advance at right angles to the course she had taken.

Since sound does not travel well over a ridge, I now proceeded much more rapidly up the east side to the summit. The west face was quite open. Not a thing was to be seen. Beyond this was another ridge, thickly covered with spruce and hemlock. In the bottom was an old log road overgrown with grass. The light had become dim and a deep stillness now lay on the land. Just as it is difficult to see well from an open lake into the deep woods, and easy to see from the woods any movement on an open lake, so does this matter of comparative light often determine who sees who first, the hunter or the hunted. Nevertheless it was a magnificent place for deer.

I crept down the open hill to a big runway. Starting along it, I found myself too high to see well into the black timber across the way. So I retraced my steps until a series of jackstraw logs offered silent access to the old lumber road below. Now was my final chance. Two or three careful steps were followed by the inevitable searching pause. Another two steps and another two, and still another. If only I could advance like a shadow. It was as if my whole being were in my eyes. Presently there was one slight movement — the nervous flick of a deer's tail deep in the evergreens. It was a doe. In one slithering dark brown glide she slid over a log and was gone. Had she seen me?

For a very long time I waited motionless in a motionless world. And yet there was a certain movement in it. It was the slow movement of darkness sinking into the forest. You could feel it descending.

Then out of that gathering gloom it suddenly happened. An enormous buck head literally popped into view as if by magic about eighty yards away. He was in an opening beyond the hemlocks, and the waning light shone full on his gleaming white-tipped antlers. So intently did he look straight at me that I felt sure he must see me. I dared not move. There was so much intervening brush it was impossible to count the points. Only his horns shining through the fading light were clearly visible. Then they disappeared.

Very slowly I sank onto my right knee. My left elbow fell on the other knee. Automatically, the sights came into line. Now my heart stood still, for I began to feel I had seen the big buck. But I was not yet sure. Was he really as big as he looked? Would he work out of that heavy cover before the light was hopelessly gone? For just a fraction of a second the horns showed again. Seen through the deep darkness of the hemlocks they were startlingly large and bright. Then suddenly I knew that it was he. He was in such a rough spot, such a heavy tangle of brush and fallen trees, that there was little chance of a better view. It was a sporting shot, and I decided to take it if ever those horns appeared again. Now the decision was made, my heart was pounding with excitement. In full readiness I aimed where I thought his horns would show. It was a long, long wait. Had he followed the doe and slipped away? Then like a flash the moment arrived. Up came his head, looking right at me. From the way it was turned, one could guess where the shoulder was. I drew a bead, let it drop low and to the left, and fired. Death struck instantly. He never knew what hit him. Success had come in a matter of seconds — not from a long and careful stalk, not because he had been outwitted, not because he had made a mistake, but purely from the luck of a chance encounter in the very last few moments of fading light.

When I came up to him, there was the strong smell of deer and blood. The very symbol of pride and grace and beauty had collapsed into a crumpled and bleeding form. To witness this sudden degeneration is always the fate of the successful hunter. It is a desperate thing to love wild animals and yet to kill them.

If the deer hunter needs any solace for his act, he can recall the well-founded claim of the biologists that where there are no wolves and no mountain lions, man should harvest 25 to 35 percent of the deer crop each year in order to prevent starvation on the winter range. That is at least one answer to the oft-repeated question: How can you bear to shoot such a beautiful creature?

"And where man has killed the last wolf and mountain
    lion the
deer increase until they eat the forest bare and begin
    to die
of hunger, weakness and disease."

PART TWO

7

On the Sino-Mongolian Frontier

"In China, centuries ago, hungry multitudes stripped bare the hills of the North. Down gullies yearly more cavernous floods poured . . ."

THE RAIL that brought us to the station of Kwei-hua-cheng pinched out into the dust and loess banks some miles beyond. It was frontier country — bleak, primitive and forbidding. But there was a fascination about it that made us want to cross the western mountains and explore the other side. To the eastward in the near distance, the ancient walls of Kwei-hua-cheng raised their glowering battlements against a stormy evening sky. A camel caravan, fresh from the Gobi Desert, trailed across the barren flats toward the city. The dust from their padded feet drifting over the plain blanketed a portion of the crenelated walls.

It was 1922. Mason Sears and I had just graduated from college and were seeking adventure in the Far East. Roy Chapman Andrews, whom we met in Peking, had painted such an exciting picture of hunting on the Mongolian border that we responded immediately to the idea and had now arrived in this remote section of northwest China.

With the approach of night, the gates of the city would soon be closed. If we would seek safety within, there was no time to lose. Leaving Chu, our Chinese "boy," to handle the luggage, Mason and I headed on foot across the bleak and level plain. Darkness descended and the gray-black walls loomed ever larger against the gray-black sky.

There is a sense of mystery about an old walled city that both repels and beckons. On that dark evening, it clung to the stark battlements of Kwei-hua-cheng and lent a fascinating aura to all the unknowns that lay ahead. We moved forward into deepening shadow. Finally we stood in the gloom of the great gate itself. Then a frightening sight hit us right through the middle and left us shaken. High on either side of the ponderous double gate were cages of iron set into the masonry. In these cages were pointed iron pikes, and impaled on these pikes were decapitated heads — gruesome reminders to all comers of the law of General Ma, Tutung* of the buffer state of Suiyuan. That was our welcome to the city of Kwei-hua-cheng.

Marco Polo had been a lonely speck of foreign matter in a land of incredible strangeness. This was a moment when we, too, felt the loneliness of strangers in a strange kingdom. Weird music and falsetto cries drifted from behind compound walls and through the gates.

Above us the giant arch towered into the gloom. The gates themselves were of massive thickness with great handwrought hinges and huge studding. In a few minutes they would be bolted and barred for the night.

It was the time of the Autumn Festival, and once inside the gates we were engulfed by the seething commotion of narrow choked streets. Like Red Indians, a few purple-coated, high-booted Mongols passed haughtily and silently by. Their entire as-

* "Governor of absolute power" (he had his own army); pronounced Dutung.

pect suggested the wild and woolly land from which they had come, a land of endless plains, broad steppes, great deserts, and fossil dinosaurs. It was the land of the living Buddha. It was also the land of the great Asian sheep, the famous Mongolian argali, which we had come so far to pursue.

At the inn that night we met two Chinese-speaking Englishmen of the English-American Tobacco Company. All the talk was of bandits said to be marauding the very hills we were about to enter. In the China of 1922, bandits were well recognized and vastly preferred to the tax collector. Usually referred to as *"Hung-hutze,"* bandits were for the most part ex-soldiers. A man would join any one of various armies, obtain rifle and ammunition, then desert. Sometimes when soldiers had not received pay for a long time, they would be warriors by day and bandits by night.

Suiyuan was a buffer state between Mongolia and China proper. General Ma ruled it with an iron hand. He had been informed of our arrival and had assigned us two soldiers as a bodyguard. However, fearing lest bandits capture their rifles, they were careful to leave them behind. It was a face-saving maneuver and both the Tutung and the soldiers were thus well prepared for any event that might befall us.

For the next few days it was bitterly cold. The north wind blew a gale out of Mongolia. With all the clothes we could muster, Mason and I were never warm. The thermometer must have gone to near zero, for the rivers froze over in a single night.

After a miserably uncomfortable sleep in the tiny hamlet of Jirgo, we continued to work our way westward, deeper into the hills. Here the precipitous walls of a dark canyon gave way to a little side valley with a bubbling ice-filled stream. A tiny mud-hut village nestled against the base of the mountain. A few scrawny cattle stood forlorn and foodless in this grim setting. Then we saw work on the threshing grounds — barley thrown high into the air to be sifted by the wind, the whirligig sticks in the hands of two men alternately beating the grain while a blindfolded mule pulled a stone roller in a never-ending circle. It was as though we had turned back the pages of time, for here was a China that had scarcely changed in five thousand years.

At our approach all work stopped. Children, naked even in the cold wind, scurried around corners and peered at us through crevices. Women on bound feet hobbled out of mud hovels to stare. The men rested on their implements to pass a few words with our donkey coolies. And all the time the blindfolded mule continued his endless circle. He, alone, had no rest. He seemed to symbolize China — going on and on forever in the same old way.

The next day we crossed a pass in the mountains. The wind was stronger than ever and the cold severe. At the very summit was a tiny shrine chiseled out of the naked rock on the edge of the trail. Nearby, sheltered from the blast, were four Chinese coolies resting from their long climb. Their loads, a hundred pounds each, had been set to one side. They were passing a long-stemmed pipe with a minute bowl good for about three draws. And they were truly enjoying themselves, their fine rugged faces wreathed in smiles and laughter. One of the men had a wooden stump for a leg. He, too, had a hundred-pound load, yet in this brief moment of respite and leisure, his laughter was the most contagious of all. Here, again, I thought, was an incredible aspect of ancient China — the capacity in a long life of travail and pain to enjoy to the full the few moments of relaxation in a day of endless toil.

Often we stopped to survey the mountains with our field glasses. Only once did we see sheep in the distance, and that first introduction to the great argali was no more than a fleeting and exciting glimpse as these magnificent creatures bounded over the skyline. But our appetite was whetted, for we now knew that wild Asian sheep did truly exist in these hills.

Toward evening, with ninety hard-won li (thirty miles) behind us, we reached a little village near the base of a canyon. No foreigners had ever been there before. One inhabitant harangued the crowd; evidently we were birds of ill omen, for he objected strenuously to our spending the night in the village. Whereupon one of our soldiers flew into an extravagantly voluble rage and beat him with his whip. After that there were no more objections and we were received docilely by the owners of what was undoubtedly the smelliest little mud hut we had yet stayed in. We were so cold and miserable we requested a fire. The Chinese made their fires from grass or *argol*, for there was not a stick of timber in these hills. It was built under the great family bed or k'ang, which stretched along one entire wall of the room. The firebox itself was an immense oven — the thick earthen roof of which was supposed to transmit a pleasant radiant heat to the sleepers. But it was difficult to operate, requiring constant attention from the Chinese who squatted on his haunches on the hard dirt floor and fed grass to it incessantly. The result was something less than perfect. Smoke poured into the room — smoke in such suffocating quantities that it drove us out into the filthy courtyard. Fortunately, there were enough tears in the paper windows for the smoke to escape so we were able to return with orders not to repeat the experiment. From there on, we had fireless evenings.

But Mason was able to rise above all these ills. With a ready sense of humor and a deep interest in everything Chinese, he was endlessly intrigued by the village life around us. Yet even in the wilds of the Mongolian frontier, Mason felt happier in his Harvard Square business suit, white collar, and tie. My most persuasive efforts failed to part him from these symbols of home.

Mason and I spent many long, miserably cold evenings chatting together. We were both dispirited. Each day we climbed hard and spent endless hours scouting for game — all to no avail. However, the rewards of the chase are often indirect, and by bringing us in close contact with ancient, unchanged China, our pursuit of the ghostlike argali had given us a glimpse of Chinese life never seen by the ordinary traveler.

We stayed in this village for several days, combing the hills in every direction. Every night we were disturbed. Donkeys brayed and woke up the whole village. Dogs barked monotonously for hours on end, and conducted midnight fights up and down the courtyard. Cats squalled and crawled through the paper windows hoping to go to bed with us. Unearthly moanings came incessantly through long hours of the night from some sick and unattended creature in an adjoining room, and the shrill squealing of a pig often added to the disturbance. Or possibly a wolf howled in the distance, thus stimulating the village pack to exercise its vocal chords. But it is not in the nature of the Chinese to be disturbed by mere sounds. They simply accept them as they accept the filth of the courtyard that blows into their houses.

In a Chinese village, no privacy of any kind can be enjoyed. Men, women, and children came to watch everything we did. And if a peephole was not available at just the right height for some newcomer, a wet finger deftly applied to the paper soon provided a comfortable aperture for another spying eye. Since there was nothing to be done about it we, in our turn, accepted these minor annoyances.

Reports of the villagers supported our own observations that game was scarce, so we continued on our way, traversing the broken escarpment that fell abruptly from the high plateau of central Asia to the plains of China. Canyon after canyon afforded magnificent terrain for the great sheep, but these fine creatures had been so hard-pressed by incessant and lawless hunting that few remained.

Through these discouraging days, Chu, our smiling thirty-year-

A typical frontier village —
our rest house at left.

old "boy" from Peking, was a great comfort to us. Everlastingly good-natured, gay and attentive, penny-saving and humble, Chu was cook and bodyguard and interpreter. His whole life seemed to be consumed by one desire only — to fulfill his masters' every wish and whim. Chu's pidgin English was sometimes disconcerting. It was several months before we learned that his oft-repeated phrase "Pleasy Masta, guadidooloo" meant simply "very good."

Being well above the coolie class, Chu had a great aversion to walking, and on travel days when not searching for some appalling scraps wherewith to concoct our next meal he was certain to be found — perched like a teed-up golf ball — on top of the biggest and softest load on the smallest donkey. Whenever I stopped to watch the caravan go by, Chu, with legs dangling foolishly and an enormous self-conscious grin, would always say, "Pleasy, Masta, walking much trouble." And judging from Mason's similar method of locomotion, I became convinced that he too, though he would never admit it, shared Chu's views on the principle of least effort.

In the morning we heard rumors that bandits had raided the next village on our route. Overcome with curiosity, we pressed forward fast. In the late evening, we arrived at a cliff village in which homes had been excavated from the sheer walls of loess. Loess is an eolian deposit of loam. Like the topsoil of our own dust bowls, it is a wind-driven product derived from the desiccation of Central Asia. In certain places, loess has accumulated into great strata of enormous thickness which the Chinese have honeycombed with apartments. Looking down the main street at this façade of doors and windows that stretched for a quarter of a mile, it was odd to see the farmers and donkeys directly overhead, tilling the fertile soil.

No sooner had we arrived than we were summoned to take care of a man shot by the bandits. He had been hit in the intestines and was in bad shape, but it was evident he had a miraculous confidence in foreign medicine. Not speaking Chinese, and not being able to give any sympathy, made me feel deeply uncomfortable in that room of pain. I prepared an iodine wash and showed the women how to use it. They pleaded desperately for a purgative, and though it was hard to conceive how such drastic treatment could help an intestinal wound, I gave them all the castor oil we had.

That night, Mason and I slept in a temple. The icy air creeping off the Mongolian plateau forced us to retire early. Chu built a fire on the dirt floor and fried some eggs we had been lucky enough to pick up in the village. The smoke was intolerable. Lighted candles recently placed on the altar revealed a bearded gilt Buddha frowning down upon us. This hideous image seemed out of keeping with the stark wilderness of its mountain setting. The surrounding paper windows were torn and frequently chirping sparrows hopped in to seek refuge on the beams overhead. When I stretched out on my cot, I found my revolver under the pillow — loaded! I pulled it out and looked at Chu with an accusing eye. In response he said simply, and with a disarming grin, "Pleasy, Masta, maybe-so littey sneak tief come night-time." But we were unmolested.

Then came a day when we decided to move back eastward to the border village of Tung-wu-shi-tu, a name meaning East-West Village.

By this time, my hunting instinct was thoroughly frustrated. The days had been too uneventful and since the country looked wonderful and harbored both the goral and the wily Asian roe deer, my feet were itching to be off. So leaving Mason to continue with the caravan, I determined to strike out alone. Someone gave me the general direction of Tung-wu-shi-tu and estimated the distance at eighty li, about twenty-six miles. With that threadbare information, I moved off into an exciting dawn, planning to re-join Mason that night.

Starting at the very first light, and knowing there would be many long and tiring hours ahead, I deliberately chose a pair of Chinese felt slippers that gave the wonderful light feel of mocca-sins I had been so accustomed to since childhood. The day was fine and the air cold and sparkling. After eight or nine miles, I came into some terrific country. Just the place for some game, I thought, for here was a valley broken with many small side can-yons offering endless hidden pockets for any creature that wished to remain unseen. Presently I spotted a roe high on the far side of the valley. Field glasses indicated a small buck, and I went after him.

The descent into the bottom was extremely precipitous with an equally stiff climb on the far side. It had been my plan to strike for the summit, work along it, and come down on the roe from above, with the daily up-mountain wind in my favor. However, when I finally reached the top of the ridge, I stopped in unbeliev-ing wonder. In all the days we had been wandering through these barren hills, not one word had been spoken of the Great Wall of China. So far as I knew, it was hundreds of miles away and yet, as I topped that final rise, there it was — crawling serpent-like up and down the ridges and into the distance as far as the eye could see. Here and there watch towers, magnificent in their decay, dominated the bleak and rugged landscape. Portions of the wall's sides had collapsed, but for the most part its perfection seemed to be unmarred by two thousand years of the erosive forces of wind and rain and snow and ice. Truly this must be the greatest archi-tectural wonder of the world. In man-hours of effort, it dwarfs all the pyramids combined — and yet at the same time, it presents as gigantic a monument to human folly as does the Maginot Line.

[95]

I sat down and gazed in awe at this prone giant that marched for over fifteen hundred miles across the plains and mountains of North China. Seen in the remoteness of these barren hills, the Great Wall was a structure of infinite beauty and sadness: beauty because of its consummate perfection of form; sadness because of its lonely traverse of great wastelands and because the picture this colossus conjured up was that of generations of millions in human bondage.

Forgetting all about the roe deer, I just sat there, munching a sandwich, looking and thinking and wondering at the devastating power of man over man and of how slave labor could have been forced by the whip to perform such herculean tasks.

That afternoon as I resumed my hunt, an elusive buck proved so absorbing that dusk gathered before I knew it. Fascination for the Great Wall and for the hunt had made me oblivious of time. With a sudden shock the thought struck me that I still had a whole day's journey ahead.

Already heavy clouds rolling over the ridges wore an ominous purplish aspect. The forces of darkness seemed suddenly to be gathering against me. The time had come to move fast, to take advantage of every last second of daylight. Choosing the river canyon rather than the mountaintop route, I plunged down into a deep gorge. In half an hour I had reached the bottom and almost immediately the precipitous confining walls narrowed sharply on either side into a true defile. Though the water was low, the river itself raced back and forth from wall to wall, forcing me to wade the rapids again and again. After a while, I stopped to take stock of a situation that was growing ever more unpleasant. In this narrow bottom the light was already very dim. I looked at my watch. It was 4:30. I had been on the move since before 7 A.M. My sandwiches had all been eaten. I had not the slightest idea where I was or how long the canyon would continue or how deep the river would get. There was no possibility of lighting a fire and sitting it out until daylight, and without a fire it was much too cold to remain motionless for long.

Standing there in that darkening abyss — hemmed in by sheer walls of rock as if in the bottom of a long and narrow well — gave me a feeling of unutterable remoteness from the world. In that deep pit, the roar of re-echoing waters consumed all space with a mighty reverberation that destroyed inner calm. I found myself thinking about the bandits, wondering if this was their regular passage and what I should do if I should meet them.

There was no choice but to continue a blind and uncertain trip down the canyon. My predicament was entirely of my own making and I would have to suffer the consequences. And suffering it was, for not only was there no moon but the clouds were low over the top of the canyon, as if sitting on its lid, and soon I was in almost pitch blackness. Fortunately, I had a balloon-silk parka from Alaska and I stopped and put it on. There was comfort in its light warmth.

After wading and rewading the river again and again, the real trouble began. Never were submerged water-smooth rocks more slippery and slithering. Never were deep pools a more formidable and icy menace against one misstep. But these hazards were as nothing when compared with the disintegration of my footgear, for my beautiful Chinese felt slippers began to soften like wet cardboard. They kept coming off and there was great danger that I might lose them in the rapids. Fortunately, I had a piece of rope around my waist and this I cut up and used to tie on the slippers. I could no longer see my watch and had no idea of the time. But deep weariness had set in and aching muscles clamored for rest. For a while I sat on a boulder and thought how wonderful it would be to build a fire and lie down beside it. But after a brief moment a chill crept down my back and my soaking-wet legs began to stiffen. So I was forced to struggle on — not just for a few minutes but for hour after hour.

Each curve of the canyon, it seemed, must surely be the last. But always there was another and still another. Now I was stumbling badly in the rapids and my toes were in such pain I knew they must be bloody and blue. Exhaustion was approaching. I stopped and struck a match. It was close to 11 P.M. I had been on the move for about sixteen hours, six and a half of them stumbling down the black canyon. After the brightness of the match, it was a long time before my eyes adjusted again to darkness. Then I began to wonder if I had been properly directed. Was this the right canyon and if not, where did it lead? But dismal thoughts did not last long. It took too much concentration to remain upright and to keep going. And somehow, I did keep going — just fumbling along till at about 12:30 A.M. the canyon debouched abruptly onto the broad plains of China. I couldn't see the sudden breadth and opening but I could *feel* it. The sound of the rapids, no longer contained within the walls, drifted off into open space. The degree of blackness diminished a little. I had the feeling I could go in any direction, but I had no idea which was the right one. So I just continued following the river but at some distance from it.

I was on a broad alluvial flood-plain with nothing but gravel and boulders underfoot. Presently, I can't possibly explain why, I had the sudden sense of emptiness in front of me and I stopped dead in my tracks. I slid the rifle off my shoulder and probed ahead underfoot with the stock. The stock disappeared into nothing. I knelt down and still felt nothing in front of me. Then I lay flat and reached down with the rifle as far as my arm would stretch but could feel no bottom. Obviously I was on the very edge of a recently formed river terrace. Some deep self-protective instinct had warned me in the nick of time. After that I retreated from the river until the sound of it grew quite dim. For a long while I felt completely lost and I just listened and listened, wondering what to do next. Suddenly a dog barked. Immediately I pinpointed the direction in my mind and moved cautiously toward it. After about ten minutes of the most careful progress, I found myself confronted with a mud wall. Gradually I followed the wall around till I came to a gate. Then I called. Immediately the dog barked again. I kept on calling, louder and louder, and finally a candlelight appeared in the hands of a little boy. He came out to the gate and held the light to my face. He recognized me as a foreigner, but instead of being frightened he opened the gate and motioned me inside. In a moment I was surrounded by friendly Chinese farmer faces. The whole family, including even the aged grandmother, were reclining on the k'ang. Why they were not all asleep I could not imagine. Immediately, with the kindness and hospitality of good, simple people all over the world, they offered tea and biscuits and seemed quite amused by my strange appearance. When I showed them the dilapidated condition of my Chinese slippers, holding them up for inspection in the candlelight, their enjoyment knew no bounds and they fairly rocked to and fro with sheer pleasure.

Then, taking out my small moneybag, I produced a gleaming Yuan-shi-kai silver dollar and indicated by pantomime that whoever would conduct the *weigerin* (foreigner) to Tung-wu-shi-tu would be the recipient of that fine piece. Though it was already well after 1 A.M., the little boy was promptly elected. I tied on my fragmentary slippers and after another cup of strengthening tea and profuse thanks delivered mostly in English, I found myself on the trail again, this time with a guide. The candle carried inside a lantern had a steady light, so we could see well. Presently I noticed the youngster kept stopping to pick up stones which he stuffed in his clothing. When he had filled his pockets, he gave some to me. I could not imagine what this was for until we reached the outskirts of the village when we were suddenly attacked by an army of savage dogs. They surrounded us and moved in close with bared fangs and rushing snarls. Without the stones I don't know what would have happened. By constant flinging at the closest animals, we managed to hold them off and continue our way until I reached the inn, where I was mighty glad to rejoin Mason.

The little boy received his dollar with a very polite bow. Thereupon once again he armed himself with more stones. What a very brave little fellow, I thought to myself, as he headed off again into the darkness, swinging his candlelight.

It took an entire day to rest and patch up my battered and swollen feet and purchase a new pair of Chinese shoes — this time a pair that came up well above the ankle. That day the greatest hunter in the mountains of the Mongolian frontier came to see us. He had heard of our failures and decided to offer his services. His name was Na-mon-gin, a shrewd ex-bandit and a big solid man with patience in his eyes and a sureness of manner that lent conviction to his words.

As a Mongol, he was racially so close of kin to the red Indian I felt on familiar and sympathetic ground. He was a rugged, tough, thick-set man and though unable to speak to him, I succeeded, with Chu as interpreter, in conveying the idea that the shooting of a big ram would yield a handsome reward in the form of ten silver dollars. Thereupon enthusiasm lit up his broad audacious face and immediately he was ready to start. Mason had decided to revisit Kwei-hua-cheng and the following morning, as the great Mongol hunter and I took off together into the hills, I turned and saw Mason on the back of a little burro headed down the main street of Tung-wu-shi-tu. He was wearing clothes appropriate for a

*The barren threadbare
hills of the Mongolian frontier.*

Boston week end, and his long legs dangled right to the ground, but I felt sure he was smiling to himself at the prospect of such an inviting change from the long discouraging days we had been through.

As for Na-mon-gin, there was evidently no doubt in his mind about where we would go or what we would do. It was almost as though a meeting with a great ram had been prearranged.

The mountains here were for the most part beautifully rounded with mature and gentle outlines, but even though the climbing was not steep, we had hard work for several hours. The Mongol climbed slowly, like the seasoned mountaineer he was. He had enormous feet encased in still more enormous Chinese slipper-like shoes, and I found it quite relaxing to place my feet in his very steps. This was one time when I enjoyed following in the footsteps of another man. He wore padded gray trousers, baggy over the behind and narrowing to the ankles, and a big padded coat which he very soon loosened to avoid overheating. Every once in a while he would say something to me. When I looked blank, he would seek to penetrate my understanding by talking extremely slowly and enunciating each syllable extra loud. I could see him thinking "How can anybody be so dumb?" Then suddenly the absurdity of the situation would strike us simultaneously and we would both end up in laughter so hilarious that a certain warm companionship quickly developed between us. Though the old bandit and I were derived from utterly different backgrounds of race, creed, custom and language, our paths had crossed for a few brief hours, and it became evident that we were both going to make them as pleasant as we knew how.

When we reached the summit of the range, Na-mon-gin crawled across the skyline and stretched out languidly against a big boulder. He was settling down for a long wait. Below us was a gaping exposed valley — peaceful and still. I could see every bit of it at a glance. Yet Na-mon-gin was content to remain propped against his rock, gazing into nothingness. It was a colossal example of patience in the hunting field. Soon after arrival, I was cold and miserable and after an hour of constant hard searching with field glasses, I was certain beyond all doubt that no Mongolian argali existed in that whole broad expanse. Yet at that very moment I felt a finger on my back. Na-mon-gin pointed. For a long time I looked, following the direction of his finger. Then, down toward the bottom of the valley, I saw a single ewe and a moment later, another. They had both just emerged from a hidden ravine. Then the field glasses revealed a young ram that mysteriously stepped into view like a conjurer's rabbit, and a few minutes later, another. Finally, a real old-timer appeared, the proud bearer of magnificent horns. With neck thick-arched, he strode proudly up to the peak of a minor pinnacle and stood there, surveying his wild and rugged home.

One glance at that fine ram through my field glasses and Na-mon-gin motioned to me and immediately started to slither from rock to rock down the steep slope until an intervening spur cut us off from their view when we rose and moved fast. Three quarters of an hour later we were within three hundred yards of six ewes, who soon disappeared over a ridge. They seemed restless but not too disturbed. Thinking the big ram might appear at any moment, I put up my three-hundred-yard sight, but he did not show.

The sheep were now on the move, and we followed at a distance of over half a mile, being infinitely careful to keep ourselves hidden from their telescopic eyes. The big ram was nervous, apprehensive. He led his flock to the crest of the range. Na-mon-gin showed no emotion whatever. Ever since we had sighted game he had not spoken a word. He personified the patient hunter — watchful, silent, waiting. After a sharp climb, he wormed his way to the very edge of a steep bluff and peeked over. Then, with extreme caution, his head withdrew slowly, turtle-fashion. I knew he had seen something worth seeing. He waved frantically. Filled with excitement, I crawled up and peered over the knife-edge. Almost directly beneath us the same grand old ram we had previously sighted was moving forward on a narrow ledge, about to pass out of sight. I fired quickly, aiming a little low, but I had neglected to put down the three-hundred-yard sight. The bullet spurted dust just over him. The next second, he plummeted down the ravine out of view. I rushed forward to a point of vantage and in a moment the ram reappeared with two ewes, racing up the opposite slope of the valley. Na-mon-gin, the enigmatic Mongol, was suddenly transported with excitement, nudging me in the elbow and screaming the one English word he knew, "Shoot — shoot." I saw my first two bullets hit the dusty slope — one just over the ram, the other just ahead. I fired my third; the ram was within a few yards of the summit and about to be gone forever. I never saw the bullet hit, but as I was slipping in my last cartridge, he stumbled, reared up, and plunged headlong down the ravine. Na-mon-gin and I just grabbed each other and shouted and danced with joy. The kick of the gun plus the altitude had given me a violent nosebleed which the old bandit clumsily tried to stop up with his fingers.

After we reached the ram, a descent of a hundred and fifty yards, we examined his fine horns and sat for a while, thinking back with satisfaction over the details of the hunt. There had been great patience and sureness in every move the Mongol had made, and there was much to be learned from the fine deliberateness of his timing. Before starting skinning, I offered Na-mon-gin a cigarette. From the folds of his padded clothing he produced a very long-stemmed pipe with a tiny silver bowl. Then, very carefully, he tore the cigarette into pieces and stuffed the tobacco tight into the bowl. When I held a lighted match for him, his big rugged face broke into a broad grin and I felt sure he must be thinking of those ten Yuan-shi-kai silver dollars he had earned so quickly. After smoking, he brought out his antelope skin bag that all Mongols use for carrying their buttered tea. It was beautifully made of the softest smoke-tanned leather and I could not help showing my admiration for such fine craftsmanship.

The following day, Na-mon-gin again proved his capacity as a hunter. He brought Mason Sears to a near-record head. Mason made a magnificent shot and he has the head to this day. In two days, our guide had no doubt earned more money than he had made in many moons. On our part, weeks of hard work had borne no fruit and now suddenly, under the genius of our Mongol friend, we had each secured a marvelous trophy. Though we had been with him such a short time, there was a certain sadness to our leave-taking. Under the observant eyes of Chu, we counted out twenty silver dollars and placed them on the table in two piles of ten. Na-mon-gin stood there, solid as a rock, watching with no change of expression. I motioned with a sweep of my hand they were his. Then Na-mon-gin did a very surprising thing. He reached into a pocket and produced the smoke-tanned tea bag I had admired so much two days before. Stepping forward, he placed it on the table, indicating it was for me. He picked up the twenty dollars, bowed ever so slightly, and stalked off in long shuffling strides. That tea bag I have treasured to this day, carrying in it shaving equipment and medicines on all subsequent hunting trips as a reminder of a remarkable man.

The next day when we returned to Kwei-hua-cheng, we found an invitation from the Tutung to visit his yamen. It is not often that the casual traveler is so honored, and Mason and I promptly accepted. Rickshaws were ordered and we proceeded on our way,

Left:
Mason Sears at Tung-wu-shi-tu
with near record head of Ovis ammon.

Right:
Na-mon-gin
with Mongolian argali.

wondering vaguely what manner of man could do justice to no less than thirty-seven concubines.

On arrival, the Number One boy, soberly dressed in white, ushered us into a small room. The only person to greet us was an interpreter who, with hands tucked in sleeves, bowed deeply and in very hesitant English advised us apologetically that the Tutung was shaving.

In a moment the great man appeared. By Chinese standards there was no question about his greatness, for the Tutung was well over six feet and boasted a colossal girth over which hung a fine silken robe.

After serving tea with the usual perfunctory compliments, the Tutung plied us with questions. Why had we come to China? Why did we want to hunt? What did we think of his country?

Mason and I replied that in college in America we had studied the history of China, had become fascinated by the most ancient culture in the world, and had felt a longing to visit the land of the Dragon Flag. We said we had just graduated and believed that travel in China would be more stimulating and educational than anything we could do. The Tutung seemed well pleased with our answers. Then suddenly he asked to see our firearms. We told him they were back at the inn, but he was so anxious to examine them that a messenger was immediately dispatched to Chu to produce them at once. Meantime, while awaiting their arrival, Mason and I kept a weather eye for a glimpse of a concubine, but we were disappointed. Not a female figure appeared. Then came the arms — a Mannlicher, a Mauser, and my revolver.

I can still remember the pleasurable smile of disdain with which the Tutung snapped my treasured .38 Smith & Wesson. After quickly sizing up the situation, he challenged us to a shooting competition. His Excellency had given us permission to hunt in his mountains and the least we could do was to accept a sporting proposal. Thereupon orders were immediately issued and in a few minutes a band struck up some Chinese martial music outside the yamen. We sallied forth to a waiting car and before I knew it I found myself — feeling very wormish — in the back seat with the enormous Tutung. It was an open touring car. The Tutung spread his fat legs wide. He sat bolt upright to attract attention and occupied at least two thirds of the seat. Mason, the lucky one, rode comfortably in front.

Already I had begun to suspect that this whole thing had been planned with malice aforethought. More and more it looked as if we were being led like lambs to the slaughter, but there was not a thing to be done about it.

In 1922, the primary object of every Chinese chauffeur was to drive through the narrowest streets at breakneck speed with horn screaming. If a man was killed, his wife received ten silver dollars, and it not infrequently happened that the husband of an impoverished family would hurl himself to death in front of a speeding car so his wife and children might have the money.

Naturally, as a pure matter of face, the Tutung's chauffeur had to break all records. It was a hair-raising ride. We didn't know where we were being taken, but wherever it was we went there mighty fast with the horn endlessly tooting and swarms of pedestrians diving out of our way. The ride was so compelling I didn't see much, but I did notice at frequent intervals gangs of workers in chains. Brief as it was, the fleeting glimpse of these unfortunate creatures left in our minds a vivid image of ancient barbarism.

Finally we arrived at an empty corner of the city. A fire had evidently destroyed this section, and the land had been cleared for a parade ground. Our car swept up to a raised dais over which a colorful canopy had been stretched. On the dais were various tables and chairs over which leopard skins had been placed. Beyond the dais, a portion of the Tutung's army was lined up at attention, with their backs to the gray walls of the city. As soon as our car stopped, a band struck up to celebrate our arrival. One glance down the parade ground indicated trouble ahead — for there, all set up at some two hundred paces, was a fine target with about a four-inch bull's-eye. My worst fears were realized. It was now completely evident that the whole reason for the Tutung's invitation to his yamen, his examination of our firearms, and his subsequent challenge was purely and simply for the pleasure of gaining face at the expense of the foreigners. Such a fine opportunity was not to be missed.

After some well-aged and very strong rice wine had been served in tiny china bowls, the Tutung through his interpreter invited us to shoot first. We had not yet seen his rifle but I was already wondering what he was going to produce. When I asked to see it, the great man snapped his fingers and immediately there was placed in his hands the finest target-shooting rifle I had ever known — a Ross with telescope sight. I knew the Ross well, having won a small shooting competition with one in Scotland many years before. It fired a very flat trajectory bullet and it had the most sensitive trigger-pull then made.

Meantime, I had been glancing at Mason. He was not looking at all happy. It is no insult to say that if there was one area of effort Mason did not pride himself on, it was target shooting. So when I suggested that he shoot first, Mason wondered if it would not be a whole lot better if he just didn't shoot at all. When he said this, he was fingering his Mauser and looking over at the army still lined up at attention. Then he turned to me and just grinned from ear to ear while reaching for another drink of rice wine.

I told him he could not get out of shooting — that the challenge had been made to both of us and that he might just as well go ahead and do the best he could. The Tutung, meanwhile, certain of success, was chatting with his attendants and enjoying himself immensely. He thereupon announced that we were to have seven shots apiece.

Mason now got down to business and, as he did so, the army was given the order to stand at ease. Putting in the first bullet, Mason fired deliberately, using the arm of his chair as a rest, but there must have been a very strong gust of wind the moment he fired, for his shot went wide of the black bull's-eye, ending well off in the white. We knew the result all too soon for an attendant standing at one side ran in and indicated the shot with a marker. As he was putting in his second cartridge, Mason looked up at me with his most attractive and embarrassed grin. He was muttering to himself and I could not hear what he said. The second shot was little better than the first. Before firing the third, Mason glanced at the Tutung, who was now wreathed in smiles. "Come on, Mason," I said, "you've just got to hit that bull's-eye once." Whether he did or not I can't remember and I doubt that he can either, but I do know that when it ended up, his total scored allowed a wide margin for improvement.

Now it was my turn. I was using a 9.5 mm. Mannlicher with open leaf sight. Though my shooting was somewhat better than Mason's it was certainly nothing to boast of.

Thereupon the Tutung squatted on the floor in the most approved sitting posture with elbow on left knee and proceeded calmly and rapidly to hit the bull's-eye with all seven shots. No sooner was the seventh shot fired than the army sprang to attention and the band began to play.

The Tutung arose and very solemnly bowed to each of us. After that, we were driven — in considerable disgrace — back to our inn, where we suddenly felt ourselves badly in need of a fiery drink of rice wine.

The next day, when emerging from the great gate of Kwei-hua-cheng, we glanced up at the cages on either side of the entrance and noted, not without a sickening shudder, that a new series of fresh heads adorned the pikes. It was almost as if, properly to impress us, the Tutung had ordered the decapitations for our special benefit.

8

Glimpses of the Jungle

"This earth is ours, to love and live upon,
and use wisely down all the generations of the future."

WE HAD crossed the fever-breeding red ground. We had passed through tremendous rubber plantations and now, on a hot January day in 1923, we were afoot following an old lumber road into the heart of the Indo-China jungle.

Fifty kilometers from Saigon an engulfing wilderness stretched northward for many thousands of square miles. It was an area of aboriginal tribes and aboriginal animals; of long primeval struggle of beast against beast and of primitive man as hunter seeking a hazardous survival against them all. The American Museum of Natural History wanted to add to their collection of Indo-China mammals and I was there for that purpose. Our bullock carts had gone ahead to set up camp in the palm tree country, and Mason Sears, F. J. Defosse and I followed at a comfortable pace.

Defosse was then the great white hunter of Indo-China. For eighteen years he had made his living with his rifle and he had an intimate knowledge of wild animals that few men possessed. Already at forty-two he was drawn-looking and fever-ridden and his eyes were heavy, but when his rifle was at his shoulder, steady as a rock, he was beautiful to see. As a young man, Defosse had been first shot of his regiment. When discharged from the service, he elected to stay in Indo-China and live the life of a hunter. His skill with the rifle had been increasing ever since. Yet even Defosse's superb marksmanship had not saved him from many rugged encounters.

In the early days of his hunting, he had been gored by a wild boar, and run for his life from a wounded tiger. He had been caught by an elephant and somehow survived. But his most frightful encounter was with a wounded water buffalo on the Lanya Plains. One swipe of those formidable horns pierced his lungs and another drove clear through his right thigh so that he hung from the horn. Yet when he was finally shaken off, he had the presence of mind — whenever the buffalo tried to scoop him up again — to keep rolling ahead of the horns until finally the wounded bull retired. Somehow, this history did not fill me with confidence in the effectiveness of a small-bore rifle. Yet oddly enough Defosse considered the double-barrel Holland Express, one of the great rifles of Africa, much too unsafe to use.

A little farther along, we came to a spot where Defosse had shot an elephant many years before. The bleached skull was still there and he took advantage of it to point out where in that massive head the brain was located. To be sure of killing an elephant with a small-bore rifle you have to hit him in the brain. To do that, you must know exactly where it is so that you can aim at it from any angle. He twisted the skull this way and that and showed in relation to ear and eye where best to place a bullet.

I asked if it was possible to stun an elephant with a head wound that failed to hit the brain. He said it was and that he had once shot a bull and sat on his back while eating lunch only to find him gone when he returned later with help from a nearby Moi village.

Defosse suggested testing our new 9 mm. Mausers. He was a

great believer in accuracy with a small bore as opposed to the heavy-duty rifles the English used in Africa. To him we were complete unknowns and it was essential that he gauge our capacities, so he nailed a leaden coin — about the size of a fifty-cent piece — to a tree and paced off a hundred meters. Then he invited us to shoot. Mason, foreseeing the result, grinned broadly, commented under his breath, and failed in several shots to come anywhere near the minute bull's-eye. I, too, failed completely. Whereupon Defosse, with left elbow on hip and left fingers elongated, drilled two bullets from his long-barreled Lebel plumb through that tiny target. It was the finest shooting I had ever seen. We were properly impressed and from then on we knew what he meant by accuracy.

Camp, when we reached it at dusk, was something completely different from anything I had experienced before. A roof of interwoven palm leaves extended downward to hip height and under it the walls were left open to admit any prowling animal and every cooling breeze. Already our canvas cots were up and mosquito netting strung over each one.

Our wonderful Chu from Peking served us supper and during the meal Defosse talked about the jungle. He told us briefly of the various animals we might encounter — elephant, tiger, leopard, rhino, water buffalo, seladang and banteng, the many species of deer, python, cobra, gibbons and frigate captains, peacock and jungle fowl and all the various small animals that prowl the forest by night. He said that in the morning he would take Mason one way and that I could go another, following the Sand River, with two Mois at my heels. Since lead bullets have little penetrating power against animals with heavy hides, I was instructed to carry lead in the barrel and magazine of my Mauser but to change immediately to steel if we encountered buffalo or elephant or the very scarce rhino. The Mois, he indicated, were poor hunters

[113]

and bad at finding their way, but they believed firmly in the magic of the white man's compass which always pointed back to camp, and if they showed any fear of getting lost, I need only tap my breast pocket where the compass resided.

The Mois were a primitive and fascinating people. During our two months in the jungle they were constantly with us, serving as porters and trackers. They are the original Malays of Indo-China and as far back as their people remember they have lived in the interior. To the Mois, the jungle is the whole world. In their early history, a mud wall had been erected as a boundary and defense against the Annamese who were invading the seacoast. The wall still exists, and so successfully has it landlocked the Mois that even today they have no knowledge of the sea.

The Mois have one great god of the jungle and subordinate gods for each species of animal. When they make a killing with their crossbows and poisoned arrows, a propitiation to the god of that species is necessary. In the case of an elephant, it lasts eight days and the ceremony takes on the from of a *"kaniau"* or drunken debauch, held about the carcass of the dead animal. A Moi will never give any information as to the whereabouts of dangerous game, for surely the animal would know and revenge himself on that Moi. Thus when the Mois found a fresh tiger's kill a short distance from one of our camps, they did not tell us about it until three days later when the kill was devoured and the tiger gone. To the Mois a tiger is *"Ông Cop,"* Mr. Tiger, and is spoken of quietly and with great respect; Mr. Elephant, *"Ông Bô,"* is rarely even mentioned.

After supper we turned off the acetylene light that was attracting countless moths. The Mois were sitting around a fire about thirty yards away; Chu was washing the dishes. I was standing out under the stars, listening. Ever since reading Conrad's *The Heart of Darkness* I had longed to be in the jungle and now I found the fascination of that first night totally absorbing. There was a rustle of air through the palm leaves that made them rattle. A gecko lizard gave his last call of the day — kuck-kaw, kuck-kaw — in descending volume until it seemed as if he were expiring.

Then I heard a barking deer. It was a sharp big sound repeated again and again, unquestionably an alarm call, and I could picture a tiger moving by. Complete stillness followed for several minutes. Then out of the darkness, from not far away, three short powerful blasts from an elephant.

"Now they know we are here," said Defosse, "and they are telling it to the world."

For a long time there was silence again. Then I heard Mason ask Defosse to tell him about the most terrifying experience he had ever had in these jungles. I came in and lay on my cot and let the mosquito netting down. Defosse thought for a while and then replied, "The time I was trailed by a bull elephant after my rifle had jammed. It happened not far from here. Two bulls were together and I had just shot one in the brain. The other bull did not charge, he just started to walk toward me. The action of my rifle had become frozen. With all my strength I could not move it. I turned and ran and after a while I came out of the jungle and crossed a stretch of open grass. Before entering the jungle again I stopped to see if I was still being followed. I did not have to wait long. He was right after me, his trunk glued to my trail. Each time I crossed an open stretch I stopped to see if he was still coming. And always he was there. The deliberate way in which he pursued me was very frightening. An elephant walk can be very fast and often I had to run hard to keep ahead of him. I was ten miles from the railroad station at Gia-Huynh and he followed me to within a few hundred feet of the station. Had I been a few years older or a few miles farther away, I never would have made it. I never felt so helpless and even now when I think about it I am frightened."

In the morning Chu called us long before daylight. It was quite cold. Defosse said, "Don't pull your boots on until you have shaken them hard to be sure a scorpion has not crawled inside." I asked him if he had gotten caught that way and he said yes, but not until he had been walking for half an hour, for it had taken the scorpion that long to work his stinger around and inject it in his toe.

Then Defosse said, "Be sure to wrap your puttees good and tight, there will be lots of leeches waiting for you."

We had breakfast by the light of the acetylene lantern and then, while waiting for sufficient daylight to see our sights, Defosse said, "Never load your rifle without looking through the barrel first; we have a wasp here that plugs it up with mud, and of course, you could lose your arm if you fired a plugged rifle."

A dim light was now filling the jungle. Chu brought us each a canteen of tea. Defosse kept raising his rifle to look through the sight. Finally he said, "Now it is safe." With that, we started, Defosse and Mason and two Mois in one direction, myself and two Mois in another, headed for Sand River.

Dawn had just broken and the mist lay black and heavy over the forest. A few tall trees out in the open lifted their heads to the surface. They were the trees of a dream, weird and unsupported, and their great black trunks disappeared into the blacker mist below. My route led away through the accursed elephant grass — rank, swordlike growth that cuts to the bone. It was wet and the cold clammy dew soaked us through. Very soon in a soft spot I saw the pug marks of a tiger that had passed camp during the night. In a few minutes a sickly green disk arose over the rim of the great forest. The mist began to move and drift about and the sun turned from livid orange to pale yellow. Then I heard the gibbons, huddled shivering in the top of the highest tree, greeting the rising sun with a song. It was a fascinating whistling sound that only lasted a minute or two, but from then on, near or far, we heard it almost every morning just as the sun broke over the forest.

Now the jungle cocks started crowing and the long-tailed peacocks were hurling their raucous notes through the open parks as we stepped from the grass country into deep jungle. It was dark there and cool and dripping, the floor of the jungle was brown from so little light, and I could not see my sights. Suddenly there was a great shaking of branches and a flock of little gray monkeys ran away like squirrels through the treetops. Then I saw the leeches — everywhere. They clung to stems, reached up and oozed slimily toward us, so we pushed on, the vines and giant creepers and thorny bushes catching at our clothing. My two Mois, Meen and Trang, followed silently at some distance, machetes in hand. They were so quiet, so unobtrusive, so hesitant, I felt as if they wished to vanish away and expected any moment when I turned around to find them gone. No doubt they were afraid of me and still more afraid of what might happen to them while with me. Meen, Defosse had said, was the better man — more alert, more intelligent, and a tiny bit more courageous.

Very soon we ran onto the tracks of a large elephant herd. Where the animals had passed through browsing as they went, the jungle had been torn to pieces. Small trees were smashed down, the tops of larger ones broken and the underbrush trampled. As I stepped gingerly about inspecting the damage and looking at the enormous fresh footprints in the soft earth, a tingling sensation crept under my skin.

For a long time they had just milled around. Then they had separated into two herds — one going back deep into the jungle, the other circling out over the open spaces toward Sand River. These we followed and on the way we saw the dancing place of the elephants which Kipling describes in the Jungle Book story of

"Little Numai." Over a broad area everything had been trampled and stamped to the hardness of cement. After a while, the elephants seemed to be traveling fast and finally I left their trail and cut down into the dried-up river bed.

The banks were steep and high with the trees arching over the depressed sandy bottom so we could not see the sky; there were sudden bursts of song from hidden birds. In this sandy bottom were innumerable tracks of tiger, leopard, wild boar and deer, and there were big holes where elephants had dug deep in the sand for water. Nearby was a crossing-ground where ponderous feet had broken down the vertical banks into a broad steep incline. Then suddenly we struck that strong, pungent, zoo-like smell of tiger. It hung in the bottom. Immediately the Mois were alert — apprehensive. I climbed the bank on a narrow deer trail and no sooner had I reached the top than I heard the alarm call of a barking deer, a few hundred yards away in the grass. It was the same call we had heard the night before. A few minutes later I heard it again, further away. The jungle was telling about "Shere Khan" — announcing his passage.

It was getting hot now and out in the open the sun was white and blistering. So I descended again into the shade of the sandy river bed. For a long time nothing seemed to be moving. We were approaching midday, when the jungle is at rest. Even the birds were still. A silent humid heat engulfed the land. Sweat was running into my eyes and trickling down my back; for a long time I had been taking large gulps of tea from my canteen. My Mois, on the other hand, did not show a single bead of perspiration. Nature had endowed them with many pores under the skin for my one or two, and their cooling system was infinitely more efficient.

Strapped on my back with my canteen was a small leather case with sandwiches prepared by Chu. In the shade of the river bottom, I threw off my overheated and rigid topee, devoured the sandwiches and drank more tea. The Mois had nothing, for they only ate twice a day. They sat eying me from a distance, completely silent, giving the sense that they wished to disappear but not quite daring to do so.

With the jungle so still and dead, I decided to take a siesta and stretched out on the sand. The time to be abroad was at dawn and at dusk, so there was no point in wasting energy when game was not moving. Moreover, my boots felt squdgy and soggy as if supersaturated with perspiration, so I took them off and found them filled with blood from leeches that had gotten through the eyeholes. Once the leeches were full they fell off and got squashed, so my socks were a complete mess.

About 3 P.M. I went on again. The tracks on the river bottom were endlessly fascinating, and soon I saw the curved, snaky, rope-like mark of a python. A great field naturalist, Harry Raven, had cautioned me to beware when following well-used deer trails in the jungle. "Never move along them with head down," he said, "for python lie in wait in the branches overhead."

In the soft sand of the river bed, walking was completely silent. We had been traveling for more than an hour without seeing a thing. Nothing had occurred to indicate danger when from close by came the stupendous ringing blasts of an elephant trumpeting his alarm. It was staccato and sharp. Repeated again and again, it had a terrifying effect. It came from just behind the solid green wall on the edge of the river and shattered the midday silence. He must have caught our scent.

"If you encounter elephant, change quickly," Defosse had said, "from lead to steel." Not knowing what to expect, I was watching the jungle and changing bullets at the same time. Some of them dropped in the sand. They were greasy and sand particles adhered to them. I picked them up with fumbling fingers and tried to insert them into the magazine, but they were too gritty to slide in properly.

Meanwhile, I was aware of being without company. My two Mois had vanished. A moment later I saw them; they had climbed the far bank and were shinning up a tree. That, I found, was their regular procedure whenever danger threatened.

After those screeching blasts I kept wondering if an infuriated elephant was about to emerge. Instead, the violent trumpeting was followed by absolute silence. I pictured him standing there, ominously waiting, and I did not have the slightest inclination to go and investigate.

Defosse said later there were probably four or five together and they had no doubt all sneaked away without making a sound. Their feet are like rubber and their capacity to move silently is unbelievable. As I calmed down, I realized this was a good lesson for my first day in the jungle: it made me appreciate the importance of steady nerves.

We headed back to camp in that magic hour of growing dusk when game is on the move. All I saw was a sambar hind standing at the edge of the jungle. Then as we passed a small batch of palms, we stumbled on a kill. A small sambar had been strangled by a python. The big snake had then made the mistake of starting to swallow the deer by only one hind leg instead of both together. He had gotten as far as the crotch but had been unable to withdraw because of his sharply recurved teeth. So the snake was waiting for the sambar's leg to rot off. Until then, he was a prisoner and unlikely to survive, for the putrefying meat would be certain to attract a tiger. As it was, the Mois chopped off the helpless python's head, pulled the half-digested leg out of his stomach, and carried the snake home for python steak. Only Mason had the courage to try it, but it was too tough for his teeth.

My primary job in Indo-China was to collect for the American Museum of Natural History, so a few nights later I got up at 1 A.M. and went into the jungle with an acetylene light on my head. It is easy to get lost and my two Mois were loath to follow, but Defosse prevailed upon them.

The jungle at night is very still and weird, full of sound and full of eyes. Civet cats look at you out of the darkness with their steely blue eyes. All kinds of deer watch you, their big yellow eyes shining like lamps. Great round red eyes fly overhead as the night birds pass on soft-beating wings. Then there are countless little bright bead-points of reflected light — the eyes of spiders, moths and snakes that shine above, below, and on all sides. The very stars are eyes that peep down between the leaves. The whole great forest is made of eyes that look at you out of its very depths. Even the old stalwart tree trunks have eyes that are black and round and hollow.

I stayed out until 4 A.M. and shot a civet cat and a hog deer. In my light, a burnt stick gave me a start for the blades of grass moving over it made it seem so alive I was sure, for a moment, it was a black cobra. Then, while circling back to camp in the waist-high grass, I came within a few feet of an enormous wild boar. Pig eyes do not shine at night and I had no warning of his close presence until he suddenly charged so fast across in front of me I did not have time to shoot. He was so powerful and huge I could well understand why they sometimes emerge victorious in their battles with tigers.

Defosse had told us that because of scarcity, the seladang (*Bos gaurus*) was by all odds the most difficult big game animal in the jungle to get. The seladang is a magnificent creature — the tallest of the bovine family in the world. He is courageous, wary, fast and much too savage to be tamed.

One day when Mason was with Defosse he encountered a herd

of seladang and got several. One of these was left as tiger bait and it was decided that I was to approach the blind at dawn the following morning to see if a tiger had "arrived."

Approaching a tiger blind isn't a thing you do every day, so I asked Defosse about it. "The blind," he said, "is a little leafy barrier of interwoven branches attached to two upright stakes. It is about three feet wide and six feet high and at the right spot there is a peephole to poke your rifle through."

"How far is the blind from the bait?" I asked.

"About fifteen feet," said Defosse.

"Why do you have it so close?"

"Because the only way you can be sure of stopping a tiger in his tracks is to shoot him in the brain."

"Well," I said, "what is to prevent the tiger from leaving the bait and walking around the corner of the blind just as you are reaching it?"

"Oh, nothing at all," said Defosse, "and of course, that does happen. It has also happened that the hunter has missed the brain and that on his first spring the tiger has gone right through the blind, rubbing blood off on the hunter's trouser leg."

"But be sure," he added, "not to do what Major C—— from the Philippine Islands did. Just as he was placing the muzzle of his rifle through the peephole in the blind the tiger saw it, jumped over the bait and walked up to investigate. Whereupon the major withdrew his rifle and simply stood there. The tiger was on one side of the blind, the major on the other. They were about three feet apart and one little flick of the tiger's paw would have completely demolished the blind.

"Yes," said Defosse, "all kinds of things can happen when approaching a tiger blind. We always make a very nice clean trail right up to the blind so one can arrive silently. Naturally, tigers like to use that trail."

[122]

"Yes, I see that makes it very cozy," I said.

"I remember so well just two years ago," Defosse continued, "when Babe White, the great All-American football player, was with me. He had shot a buffalo on the plains and built a blind that was too low to walk up to. So Babe got down on all fours and started to crawl toward the blind, a distance of a hundred yards. I, meantime, stood my ground and, so to speak, covered Babe's rear — which, incidentally, was enormous, even for a two-hundred-and-fifty-pounder. Babe was making good progress in the dawn light when suddenly a tiger jumped out into the trail a few yards behind him. Babe, scrabbling along on all fours, had not heard a sound whereas the tiger, sighting such a fascinating object, was so intrigued he immediately pursued it. I did not dare shoot the tiger because he was directly in line with Babe. Neither did I dare yell, for Babe would have had to turn and aim in my direction. Meantime, the tiger was advancing so rapidly on Babe's posterior that immediate action was necessary. So I simply fired into the air and by the time Babe glanced around, the tiger had already bounded off into the sword grass. You see," concluded Defosse, "a lot of things can happen."

With this grounding, and after a rather sleepless night, I started on my first tiger hunt. Shortly after dawn I reached the beginning of the trail. About a hundred yards away I could just see the small leafy blind. The jungle was dark and dripping and I felt sure a tiger must be there. Meen and Trang patted themselves lightly on the chest to attract my attention and asked permission to retire. I nodded and they quietly left. I felt horribly deserted.

I checked my rifle and removed the safety catch. For a while, I crept along the trail without making a sound. My own stealth played havoc with my imagination. I felt as if the tiger would catch me trying to out-sneak him. For a long time I stopped and listened and held my breath. That made things much worse for I was sure now that I could hear him. An old hunter had said to me, "If you go tiger hunting, be sure that you want to meet him." At that moment I was not at all sure. I wondered if I had buck fever. I stopped and lined my sights on a tree and was amazed to find they were quite steady.

Now I was getting close and I began to picture the tiger stepping around the edge of the blind and meeting me face to face. What would I do then, at such close quarters? I stopped and listened again and now I was truly excited, for there was no longer any question about it — something was tearing at the meat. At that point I remembered Defosse had said that many sensible hunters simply refuse to go to a five-yard blind alone. "It is not often," he had added, "that a man has serious trouble, but if he has it once, he never has it again." I had not asked him to amplify that final comment but it had left an unpleasant impression.

As I drew close to the little screen of leaves, I began to wonder whether to peek through the peephole first or to put the rifle barrel through first. I was stooped well over so that the tiger could not see any movement through the peephole and I now raised my barrel gingerly and pushed it through the hole. It made a tiny rustle against the leaves and immediately I held my breath and listened. I could still hear plenty of noise at the bait so I now started very slowly to raise myself to the proper level. Bit by bit, as my head went up the barrel of my rifle was depressed until finally it lined up with the large swollen black carcass of the seladang. And then came the biggest letdown of my life — instead of a tiger it was only a large monitor lizard feasting on the bait.

The next day Defosse and I hunted together. By midmorning I was scorched with the heat and needed rest. We were passing an island of jungle surrounded by open grass and I suggested we rest in the shade for a few minutes. Hardly had I lifted the canteen to my lips when we heard a loud crashing close by. Defosse's eyes caught mine. "The elephants," he whispered. The Mois did not hesitate a moment. They scrambled up a tree and grinned down at us from their perch like a pair of monkeys. Before taking another step, Defosse and I changed very quietly to steel, muffling the metallic clicks as best we could. Then, with infinite care, we made our way toward the sound.

In Defosse's language I knew we were "attacking the elephants." Working cautiously into the interior of the patch of jungle, we found that it opened up for about forty yards. The elephants were not thirty yards beyond the end of this little glade. We could see the trees shaking and hear the breaking branches and the full flap of elephant ears and even their digestive gurglings. We made a circle back through the jungle to make sure no elephants were behind us, and then we returned very close to where they were noisily browsing.

Defosse whispered that elephants hate to get caught in the open so my first shot would not drive them ahead into the plains but would bring the whole herd racing back through the jungle in our direction. It struck me he was alerting me to the probability of a charge. "Therefore," he continued, "as soon as you shoot, we will run back to that big tree and that will give us thirty yards of clear jungle to kill in. Don't stop shooting until there are no more elephants facing us and remember: not below the line of the eyes!" Defosse's whole expression had suddenly changed. He was leaning forward from the waist with intent eyes, his knees were flexed, suggesting the necessity for quick movement. His rifle was held in both hands, ready for instant action. "Take off the safety catch," he whispered.

It was getting exciting, but all I could see was an occasional trunk reaching up to grab a branch, or part of an ear flopping —

certainly nothing on which to risk a shot. Then, after a tense wait, the wind changed. Just a puff of air was wafted through the jungle toward the elephants. There was a moment of silence. Even their noisy digestions seemed to stop. Defosse swore under his breath. Then, with a sudden startling impact, the whole jungle seemed to break apart. With one accord, the great gray bodies hurtled out of the forest, smashing through everything in their path. A moment later, the shattering sound ceased and in its place we could hear the swish of long legs racing through tall grass. "Shoot in the air and run to the big tree." I fired two shots and Defosse and I ran for the tree. At the sound of my shots the elephants wheeled and hurled themselves back into the jungle.

The terrific crashing grew louder; we stood by the big tree, tense and ready. Then the elephants stopped and there was again silence. "They are looking for trouble," whispered Defosse. One moved on. He was not coming directly toward us, he circled and passed beneath the tree the Mois were sitting in. We could see the Mois but so thick was the mass of creepers below, we could not see the elephant, and we did not dare go into the thick jungle to try to "head" him. I could see the Mois looking straight down at him. For a moment I had visions of the elephant reaching up with his trunk and grabbing them. He could have done it so easily. But he passed around us leaving behind an open trail through the mass of creepers.

Now the others followed and for a while there was a rending and crashing both in front and behind as they smashed their way through. But they had located us perfectly by that first puff of wind and they all circled by and moved on. The island of jungle wasn't more than seventy yards wide and we were in the middle of it, and yet it was so dense that five elephants passed us in that narrow strip and we were unable to get a shot.

There was no use following them on foot, so we started for

camp. The sun was hotter than ever and the miles were long. From intense excitement we now passed to unutterable boredom and the discomfort of sweating along through the accursed sword grass and the doubly accursed broiling sun. Defosse stopped to light his pipe and I hated him for it. How any man could stop to light a pipe under such a sun I could not understand. But it had been a great experience. The spectacle of gigantic bodies smashing their mighty way through primeval jungle was unforgettable.

On two successive days there had been complete failure in pursuit of the two greatest animals in Indo-China — the tiger and the elephant. On the other hand, my Museum collection was progressing. I had obtained a fine banteng, the big red cousin of the seladang, usually referred to by the French as the *"boeuf sauvage."* I had also obtained a group of sambar and barking deer and hog deer and wild boar and many smaller nocturnal species.

Therefore, since I was most anxious to visit the high mountain country of Annam and to collect the famous Elds deer, I decided to head off alone on a new adventure.

Elds deer (*Cervus eldi platyceros*), called by the natives the *"conquatant,"* lives in the mountains of the Lang Bian in Annam. Since Mason and Defosse were planning a big tiger hunt on the Lanya Plains they would not miss me, so I made the two-day journey partly to get the deer for the Museum and partly because of a longing for some good cool air at five thousand feet. The country was like a bit of Scotland tucked away in Indo-China and the hunting was reminiscent of deer stalking with beautiful rolling hills partly open and partly pine-clad. The air had a bracing tang and the rocky streams ran clear and cold — a glorious contrast to the heavy-laden heat waves and warm smelly waters of the bottomland jungle.

With six Mois, I camped out under some pines and as the cold night air settled down, an open fire became a glorious necessity. One Moi spoke a few words of French. He was my only contact with my Mois and a very tenuous one at that.

Late the second evening, after hunting hard for two days, I saw a large herd of *conquatant* working down out of the timber. Though it was getting quite dark the situation offered real hope, for the deer were moving over a ridge into a deep gully. As soon as they were well out of sight, I had only to circle above them and run down the ridge they had just crossed. When I thought I had passed them, I swung off the ridge into the gully and waited on a rock. It was only a minute before they appeared. The up-mountain wind was right. The sun had long since set, and the shadows had grown deep and heavy. If I remained immobile, they would not see me. Some twenty of them worked their way along below me — does and fawns and a couple of young bucks. Then two fine stags appeared. Even in the dim light I could see that one of them carried a very fine head of horns. Though it was too dark to count the points, the general swing and shape of the head was unmistakable. However, when I drew a bead on the big stag, I found that the dark gray-brown background so exactly matched the color of the animal it was impossible to tell where I was aiming — whether at some portion of the animal or the land beyond. It would have to be a chance shot, and I waited until he was not more than fifty yards away to take it. The blurring of the sights made an overshot very likely, so I deliberately aimed low and fired. He reeled and staggered and went down. With surprising ease I had obtained a fine example of that unique, almost caribouhorned variety of the typical deer.

However, during the warm afternoon I made a serious mistake by jumping into a cold mountain stream. That chilling of the blood brought on the fever. It hit me in the middle of the night and a roaring fire a few feet away could not keep me warm.

The next morning, with a body full of aches and no breakfast, I started out to try and get a hind and fawn to complete the Museum group. The deep valleys were filled with white mist. Three Mois came with me and did not seem to understand what was the matter as with thumping head I made my way slowly along.

Then I found a hillside that commanded a good view of the country and I stretched out in the sun. I kept one Moi to watch and sent the two others to look for deer, telling them to signal if they saw any.

I had been lying in a sick daze for about an hour and a half when the Moi at my side called me and pointed. On a distant slope I saw my two men standing together. Field glasses showed they were waving. The walk to the other hill was one of the painful events of my life. My eyes were bleary with fever. My sense of balance was gone and I fell repeatedly. But the animals were there and somehow I managed to shoot them.

For the trip back to Dankia, I obtained a mule. We passed through several Moi villages and distributed meat. In one village I got off the mule for a moment. Whereupon a tame water buffalo promptly displayed the hatred of his race for all white men. He immediately came for me. Fortunately a youngster who could not have been more than six or seven, seeing what was happening, rushed at the brute and turned him away simply by slapping the great neck with his bare palm.

Finally, long after dark, I located the home of *Monsieur le Docteur*. He was not there, and I lay down on the floor of his living room with a splitting head. When he arrived, he took one look at me and said very simply, "*Ah, mais oui, vous avez le paludisme.*" Then he gave me a big shot of quinine and took me to the mountain town of Dalat. There I remained, alone in a room for ten days. I had nothing to eat and saw nobody except the doctor, who came once a day and shot me full of quinine. I lost thirty-five pounds and was reduced to a rack of bones.

On the eleventh day, I left Dalat and returned in two days to Saigon. Malignant malaria is tough to cure and I still had a fever of about a hundred. However, a doctor in Saigon was very helpful. He gave me a combination of arsenic and quinine which he said would strengthen me. He assured me it was perfectly all right to return to the jungle.

The next day I managed to obtain a little stallion at Gia-Huynh and rode him a day's journey to Defosse's camp on the Lanya River. On the bank above the river was the palm hut. Defosse and Mason were sitting at a table as I came quietly up at dusk. Mason had procured some beer from Saigon and brought it out by bullock cart. They were having a bottle and as soon as I arrived the faithful Chu rushed down to the river and produced one for me. It was a joyful reunion and deeply relaxing to be among friends again — particularly with the tender care of our wonderful Chinese boy.

Mason and Defosse said I was "a sight to look at" and they seemed more than grateful at my escape from malaria. Chu brought me food, as I had had nothing since six in the morning. After supper that night I learned that Mason had been hunting tiger steadily and had seen six. His marksmanship had not yet produced results, but his courage and determination were so great that he had even approached a tiger blind by moonlight — something I would not have considered doing. Mason had also had the good fortune of running into a solitary seladang, which he had shot. The old outcast's horns were twice as big as those of the herd bull he had already obtained.

Before retiring, I went out with Defosse and we stood on the bank of the river. The Lanya flows into the Donai and the Donai flows into the sea. As I saw the Lanya first, it was a ribbon of silver beneath a young moon. Close by were the campfires of the Mois, their dark figures stretched out on the white sandspit. I heard fish splashing and the deep grumble of crocodiles. There was a great rounded black rock in the middle of the river that reminded one of the council rock in the Jungle Books. The passing ripples soothed it gently and flowed away into the gloom around the bend. A deep gurgling of moving waters filled the stillness.

Defosse said the elephants had been roaring every night and that there were plenty of buffalo on the open plains but that the Mois had not yet burnt much of the grass and the hunting would be hard and dangerous.

That night the fire ants attacked me. I got some firebrands from the Mois' fireplace and tried to ward them off with a smoldering barrier but my efforts were unsuccessful and I finally had to move my cot well out under the stars to get some sleep. A bird in a cage suspended from the roof was killed by the ants that night.

At camp there was a mare in heat and the next morning the Mois, showing an uninhibited interest in such matters, reported that my little stallion had served the mare fifteen times. During breakfast, it became evident he was still far from exhausted. The Mois' concern for matters biological brought to my mind a story of Merian Cooper's that took place in northern Siam.

Coop had a letter of introduction to the rajah of a certain town. When Coop arrived, he found the town remarkably empty and the rajah, who had been expecting him, pacing restlessly up and down. After a few brief words, the rajah could stand it no longer and invited Coop out to see the show — in this case consisting of the breeding of elephants. The whole town, including the children, had turned out to watch.

In a dugout early in the morning when the mist still lay thick between the banks, we floated down on the quiet Lanya and I saw the beautiful crested long-tailed peacocks sitting in the trees, fairly hurling their calls across the water. I watched a flock of monkeys scrambling up and down some vines and creepers that dangled from the spreading branches of a rubber tree. And there were all kinds of birds — egrets and near egrets, snakebirds, adjutant birds, cranes and hawks and the little kingfishers, those veritable jewels of the jungle.

We saw the crossing-places of the elephant and the buffalo where the vertical banks were worn down to a gentle decline. Crocodiles had been dragging their tails all over a sandspit and there were fresh tiger tracks there too. Here was a big crocodile that rattled off the bank to glide out into midstream, the three black points of his eyes and nose moving without a ripple over the water before he disappeared, submarine-like, into a deep pool.

Then a hog deer tried to swim across and a croc caught him from behind. The little deer struggled and squealed as it was being dragged under. The Mois paddled fast and drove away the croc. Then they grabbed the deer and took it themselves for meat. The toothmarks on his hindquarters were ugly to look at.

A dugout came around the bend, a frizzly-haired Moi standing in the stern, paddling. He had a boatload of naked women suckling their babies. Quietly they came around the bend and quietly they passed by and went on upstream. Not a word passed between the two boats.

So we came to Mason's tiger country. For the past two days he had been watching the animals. They would not come to his bait and because of swamps and pools he could not get closer to them. For hours he watched them moving in the grass and wallowing in the water playing with each other, then finally risked a shot and missed. I could well imagine his frustration.

After that Defosse and I returned to camp over the heat-laden plains. We saw elephant trails and more fresh tiger tracks and lots of buffalo tracks; we saw hundreds of hog deer, those little fools that squeak and scurry around in the long grass and run into the open mouth of a tiger.

While crossing a patch of jungle just before reaching camp we stopped at the sound of shaking branches. One's first thought is always elephants, but the sound was too high. I looked up and saw big monkeys traveling at a wonderful speed through the trees — their long arms reaching out and seizing branch after branch as they swung themselves along. "Shoot," said Defosse, "the frigate captains." I saw one stop and I fired. He held on for quite a while, swinging from one hand, and then fell dead. The others were already gone and we only heard a distant rustle in the treetops that rapidly faded away.

For many miles the Lanya flows through the plains, eddying and circling back on itself in great bows before it swings again into the jungle.

On either side of the river extend plains covered with sword grass and dotted with pools and wallows. It is the home of the wild water buffalo about whose fierceness we had heard before we came to Indo-China. In danger, Defosse rated the buffalo second only to the elephant and well ahead of tigers; a buffalo bull is quite capable of killing a tiger in fair fight. Some buffaloes have even been known to go after tiger every time they have a chance.

The Indo-China water buffalo is the finest there is, and I was most anxious to get a good group for the Museum. So the next morning Defosse and I started after them. On our way we followed a narrow strip of jungle between two plains. Evidently that strip had been the home of the elephants for a long time for there were broad trails everywhere and glades with no underbrush left. I heard a little bird chirp airily. It was the Moi bird of good omen and quickly our two Mois called out in answer and made their wish. Defosse told me it was for the elephants that they had wished. Once again we heard him and once again the Mois made the same wish in a curious singing voice.

There was a tiger somewhere ahead of us and several times Defosse smelled him but the leaves were dry and it was useless to bother.

Presently we came out onto the plains. They were ashimmer with heat waves that danced and trembled so that in the distance everything was in a haze and seemed to be moving. I looked around at the mountains that all but encircled the plains and cursed them for cutting off the breeze. The burned ground underfoot was at broiling point and a blast of hot air smote our faces and the sweat dripped from our pores.

Then we saw nine young buffalo bulls. They saw us at the same time and immediately fronted and stood flank to flank, tossing their heads and pawing the ground, now and then advancing a few feet. "These bulls must come from downriver," said Defosse. "I don't believe they have ever been shot at." We made a half circle in order to give them our scent. The Mois did not like the look of things and headed for the jungle.

As we circled, the buffalo seemed to be getting more and more impatient. One in particular stamped the ground and threw his head about, showing the others, as Defosse suggested, what he was going to do about it if we came any closer.

When our scent was blowing directly to them, it seemed only to increase their nervousness and anger. They were less than a hundred yards away and could see us perfectly. Their noses were stretched high in the air, their horns sweeping out and down against their flanks. They bristled audacity, and I felt sure that could they talk they would be saying: "We hate you. We are not afraid. Get out of here. If you come an inch closer we will charge." I saw no more magnificent sight in the jungle than this formidable array of wild buffalo in battle formation. Not only did they refuse to give ground, they kept advancing toward us with increasing uneasiness until Defosse finally remarked, "We had better be moving along — we can't keep teasing these boys any longer."

So we left them and returned to the jungle. At the edge of the timber was a large pool full of fish left from the flood of the last rains. Some twenty Mois were fishing there with nets and spears. They were giggling and laughing and playing tricks on each other, catching hundreds of fish and occasionally, with an apt flick of the wrist, scooping up mouthfuls of foul water. Altogether, they were having a hilarious time — like so many children at recess.

After lunch, we went into the open to light fires. At midday the grass was thoroughly dry. With snap and crackle and rip and raw, the flames tumbled over each other high into the air and like a prairie fire swept down the plains. But fire and smoke do not seem to bother the game of Indo-China. Swallows and flycatchers dive in and about above the lick of the flames, but the game moves calmly and easily out of the way. There are good reasons for lighting these fires on the plains. The burn not only clears away the long grass so a hunter can see — it also provides fresh succulent shoots that bring out the game. The fire stops dead at the jungle wall which it is unable to penetrate.

We circled the edge of a pool through long tufted grass. I did not quite like the feel of it and Defosse said it was the best way he knew of "getting caught by a tiger." At the lower edge of the pool a large croc was basking in the sun, his great jaws open as if anticipating a huge mouthful. His eyes were hidden by the open jaw so we were able to walk up very close before he heard us and rattled off into the pool.

Defosse now told me that he felt an attack of fever coming on and that he would have to head back to camp. Since the afternoon was still young, I elected to continue in search of a big water buffalo bull.

A little later, I saw where two bulls had come out of the long grass on my left and circled back in again. The tracks were fresh and I changed quickly from lead to steel. The animals had been feeding on the young shoots of some recently burned ground. Further on were the tracks of a large herd that had also cut back into the long grass on my left. To my right was a narrow strip of unburned grass and beyond that a big pool where I had seen some cows and calves a few days before. I wanted very much to get a look at that pool and accordingly cut through the sword grass; as I emerged on the far side, there — standing by the edge of the pool a hundred and fifty yards away and looking straight at me — was a magnificent bull. His head was up, his nose reaching high into the air, twisting this way and that for a telltale scent. The eyesight of a buffalo is poor but his sense of smell is excellent, and after he has been shot at a few times the merest whiff will send him away on a lumbering gallop that swallows up the plains.

With my left elbow on my hip — Defosse style — I took careful aim just below the bull's nose and ticked off the trigger. My rifle misfired. It had misfired twice the day before when shooting hog deer for meat and I was rapidly losing confidence in it. Quickly I reloaded and fired again and this time the bullet whizzed away in a screaming ricochet off the bull's thick hide. The animal recoiled from the impact and made off broadside. As he did so, I fired again and heard the thick plunking impact as the bullet went home. Before I could fire again, he was out of sight in the long grass.

Then I became conscious of a deep roaring rumble that rapidly grew in volume. It was the pounding of hundreds of hoofs coming closer. A moment later a whole herd of cows and calves burst out of the grass and swept by close in front of me. It was a wild,

Top:
Mason Sears going down
the Lanya River after tiger.

Bottom:
The solitary water buffalo bull.

thundering, wonderful, and quite terrifying sight, and I was happy they were not headed my way. They ran for perhaps three quarters of a mile, then the entire herd swung around and faced me and I could see clearly the long line of their tossing black heads. These were wonderful animals.

But what was I to do about my bull? The idea of going into the long grass after a wounded buffalo with a rifle that misfired and bullets that ricocheted had no appeal, so, after reloading, I made a wide detour around the sword grass to see if he had come out the other side. He had not done so. Somewhere in that patch of grass he was either standing waiting to charge, or sick enough to be lying down, or perhaps even dead.

If he were down, the vultures would come. I would not have to wait long to find out. Meantime, I sat in the middle of the broiling, blackened ground and waited. The longer I waited the safer it would be to go into the grass. My Mois were nowhere in sight. It was a hot and lonely vigil and I kept wishing that Defosse were with me. I remembered that he had said that buffalo hunting would be dangerous on the Lanya Plains because so much grass was still unburned. I knew now just what he meant.

The next time I looked up the vultures were there. They were circling high above the grass — a few at first, then more and more appearing out of nowhere.

Finally I knew the time had come to go into the grass. I pushed off the safety catch and entered. Once inside, the grass seemed shorter than I had expected, and I felt sure I could have seen the bull had he been standing. The thought of his being definitely down was comforting. I moved with the greatest of care, cutting diagonally across the island. I saw nothing. So immediately I started back a few yards further up. Well out in the middle of the grass I suddenly saw the white tip of a horn between the grass blades. For a long time I stood absolutely still, watching for the slightest movement. There was none. I advanced a step and looked again, and then another. Then I saw that the horn was tilted well over to the side and it seemed certain that the bull was dead. A moment later I was standing on his back and saw my two fine Mois approaching over the burned ground. Evidently they had been watching the proceedings with great care.

On my first trip through the grass I had passed within ten yards of the buffalo and failed to see him. The bullet had entered low down behind the foreleg where the skin is less tough. Buffalo can absorb quantities of steel and it was nothing less than tremendous good luck that one bullet had killed. My little camera was on my belt and I showed Meen just how to look through the finder and click it. It took at least half an hour of painstaking work to get him to hold the camera still while clicking it. I was mighty proud of that bull and wanted to have my picture taken with him. After that the three of us started the skinning.

The next day I got a cow and a calf and then we moved our camp back into the jungle again, as Defosse still had hopes of meeting up with the seladang.

Of the months spent in the Indo-China jungles in 1923, my most vivid recollection concerns a sound I heard late one evening a few days before we left. It is the most dramatic and formidable wild animal sound in all the world; once heard it is never forgotten. Its deep, thunderous reverberations still ring in my ears.

I had been out since dawn with my two Mois, looking for seladang. We were in new country and the Mois were very fearful of getting lost so it became necessary from time to time, when their anxiety mounted, to examine my compass, the magical properties of which they never failed to respect.

In the late afternoon, I ran onto a herd of banteng. They had not seen us and the wind blew strong and steady in our favor.

Hoping there might be an old bull with a really big head, I sig-
naled to the Mois to stay where they were and began the stalk. A
cow was on the watch, so I had to crawl belly down about fifty
yards through short grass till I got behind a tree. The banteng
were only a hundred yards away on the edge of some long grass
and bamboo thickets. I could see five of them — all cows and
calves. In front of me it was very short grass, so a closer approach
was impossible. The animals were partly concealed and I was sure
there were more so I waited. During the next fifteen minutes several more cows appeared but still no bulls. Then suddenly a very
large boar grunted and rooted his way out into the open ground
to my left. He was a good solitary — bigger than anything I had
obtained. So I turned and fired and immediately looked back at
the banteng in hopes that a bull would come into view. I had a
glimpse of ten or twelve twirling tails and that was all. But at that
moment I noticed out of the corner of my eye a black object
streaking across the clearing at terrific speed. I threw my gun
around and fired and had the satisfaction of seeing the boar turn
a series of somersaults and lie still. Evidently my first shot had
only wounded.

Meen then ran up with many exclamations of disgust. Knowing
nothing about collecting, he could not understand letting the
banteng go and shooting a mere boar.

It was getting late and we were a long way from camp. So we
started home, the Mois carrying the boar on a long pole. To
make travel easier, I followed an old lumber road. Curving lumber
roads can be very deceptive, but although I was on a road I had
not previously traveled, I sensed no anxiety — a state that scarcely
applied to the two Mois. However, I could not build up too much
concern for them, for I knew if the least thing went wrong they
would shin up a tree and if necessary spend the night there.

What I did not know was just how long it would take to get

back to camp — and in the jungle this is an all-important matter, for when tigers and leopards move abroad in the dimming light, it is a very serious mistake to be caught out beyond that time when the sight of a rifle can be clearly seen. But it sometimes happens that a particular situation is so intriguing, so compelling, that caution is momentarily forgotten. This was what happened that late evening while returning to Defosse's camp.

We had come to a spot that arrested attention. Between the jungle trees to the left of the track I could see a light area and dead tree trunks against an orange sky. It looked as though a slough or marsh might be there — obviously different from anything I had yet seen. I could not resist investigating. Leaving the Mois I headed off at right angles into the jungle. In a few minutes I had reached the edge of the opening. Evidently it was an area that flooded during the rains but was now dry. Spotted throughout were great dead trees, their branches forming weird and grotesque silhouettes. Nearby was an enormous banyan tree whose vast honeycombed network of interlacing columns and passages could have concealed a dozen leopards.

At that moment I heard a loud raucous squawking and a magnificent peacock sailed through the trees and lit above me on a branch not fifty yards away. I could easily have shot him. It seemed a little early for him to be going to roost and I wondered whether a leopard had scared him.

Then I saw a hornbill flying over the dry marsh, his wings making a noisy rasping sound with each downbeat. No doubt he was headed home with a mouthful of fruit for his sealed-up mate. A woodpecker started hammering on one of the dead stubs. He made a clear ringing bell-like sound against the hardwood. A gecko, high up in the banyan, saw me and kuck-kawed his tired, sleep-inducing call.

This was the exciting hour in the jungle, when day was turning into night. Some animals were going to rest; others were waking. Everywhere there was movement and sound and an exhilarating sense of something impending.

I heard a barking deer across the marsh. It was an alarm call repeated half a dozen times. There was no mistaking the sharp message in that voice. He was telling the jungle of a leopard or a tiger. I did not know which. He might even be telling of a companion that had just been killed, for there was the feeling of insistent horror in his call.

There was such fascination in every second, I felt rooted to the spot, but darkness descends fast upon the jungle and I knew I should be on the move. I tested my sights. Much was still clearly visible, but ripening gloom was already blurring all outlines and touching the commonplace with a mysterious halo. It was the hour when the mind reaches for the inner heart of things.

For a moment stillness settled with oppressive completeness upon the forest. It was as though the whole jungle held its breath in anticipation. I was standing there alone, motionless, looking and listening and keyed to the highest pitch of awareness, when there came the thunderous roar of wild elephants not far away. First one and then another, answering back and forth and filling the late evening with a gigantic volume of low deep rumbling roars — wave upon wave of them, one after another.

The sound, as it hit me where I stood by the edge of the dried-up marsh, was galvanizing. I did not know what it meant or what they were doing, but it seemed as though they were on the move and I could picture them swinging through the forest and bursting into the open. The sheer power and might of it left me with no strength. Or maybe it was the awareness that the sound came roughly from a direction between me and Defosse's camp and the intimidating thought that to get home I would have to squeeze by that herd, not knowing in what direction they were headed.

Their temper sounded bad and from the way they took over and proclaimed themselves, it was as much as to say that the whole world was theirs. Even with rifle in hand, my stature seemed to shrink to minute size.

Unlike the trumpeting, this was a sound that came from deep in their great bellies. It was at once majestic and awe-inspiring. I wondered if they might be heralding the birth of a baby elephant as old elephants are wont to do, but Defosse said later that more probably it was a big herd saying to each other it was time to leave the jungle and go down to the watering holes.

By now darkness was really sinking fast upon the forest and I suddenly felt the same violent urge to flee that had hit me so hard many years before when I heard wolves behind me in the Canadian forest. I was keyed up — nervous about staying and nervous about going — for, as never before, I had a deep sense of the hostility of the jungle and the puniness of man.

The roaring of the elephants had stopped and there was not a sound. I felt in a vacuum. Then I wondered about my Mois and dashed back to them. I found them thoroughly frightened, for they knew that added to the danger of encountering tiger or leopard when too dark to see the sights there was now the much greater danger of suddenly coming too close upon the elephants.

I motioned to them to leave the boar and we went as fast as possible, for speed was of the essence if we were to avoid being caught in complete darkness. It was a question too of just where the lumber road would come out.

Whether you encounter game or not depends so much on timing. It was quiet underfoot, so noise was hardly a factor. But a tiger or leopard could have crossed the track a moment before or a moment after we passed by. It was too dark to see the light imprint of pug marks, so we had no way of knowing. On that fast walk I saw only two sambar — that was all. The elephants did not speak again and they had not crossed ahead of us. It was an exciting trip and we fairly flew.

When we reached camp I expected some reprimands from Defosse and I got them. He told me he doubted if the Mois would ever go with me again. He cross-questioned them, and I did not ask him to translate their uncomplimentary answers. "There is no excuse," said Defosse, "for taking unnecessary chances." He made me feel like a small boy. Yet, for the moment, it seemed to me enough that we were all safely home, and I consoled myself with that thought.

Late that night I stood out in front of our palm hut. The jungle moon was sailing a cloudy sea and the Southern Cross stood low over the rim of the great forest. The soft air flowing in among the black tree trunks brought all the noises of the forest — the bell of the sambar stag, the yelp of the hog deer, the sharp bark of the muntjac, the songs of night birds and crickets and lizards and now once again in the distance the roar of an elephant — Kipling's "pinprick of sound in the darkness." And when I heard it, I suddenly felt glad in my heart that I had not shot an elephant. It would have been an exciting experience but at least I had not been responsible for the death of one of these wonderful, intelligent animals whose survival from the great age of mammals into the age of man has given us something to admire and wonder at and even to stand in awe of.

Then I looked at Defosse, "*l' empereur des forêts*," as the French called him, with ninety-eight elephant and forty-five tiger notches on his gun. He sensed that I had been admiring the beauty of the night and the sounds of the jungle, and he waved a careless hand toward me, as if encompassing the universe, and said, "All this just for the asking and I do not have to pay."

9

Savage Abadabur

"You shall know immensity,
     and see continuing the primeval forces of the world. . . .
You shall see mountains rise in the transparent shadow before dawn."

I T WAS the lure of remoteness, the challenge of inaccessibility, as well as visions of the famed Marco Polo sheep (*Ovis poli*) — perhaps the greatest game trophy in the world — that made me dream of the High Pamirs.

This vast "roof the the world" plateau that cradles the Oxus River belongs to the true hinterland of Central Asia. A harsh, strange kingdom with primitive nomadic tribes, it is also a land of history — of earth conquerors, of Tamerlane and Kublai Khan.

The Oxus itself is a river of dreams. Where it flows northward through the Chorasmian waste "brimming and bright and large," the mighty Sohrab and Rustum, father and son, fought to the death while great hosts looked on.

To the south, the melting Pamir snows feed the Indus, a river so old it was there before the greatest of all mountain ranges reared their giant heads some sixty million years ago, a river of such power it cut through great blocks of upward-thrusting rock more rapidly than they arose. From the Indus Gorge to the heights of nearby Nanga Parbat lie more than 23,000 vertical feet. Like the Columbia that slices through the Rockies, so the Indus bisects the Himalayas with deep roaring abysses chiseled through vast accumulations of sedimentary rock.

But my dream was not to be fulfilled. The British had grown strict about their Soviet borders. First and foremost, I had to sign a pledge not to proceed beyond certain designated territory. Only then was permission granted to cross the Himalayas via the Burzil Pass and descend into the deep valley of Astor, whose bordering ravines, or nullahs, harbor ibex, red bear, shapu, and the snow leopard.

Disappointed as I was, the possibility of hunting markhor and ibex, the greatest of all goats, in country as rough as any that exists, was not lightly to be turned down and, even though the journey would have to be made alone (Mason Sears had been called home to Boston), the temptation was great.

One night when trying to make up my mind, I hired a shikara boat and slipped away noiselessly from the quaint moss-covered houses of the canal city of Srinagar, the capital of Kashmir. I needed to go where I could look at the mountains and think about my possible journey.

It was a craft for the Great Mogul himself — long, narrow, trim, double-pointed, with the tasseled canopy and becushioned divan of a sensuous tale from the Arabian Nights. Seven paddlers propelled me across the Jhelum River and into the beautiful canals beyond the city. The rhythm of their paddling was slow at first, very slow, with long quiet strokes that gradually increased in tempo — increased and increased, finally grabbing the water so hard one felt catapulted with violent strength across the shimmering surface. Then, when they must surely be exhausted by the sheer zeal of their paddling, they suddenly rested and the boat

Rahima Loon spying for ibex
in savage Abadabur.

glided quietly as a canoe between the green embankments of the canal. Only when our speed had dropped so the bow wave was the merest ripple on the glassy surface did the very slow and silent paddling begin again. It was a novel method of locomotion — the change of pace specifically designed to avoid boredom for the passengers.

Late in the evening, when well out in the peaceful country beyond Srinagar with neither a house nor a boat in sight, I told the boatmen to wait while I climbed a low embankment and walked along it. The damp earth was breathing with the sounds of early spring: sucking, watery noises in the wet sod, a slick, clinging, muddy feeling underfoot, and the frogs, like our own spring peepers, were filling the air with their singing.

I came to an opening with a view in all directions. Beyond the flat bottomland the girdling mountains all but surround this most beautiful valley.

There was a dead tree stub and I sat down and watched the gathering night. The clear, still air sparkled under a brilliant moon. What a contrast to the dusty, heat-laden plains of the Ganges! Many of the hills were dark and timber-clad, but here and there in the distance were snowy summits gleaming in whiteness. Then as the night shadows deepened, the great somber barrier of mountains loomed larger and more formidable. It rose up and up until it seemed to pierce the sky, dividing the entire world into two halves.

Absorbed by the immensity of the scene, I sat there, an infinitesimal speck surrounded by distance and space, and in a moment my spirit was soaring over the mountains to the fearful distances beyond, where I had a yearning to go.

Here was the most colossal physical barrier in all the world, whose very existence, sheer size, dormant power, seemed to father the wish to investigate the other side. The hunting was the ostensible purpose, but as I think back the real craving was the age-old wanderlust — that deep instinctive stirring in the blood to go and look and see, a feeling inherited from countless generations of primitive wandering tribes. Suppressed though it usually is, give it the slightest encouragement and it demands recognition.

How fortunate to be in the magnificent valley of Kashmir at the very edge of the great Himalayas! And yet, there began a fearful feeling of what lay ahead in the strange lands beyond. It was the fear of the unknown, and on that night it was tinged with loneliness. I thought then of Marco Polo — his incredible exploits and lonely travels for so many years. What inspiration and colossal courage he must have had.

The horizon was dark velvet where the deep blue met the white crests. Never did space make man seem so minute; yet in one sitting there, it produced a feeling of belonging to a vast unifying whole. As the night blossomed with moonlight, a sense of peace and composure crept over me. I decided to head for Abadabur,* a deep and formidable nullah on the far side of the great mountains.

The next day in Srinagar, I obtained my shikari, Rahima Loon, who spoke a little English and was able to help me with the outfitting. And I needed the help badly, for nowhere on earth were there such lying and thieving rascals as in Srinagar. A well-known merchant, Bahar Shah, invited me to lunch on the porch of his store overlooking the Jhelum. When, during the meal, three maidens appeared on the far bank and stripped down for a swim, I felt sure it was a planned entertainment designed to loosen my purse strings.

Unfortunately, on the trip across India I had been unable to obtain any more ammunition for my 9.5 mm. Mannlicher. Since only eleven cartridges remained, it was necessary to decide whether to purchase a new rifle with plenty of ammunition or to rely on an old favorite with only eleven rounds. I chose the old favorite after

* Pronounced Aba'dabur, with the stress on the second syllable.

filing the trigger-pull to such a fine point that when the end of the "drag" was reached the least tick would touch it off. With such a delicate trigger-pull, I felt confident.

The next day we slid across the reflecting waters of Wular Lake to Bandipur, where we obtained porters and prepared the loads. Then the real work began — a six-thousand-foot climb to the Tragbal Pass and on down into the great valley of the Kishenganga, where we averaged close to twenty miles a day.

It was mid-April and on the steep open slopes the effect of the sun on the snow created critical conditions. Already I had seen several places where slides had come down and were now lying spent and lifeless to a depth of forty feet. One slide had entered a pine forest where for hundreds of years the huge trees had weathered mountain gales. Like ninepins they had succumbed to the primeval force of avalanching snow. What dormant power may lie hidden on a mountainside!

Rahima told me that several years before twenty-four Kashmiris struggling up toward the Burzil Pass were wiped out by a slide. It is hard to imagine anything more frightening than to hear the warning rumble of a slide above you, to look up and see millions of tons of snow thundering down and to know that escape is impossible. Only on one occasion did I hear a slide coming down behind us and then all the men came on the run crying *"Chello, chello!"* (Quick, quick!)

Ours was the first party to cross the Burzil in the spring of 1923. To avoid the danger of slides, the only safe method was to travel by night, and this we did, leaving the Burzil Chowki bungalow at 3:30 A.M. after a little sleep.

The snow was hard underfoot and our grass shoes clung well to the steep slope. In the rarefied air of close to 14,000 feet, we moved up slowly into a moonlit world of deep purple shadows and glistening whiteness. Looking back, I saw the line of porters, their eighty-pound boxlike loads held by rope cords across their shoulders, threading their way single file up the pass. The air was completely still. As Rahima and I stood there, I became aware of the high-pitched ringing of absolute silence, a sound that seems to descend from outer space. Then a quavering falsetto voice broke through the zero air, rolled loud and clear up the valley to be joined at the chorus by a dozen others. How did those men have the strength to sing while climbing under such loads? Perhaps they were rejoicing at the stillness of the air, for they remembered killing storms and bitter winds.

The moon set while we were climbing and dawn caught us on the summit. On the very top of the Himalayas, I stopped and took a long look. We were very high in an area closed to travel for a large part of the year. Away into the distance marched the spear-like peaks of the greatest of world mountain ranges. Dawn was creeping across the east, casting a warm glow on the barren wilderness of snow and rock, a mountain vastness completely removed from other worlds. I don't believe Rahima understood why I sat there so long — he never liked to stop on the march unless there was a place to lie down and go to sleep. On this occasion he kept trying to urge me on saying something that sounded like *"Pleases neetche jaiager"* (down going). When I told him to go ahead it appeared he would not dream of going before his master. So I gave in and we fairly floated down the other side of the pass. On the way I noticed the tracks of several stone marten. Finally the eighteen-mile crossing of the Burzil had been accomplished and we found ourselves mounting the snow-covered steps of the bungalow of Chillum Chowki. The chokidar immediately massaged my legs until I finally said *"bos,"* enough, thus assuring him of several extra annas of baksheesh.

The porters did not get in until five o'clock. They had been fourteen hours on the march and were absolutely done up. As I

[1 5 0]

watched them, I wondered how many more years man would be able to hire man to do the work of mules. That night Rahima and I talked for a long time. He sat there with his gurgling "hubble bubble" pipe and quietly told me of his travels with many different sahibs in the wonderful lands of Central Asia. He was constantly talking of Aksu, Muralboshi, Kashgar, Yarkand, Urumchi, Uliassitai — names to stir the restless blood in any man.

Two days later we passed through the little Dard village of Astor. From a miniature polo field we dropped down steeply to the Astor River. Then for many long hours we struggled upward on precipitous ledgy trails until we finally emerged onto a steep grassy opening. Above us was a sharp ridge. Rahima told me that Abadabur Nullah began on the other side of that ridge. I had walked some one hundred and fifty mountain miles to see this place and was filled with excitement.

I will never forget that first look. Abadabur Nullah was rock-hewn desolation — a deep trench, a raw slice cut out of a mountain as if by two giant strokes of some primeval ax. The peaks, I was told, ran up to 17,000 feet, whence the sheer cliffs plunged into unseen depths. The precipices were so steep I did not see how anyone untrained to mountaineering could possibly maneuver over them. No wonder it had been necessary to employ Jumma Khan, a Chota shikari or local guide, for only through his intimate knowledge would it be possible to move about at all in such fantastic terrain.

I took out my field glasses, and began to examine the cliffs more closely. The more I looked the more uneasy I became, for we had no rope, no pitons, and were totally unprepared for rock work, yet the vast bulk of Abadabur was raw naked rock, a fit home for that master climber, the great Asian ibex. I expressed my doubts to Rahima, who replied appeasingly, "Every day little bad — every day not very bad."

[1 5 1]

We made camp on a few feet of more or less level terrain. No sooner was camp established than Rahima suggested we "take a little look" on some markhor ground.

Markhor prefer the steep timbered precipices of the lower country, leaving to the ibex the higher open cliffs. Without bothering to put on grass shoes, we started off following Jumma Khan, attired in the usual *chaplis*, or hobnailed sandals. Presently we came to some steep cliffs, but since no markhor were to be seen, Jumma Khan scrambled lightly down. The way the Dard went down looked so easy I immediately started to follow but soon discovered there was something radically wrong. The *chaplis* were so useless I had to take them off. Rahima, I noticed, did likewise. In stocking feet I continued the descent, getting into a more difficult situation the farther I went until at last I was spread-eagled against a rock face, not daring to look down. I tried hard to concentrate on the details of the cliff face but failed to notice any cracks into which a step could be taken in any direction. It was a grim situation and not at all what I had bargained for while dreaming of the High Pamirs.

In due course, Jumma Khan, aware of my discomfort, scrambled back up to me and, by placing my foot on his shoulder, was able to maneuver my descent. Rahima, I was pleased to see, also required help. On this kind of going I felt as awkward as a child learning to walk. Later I learned that a shikari had been killed on markhor ground that same spring. The only surprising thing was that it did not happen more often.

It took some time to recover from the descent and then we crept up cautiously to look over other cliffs. Just as I peeped over I heard a strange sound and a moment later saw two female markhor plunging down the mountain. From pinnacle to pinnacle they hurtled downward at a speed that seemed to equal that of antelope on a level plain. Forty, fifty feet at a jump, straight down; their shoulder blades should have ripped through their skins, yet they were at home, enjoying the speed of their descent and their own unbelievable agility. It was one of the extraordinary sights of the animal kingdom — a great example of adaptation to environment.

Rahima told me later that unlike the ibex and most other members of the goat family the markhor, when danger threatens, almost invariably head down. No doubt these two females had caught our scent, for the hair-raising exhibition they put on was certainly impelled by fright. It was like watching skiers in a great downhill race, with disaster imminent at every turn.

Markhor are constantly on the watch, looking both uphill and down, and the smallest falling stone attracts their attention. Furthermore, they have good eyesight and a good sense of smell. It is easy to see why an old solitary markhor with his grand spiral horns, his long beard and shaggy underlock, is such a highly prized trophy. Among Kashmir big game, he ranks first. Certainly he is the most difficult animal I have ever hunted.

In the course of the next two weeks we saw some eighty markhor but only one good head. He was a wary old king with a great mass of shaggy white hair under his neck, and days would go by without our getting a glimpse of him. Once we saw him coming on the full run in our direction. Rahima suggested that a snow leopard might have scared him, but at the crucial moment I dislodged a stone that went crashing down over the cliffs and spoiled the hunt for the day.

Every day Rahima and I had our trials and troubles with rock work. I remember on one occasion we both stood aghast watching two of our Dards going down a rock face. "Same dat bear" was Rahima's comment.

Then one afternoon we saw our markhor well up on some cliffs where it would have been impossible to approach him unseen. He had been joined by several smaller males, which only added to our problem. However, toward evening he started to work down accompanied by the others. It was easy to get within four hundred yards of him but I did not care to risk a shot at that range. For a long time they butted and played with each other on the steep rock face, their little stumpy tails wiggling hard all the while. Then finally they moved out of sight into a little gully. This left us free to get quite close providing the wind held and we made no noise.

Rahima started out over a steep rockslide much too fast. I tried to restrain him by whispering *"aste aste,"* slow slow, but since these admonitions had no effect, I was forced to say severely "Rahima, behind going!" Whereupon he gave me such a disheartened and downcast look I almost changed my mind.

Finally, with utmost caution, I came up over a little rise of ground and looked down into the gully. About thirty yards away I had a glimpse of a small markhor. He had his right forefoot up holding down the limb of a tree and was feeding. He did not see me. Very slowly I crouched down again, preparing to creep up a little further. But before I had even taken a step, I heard a falling stone and on quickly looking up, saw all the markhor on the run. They had my wind. Luckily the big fellow, instead of going down, ran along a steep face of rock. I fired twice as he went and then, hard hit, he took a little jump outwards and plummeted fifty feet onto the rocks below. That leap into space gave me the same awful feeling that wakes you from a dream. His skin was mangled and his horn tips broken, but nothing that could not be repaired. Rahima was quick to forgive me. He was grinning from ear to ear and saying a lot of things I could not understand. I thanked him and we shook hands, had a smoke and relaxed, enjoying our victory to the full.

The next morning we headed for the ibex country. Well up toward the upper end and near the bottom of the great slablike V-shaped ravine that is Abadabur Nullah is a cave where we decided to camp. The porters under the guidance of Jumma Khan were to go around by a gentler route while Rahima and the tiffin porter and I planned a long climb in order to drop into Abadabur over the edge of the V.

Abadabur Nullah from the lip of the V was once again a glorious and formidable and challenging sight. We had now entered upon the second phase of our hunt, the pursuit of a fine ibex in game country as hostile as any that exists. At first we slipped down a brief grassy slope and then for a long time sat looking into a terrifying gorge. Not many minutes elapsed before we had our first glimpse of ibex. They were playing on cliffs so steep they seemed to be sheer. I watched them through my field glasses — two good-sized bucks, two does, and two kids. The ledge they were on was so narrow that as the bucks walked along it they had to cant their heads to one side to prevent their scimitar-shaped horns from striking the rock. The lead buck somehow managed to turn, and rising up on his hind legs he thrust forward, butting the other. They repeated these playful antics many times before stopping to look down a precipice of several thousand feet. Even the young gamboled along these fantastic ledges as though in absolute safety. I was fascinated by the sight and in constant suspense lest they fall.

Finally Rahima said, "Pleases down going." As I stood up I looked over at Nanga Parbat, that famous 26,620-foot mountain whose dreadful slopes have, I believe, exacted a higher toll of human life than any mountain ever assaulted. Her forbidden pinnacles were bathed in a flush of color by the evening sun. Serene and perfect, she raised her giant blocklike head above all worldly things. I could have looked for hours but the deep chasm below was already growing ominous in the depth of its shadows.

Rahima led the way. Russleon, the barefooted tiffin porter, followed with my rifle strapped over his back, while I took up the rear. I shall never forget that descent of some two thousand feet over an endless series of cliffs that were all shelving at such a steep dip that toe and hand holds were altogether inadequate. Also the rock was friable and thus likely to give away at any moment.

Hardly had we begun the descent than I was once again spread-eagled against a rock face unable to move and scared to death. For a horrible minute I had the feeling it was utterly hopeless and that I might just as well jump and be done with it. My knees were the worst. They shook as though with ague. Finally Russleon came to my rescue, showed me where to put a foot and then a hand. Thus, very slowly, I began to move again, and movement conquered fear. But my slowness consumed a lot of time and dusk was near.

The descent lasted several hours and fortunately the lower cliffs were much easier to handle than the upper ones, otherwise we never would have made it in the dark. At last we came down under a ledge of rock and up into our cave, which was only an overhang of rock. A fire was burning brightly. I was still shaken by the experience and while the shadows played on the back of the cave I sat down by the fire and told Rahima what I thought of him for bringing me down those cliffs. "Damn foolishness" I called it. I explained I had come all the way to Astor to hunt and have a good time, not to break my neck. To which he replied by way of a mild compliment meant to appease, "God always taking care of good sahibs — sahib not falling." I answered I thought that God had nothing to do with my not falling and that on no account was he ever to take me again over such ground.

Rahima tactfully changed the subject and with a light in his eyes talked of a big old ibex with a wild head that Jumma Khan had seen from the cave earlier in the afternoon. One horn, injured in youth, had grown in a circle down under his chin so that one wondered how he ever managed to eat. A gusty cold wind was blowing and the smoke was whirling around the cave at such a rate I could not even see what I was eating for supper. Since no comfort

Rahima and Russleon on
the long trek to the Burzil Pass.

was to be had, bed looked inviting. My marmot-skin sleeping bag, made in Peking, had been set well apart at the extreme end of the cave. Very soon I crawled in and in spite of the hard rock floor went right off to sleep.

I don't know what time I woke up but when I did my head was pounding and I felt nauseated and sweaty. The fire was out and everybody asleep. My first thought was that malaria had struck again. After one of those long agonizing intervals of torment and indecision, I crawled out of the cave and was sick.

When Russleon came to wake me long before dawn, I was so ill I could not move. The retching had continued all night on an empty stomach, and I was incredibly weak. All that day and the next night it continued until I was coughing up flecks of blood. I began to think I had ptomaine poisoning or that inadequate boiling at such an altitude had left me with some virulent Himalayan germ deposited by the dirty fingers of one of the long-unwashed cooks.

Rahima was sympathetic and much disturbed and at the end of a rough day he suggested a massage to offset the bruising effect of the jagged rock on which I lay. Knowing that the mountain people of the Himalayas were the original inventors of massage and having already appreciated the magic of their fingers after crossing the Burzil, I was immediately receptive to Rahima's insistent desire to help.

The massage he gave me was nothing less than miraculous. A tense, distraught body was soothed by sheer manipulation into relaxation and peace and slumber. The last thing he did was to pull every finger and toe until it cracked and after that a wonderful sleep came upon me. However, it was two more days before strength began to revive — days that were made possible only by Rahima's expert massage.

Then I said I was ready to go again. Getting up before the first streak of dawn on a cold, windy, and desolate mountain was never fun. That morning I needed help and my kindly men knew it. Russleon woke me with a cup of tea and sat there until I drank it. Then he held my clothes until there was nothing left to do but rise up and jump into them. After that I rushed to the fire where the porters spread blankets to sit on. Then, while yawning and shivering and getting smoke in my eyes, I tried to down some breakfast. Meantime, one porter massaged my legs, another tied on my grass shoes. After that, we started to climb in a before-dawn bleakness and blackness. Ascending the cliffs was much easier than descending, and with Jumma Khan to lead the way there was no problem.

As dawn came, Nanga Parbat emerged in salmon pink high above the rest of the world. Somehow the sight of that majestic mountain made climbing easier.

After a two-thousand-foot ascent, we found the fresh tracks of the big ibex. We followed them for about a mile into the snow and then saw him a thousand feet above us. He saw us, too, and after selecting a fine position that commanded a view of all the ground below, he lay down. Any attempt at a stalk was useless, so we sat behind some rocks and watched him.

Late in the afternoon he got up to feed and we made another attempt, but he caught us in the act of crossing a snow field — so we simply sank motionless into the snow, hoping he would begin to feed again, as we were a long way off. But he had no such intention and just stood there with his eyes glued on us.

So we waited, stretched out in the snow, getting colder and colder. For nearly an hour I held myself in check, for there in front of me was Jumma Khan motionless in his thin gray rags and with his bare feet in the snow and the gooseflesh standing out all over him. At last I could stand it no longer. I got up and let out a whoop and started jumping around, poking Jumma Khan. The latter was fairly beside himself from the painful wait and at each poke he let out a bellow as though all the pent-up forces of a volcano were inside. Though my unseemly behavior was frowned upon by Rahima, Jumma Khan and I very soon restored ourselves to normal human beings and we then made our way slowly back to our cave. It had been another example of the futility of trying to out-patience a wild animal under severe conditions.

With endless variations it was the same story day after day. Then came a time when we found the old ibex in a good position for a stalk. A long detour was necessary in order to get above him, but he heard the crunch of our feet in the snow and from below us he circled unseen and then suddenly peeped down over a ledge four hundred yards away as much as to say, "You silly idiots — you can't fool me." Immediately Rahima wanted me to shoot, but since we could only see his head and neck it seemed absurd to take a chance with but nine cartridges left. So I said "No" and Rahima said "Yes." But I kept on saying "No" and Rahima was very annoyed with me. I put down my rifle which Jumma Khan had handed me and picked up the telescope. For the hundredth time I gazed at the ibex's curious horns and wondered if I would ever have the pleasure of seeing them in camp. Then he went up to the summit and lay down on an open slab of rock. At that point, pursuit of this beast seemed well-nigh hopeless. From below, the roar of unseen waters racing down the chasm suddenly came up strong on the wind. For a brief moment the swelling volume of sound filled the air. Then it grew fainter and fainter until it was swallowed up in endless space and the mountainside was again in silence. Rahima did not want to look at me. He kept his eyes averted and fingered his climbing stick. Then he said, "Too many days going behind this ibex. Never before I see ibex like this. Tomorrow we go after other big ibex." Any change seemed for the best so I consented, little foreseeing the ordeal ahead.

The next morning we made our way up the bottom of the nullah for several hours. The further we went the more difficult the ground became until at last we found ourselves in a seething maelstrom of sharp rock fragments of every size and shape. Torn by expanding frost from the cliffs above, they had hurtled down and now lay inert in massive turmoil, mute witness to the tremendous power of erosion.

With every day that went by I had come more and more to think of Abadabur as a savage place where no man had a right to be. And now, as I looked ahead into the tangled confusion of rock fragments and plunging cliffs, I wondered where in the world Rahima and Jumma Khan were taking me. It was then that Jumma Khan led the way to a vertical rock chimney. Never before had I been introduced to such an artery of travel and one glimpse convinced me it was not to my liking. I asked Rahima if there were not some way around. And he said, "No, this only way, this not bad."

By that time we were at the foot of the chimney, looking up. Rahima demonstrated how to brace oneself between the sheer walls and explained that Jumma Khan would be directly beneath me if I needed help. Though apprehensive, I started up. There were hand holds and the rock was solid and for a while all went well except that we were getting higher and higher. I realized that if I slipped I would take the other three men with me, and I could not understand why they trusted me so much. Studiously I avoided looking down and just kept inching up bit by bit.

Then came a shock, for on reaching the top of the chimney we discovered to our dismay it was impossible to clamber out. An enormous rounded boulder filled the whole upper aperture. Beneath the boulder was a little ledge of sloping dirt that I promptly crawled up into like a worm seeking safety. Crouching there with my head bent forward beneath the rounding overhang, I could not

[160]

help looking down the chimney. It was a frightening sight, like peering over the edge of the Empire State building, and that horrible want-to-jump feeling assailed me again.

Obviously it was utterly impossible to crawl out around the bulging boulder. The very thought of it froze me. I didn't dare speak lest my men read my fear. I just wanted to crawl in further and further beneath the boulder and bury myself for good and all.

Finally I said to Rahima, "I can't make it — we will go down again." Then Russleon came up past Jumma Khan. They were laughing! Jumma Khan braced himself so that Russleon was able to step on his bent thigh and then on his shoulder. From there, in some miraculous fashion, he managed to clamber up over the outside edge of that dreadful boulder. It was inconceivable. Then it was my turn. I hung back while Rahima and Jumma Khan offered encouragement. I told them I could not possibly do it but they kept saying in persuasive tones that everything was fine.

To force myself off my safe little shelf of dirt into the void of the rock chimney was certainly the most difficult single thing I have ever had to do. My position did not permit me to turn around. I had to do it while facing right down the chimney.

However, Jumma Khan proved himself master of the situation. He had handed my rifle up to Russleon. Then he planted himself firmly on bent thighs with one foot on each side of the narrow chimney. Both his hands were free and with these he guided my forward movements until, while standing with all my weight on his thighs, I managed to turn around. Then he bent well down until I got a foot on one shoulder. It wobbled on his flesh but finally I managed to get my other foot on his other shoulder. When we both straightened up, I could just reach Russleon's outstretched hand over the top of the boulder. With Russleon pulling and Jumma Khan pushing, I finally succeeded in worming my way up over that desperate overhang. Rahima needed as much help as I did. Jumma Khan was a human fly. He only required a pull from above. After it was over Rahima may not have felt as weak as I did but he certainly did not object to a long rest.

And as I feared, it was all in vain — for we did not even see the other big ibex. I never mentioned the incident again and never even scolded Rahima for taking me there. He knew how I felt and there was no use rubbing it in.

That night by the fire in the cave I said to Rahima, "What doing now?" "See dem — see dem" was his characteristic reply and that was all I could get out of him.

But the next day our luck changed. After the usual early morning climb, we were unable to locate the old ibex. So we all searched in different directions. At about eleven o'clock, Jumma Khan found him. He had sought safety in the terrible chasm that divides the right wall of Abadabur Nullah into two halves. This was truly a savage place, a gorge of death into which huge rocks were constantly falling and hurtling down the shelving gneiss of the chasm floor. A reverberating din arose constantly from this raging abyss. Erosion was so rapid the bottom of the gorge was like the ore-chute of a mine, polished and scoured from the endless wear and tear of crashing rocks. Sulphurous fumes drifted out of its depths.

Rahima and I raced back with Jumma Khan to the edge of the chasm and peered down. There he was, over two hundred yards away, vertically beneath us. He had selected a spot behind an out-jutting spur that protected him from the flying fragments. His head was down — obviously sound asleep. We had been hunting him so hard he had finally turned to the protection of this wild chasm to get some rest. His had been a magnificent battle. Now he was off guard, about to succumb as a result of sheer fatigue.

This was the moment we had long been awaiting and yet, when it arrived, I felt strangely calm. In order to shoot, I had to lean right out over the edge while Rahima held onto my legs. In such a precarious position, a steady hand was almost impossible and I was thankful my trigger-pull had been filed down. I aimed between his shoulder blades. The shot was scarcely noticeable amid the rumblings of hurtling rocks. He did not stir. One form of sleep seemed to pass into another without a tremor.

Immediately several other ibex ran across the steep floor of the chasm. One was almost hit by a falling rock and I saw him jump skillfully behind a projecting ledge as the rock went flying by. Then for some time I watched them climb the steep wall on the far side. Now and then they got into tight places that necessitated careful study of the terrain followed by three or four fantastic leaps. I shouted to Rahima, "Did you see that?"

Two young ibex were following their mother until they came to a spot that was too tough for them. She waited but did not offer help. Finally they showed some initiative and, after turning back into the chasm, came up at top speed by another route, wagging their tails and seeming to be as pleased as a dog that has found its way around some obstructing fence.

When the excitement was over and I looked back at the fallen ibex, I hardly knew what to think. It would be impossible to describe the mary varied and conflicting emotions that a hunter experiences on shooting game. Sometimes it is elation, sometimes regret, sometimes a combination of pity and sorrow and a strong distaste for the whole business. On this occasion I think there was a certain satisfied feeling of "Well, at last!" And yet, regret was strong, for it seems that the longer the chase continues, the more of a friend the object of the chase becomes. You get to know him pretty well — his little tricks and habits, his favorite haunts and feeding grounds — and it is impossible, therefore, that one should experience only a feeling of glee when the big head has fallen and his battle is at an end. How my men ever got down to him and brought back the skin and head I do not know. It was a marvelous feat of mountaineering.

That night a terrible storm rolled down into the nullah. The clouds sat on top of the oven V of our valley and the lightning poured into it in an endless sizzling stream of brilliance that lit up the great precipices towering above our cave. Between the giant rock walls the thunder roared and rumbled and re-echoed in over-powering explosions as though they sought to smash the walls apart. Thor was at his mightiest that night. Never have I heard such a colossal, earth-shaking sound. It was like being in a giant kettledrum with sledge hammers smashing on every side. It went on and on and I wondered how the ibex were faring on a night like this.

In the brilliant flashes I could see up on the mountainside two old gnarled cedars shaken by the wind and battered with hail. The ibex were taking it too, standing on their narrow wind-swept ledges, waiting for the storm to pass.

Finally it moved away over the range, barking into other nullahs as it went until at last it became a deep grumbling and confused complaining of sound in the distance. It had been a dramatic night, filled with a sense of foreboding, and I became more and more pleased at the prospect of leaving this hostile place. It was a long time before I got to sleep.

At the first streak of dawn I was aroused by a curious sound — a sudden booming that startled me into complete wakefulness. All the men had jumped to their feet and with heads thrown back were gazing up the mountain. It was a slide. Millions of tons of snow, soaked by the heavy rain, had let go and were coming down, gathering force and headway, the sound increasing into one tre-mendous roar, the strength of its reverberations making the whole mountain tremble. Then it spilled over a ledge in a gigantic snowy cascade, dropping a thousand feet, the massive compacted snow

Rahima with the wild ibex head
in our cave at the bottom of Abadabur.

splitting into fragments as it fell but striking the ground again with thunderous impact. For a long time it continued in a mighty rumbling roar. Then, bit by bit, the volume slowly subsided to a trickle and finally ceased. After that there was a sudden blast of wind that whirled all the dust of the cave into our eyes. That very gully had been one of our favorite passing grounds. Then quiet and peace descended on the nullah once more. We had had sufficient display of elemental forces for one night and the thought struck me again: "Savage, inhospitable Abadabur, you have given us many warnings — it is time to leave."

In the next few days on the slopes below Abadabur, we got a fine Himalayan red bear and three magnificent sha, or urial, a variety of wild sheep (*Ovis vignei*). After that, with still two bullets left, I headed back across the Burzil to the luxury of a houseboat in Kashmir and many peaceful days of reading before returning to the heat of India.

Rahima had taken good care of me and I had become very fond of him. He was a good, sensitive, faithful man. Our parting contained the sadness of knowing that we would probably never meet again. But it was mitigated by my assurances that I would recommend him highly to Kermit and Ted Roosevelt, who were then planning their expedition to Central Asia. Immediately Rahima's mind classified Kermit and Ted as "princes" and "the sons of a king," and as he finally bowed deeply in farewell salaams, he was grinning with pleasure from ear to ear even more with the thought of the "princes" whose shikari he hoped to be than from the well-earned stipend I added to his pay.*

* Rahima Loon did in fact become the Roosevelts' shikari on their tremendous expedition to the Tien Shan, and they said of him afterwards that he was the best shikari they ever had.

PART THREE

10

The Komodo Dragon

"And you shall need the tongues of angels
to tell what you have seen."

"Allah Does Not Count the Days"

AWAY OFF in the blue of the East Indies is a tiny island no more than twenty-two miles long. It is called Komodo and it belongs to the Lesser Sunda chain that stretches eastward from Java through Bali and Lomboc some eight hundred miles out to Wetar.

The Lesser Sundas are volcanic islands built up by slow degrees from the bottom of the sea along an arc of weakness in the earth's crust known as the Sunda Fold. Not far to the south and extending northward from Australia lies the Sahul Shelf, while to the north of the chain the sea plunges to abyssal depths.

Tiny Komodo is sandwiched midway in this chain between Sumbawa and Flores and, because of this strategic position, it was not dominated by the great mammalian predators of either Asia or Australia. Tigers got no farther than Bali, while the dingo evidently never reached the Lesser Sunda Islands at all. Thus Komodo offered a fine refuge for the survival of more primitive and more vulnerable forms.

[169]

Because of Komodo's position, tidal currents backed by monsoon winds flood past it at a rate of thirteen knots. For hundreds of years these currents racing among the offshore reefs of coral have discouraged collectors. Even Alfred Russel Wallace, the great naturalist and co-discoverer of evolution, never landed there though he passed close to its shores.

Why then had we organized an expedition and traveled halfway around the world to reach this forbidden speck of land? Simply because we might find on that island an almost mythical creature — a survivor from the Pleistocene epoch when great varanid dragons prowled across Australia.

The largest of the Pleistocene lizard flesh-eaters is known to scientists as *Varanus priscus*. Though its length is not definitely established, it is thought to have been in the range of from fifteen to thirty feet. Here, then, was a giant saurian whose ancestors dated back to early Eocene times, some sixty million years ago. It was a carnivorous lizard which survived into the late Pleistocene and may have been a contemporary of primitive man. The giant was swift and powerful and rapacious, while primitive Australian man was relatively slow and defenseless.

This, it seemed to me, could well have been the creature that has given rise to all dragon mythology and even perhaps to the dragon of the Chinese flag. For certainly the aboriginal Australian could have been devoured by *Varanus priscus* as easily as the Komodo dragon devours the monkeys on the little island of Rinja today.

In the mythology of almost every country in the world, the dragon is important. Moreover, various descriptions of the beast have a striking resemblance to each other; so much that it seems incredible they could have arisen independently. The dragon was usually conceived as a monstrous fire-breathing lizard — the very personification of evil. As the national symbol of China, the

[170]

*The volcanic
pinnacle country of Komodo.*

dragon plays a large part in Oriental art. In the Western world, it appeared as the emblem of Celtic sovereignty on English standards. The dragon concept girdled the earth. And so the thought struck me that dragon stories must originally have been founded on fact, on some beast that actually lived — perhaps a giant carnivorous lizard whose size and strength and rapacious behavior could impress the mind of primitive man.

My interest in the subject was aroused by chance. In a course in paleontology at the American Museum of Natural History given by the late brilliant scientist Dr. G. Kingsley Noble, he mentioned a paper written by P. A. Ouwens, then Director of the Museum in Buitenzorg, Java. The paper described a new species of giant lizard which Ouwens named *Varanus komodoensis*.

In 1912, according to Ouwens, a native brought in a single varanid skin to the little museum. The skin was over nine feet long. Obviously it had clothed an animal many times heavier than any known lizard. The collector told Ouwens that this was a small specimen and that big ones reached a length of twenty feet.

Here was a fascinating if almost unbelievable prospect. That one might find persisting to this day a creature belonging to the mythology of dragons seemed unthinkable. Yet, here was definite evidence of a nine-foot specimen. If they reached that length, might they not grow even larger?

I started studying maps and reading everything I could find on the Lesser Sunda Islands, and the more I read the more excited I became. Here was a possibility of studying and collecting a fabulous creature no white man had ever seen. Of course, it was a gamble. Maybe they were rare — maybe we would not be able to find them at all. Nevertheless, the idea gripped me. With mounting enthusiasm, I began to make preparations for a lengthy expedition.

I wrote a letter outlining my proposal to Professor Henry Fairfield Osborn, then President of the American Museum of Natural History. He was wonderfully enthusiastic and endorsed my plan completely. After months of preparation and the assistance of many people, we at last took off. In Java I saw the Governor who made available a small boat, the S. S. *Dog,* for the journey from Batavia to Komodo.

My wife Babs and I brought from Peking our wonderful Chinese boy, Chu. He had been with me on the Mongolian border, in the Philippines, and in Indo-China. A touching and sensitive character, Chu was completely reliable. At Singapore, we picked up our old jungle friend, F. J. Defosse, who I knew would be very helpful in capturing animals alive, and in Java we were met by Dr. Emmett Reid Dunn, a herpetologist who Dr. Noble felt would be particularly valuable to the expedition.

Some eight hundred and fifty miles from Batavia, we found ourselves plowing among the reefs toward the island we had come so far to explore. Before us were frothy rips, whirling currents, bare reefs — and there was Komodo itself: a wonderful island hulking out of the sea with strange and fascinating outlines and beautiful colors.

Of Linta Strait, which we now passed through, Wallace tells us that the violent tide rips cause the sea "to boil and foam and dance like the rapids below a cataract so that vessels are swept about helpless and are sometimes swamped in the finest weather and under the brightest skies." Everywhere the water was seething ahead of us as I went up on the bridge. From that vantage point one could see a great commotion in the sea and yet, though our ship twisted and turned in its grasp, we had no difficulty.

More and more I became interested in the rugged outline of Komodo. Here was a true volcanic island, older than any we had yet seen, for at least one of the great cinder cones had been entirely eroded away leaving only the durable plug, or core, of ig-

[172]

neous rock, to tell the physiographer of the volcano that once was smoldering and booming there. There was something grand about the island. With its sharp serrated skyline, its gnarled mountains, its mellow sun-washed valleys and the giant pinnacles that bared themselves like fangs to the sky, it looked as fantastic as the mountains of the moon.

As we drew nearer — now jamming through narrow straits, now skimming past strips of glistening coral sand that stretched out into the blue-green translucence of the water — we seemed to be entering a lost world. Everywhere the incredibly tall gubbong palms stood outlined against the blue. An antediluvian land, there was that about it that seemed to say: "Anything can live here, even a myth — anything can happen here." At last we coasted into the quiet, peaceful waters of Telok Sawa, or Python Bay, and cast anchor in the lee of a tiny island. Then we rowed ashore and set foot upon fabled Komodo.

It was good to stretch our legs and get the feel of solid ground again. The air was deliciously cool and we walked for miles along the edge of the bay, enjoying the sense of freedom and release from confinement. We saw tracks of deer and wild boar: there would be no problem of meat for ourselves or bait for the lizards. As we wandered back to the ship, the air was like tonic. A golden sunset painted the rocky islets and the purple sea in glorious colors.

Late at night we heard tomtoms beating across the water, incessant, monotonous, rhythmic beats. A native proa was in the bay, and with the drums the Malays were summoning the winds to blow. It is a common practice for these people on a sea voyage to drum hour after hour in order to insure a fair breeze.

Early the next morning, June 11, 1926, we started out to explore Komodo. It is an arid island, so before we could decide where to pitch camp it was necessary to find a spot that combined water with plentiful signs of the big lizards. Accordingly, Defosse and Dunn went northward along a crescent-shaped beach while I struck out straight west across the mountains. Two of the Malays we had brought from Sumbawa came with me.

Climbing in the tropics is always bad, but when the sun is blasting down on jagged lava one might as well be walking in a furnace. Loose porous boulders rolled underfoot. Saw grass cut my hands, and the soles of my boots were torn so badly they flapped with every step.

After several hours of climbing we came into a beautiful rolling park where a cool breeze seemed to descend from the sky. The transition was abrupt and remarkable. In one stride we had stepped from a sun-scorched desert into a luxurious land. For a while we rested in the shade of some bamboo. Birds were calling in the jungle — sounds so liquid that in my thirst I was reminded of clear and babbling streams. I heard jungle fowl, saw blue pheasants, and five or six different species of beautiful pigeons, turtledoves, quail, and the yellow-legged running hen that resembles the tinamou of Central America. The yellow-crested cockatoos were always in evidence, screaming raucously at each other and flying in every direction over the jungle. A wild boar trotted by within a few yards of us, and then we saw a herd of deer (*Cervus timoriensis*) feeding on a distant slope. My spirits rose. Komodo was nothing less than a paradise.

A little farther we came to a pool in the lava rock. Here was an ideal place to camp — good water, a breeze, and most important of all, tracks of the giant monitors. One large animal had walked through a muddy spot dragging his tail. At that moment I felt certain our trip would be successful.

A moment later we came upon something totally unexpected — signs of water buffalo. Their presence changed the entire scene, for I had no steel bullets and 8 mm. lead against a water buffalo is

Defosse and Burden
at thatch hut near Komodo shore.

about as effective as bird shot. Seeing these tracks I recalled that Merian Cooper had watched a tame bull step deliberately in front of a full-grown charging tiger and toss him with such frightful strength that the tiger was soon killed.

I was extremely wary as we followed buffalo trails through patches of jungle and passed clumps of thick bamboo. My two natives were begging me to kill a deer, or *"rusa"* in Malay. *"Tuan pasang rusa"* — "Please master shoot a deer." Finally on sighting a big buck, I dropped him. The men, with endless "ohs" and "ahs," expressed their astonishment at the distance of the shot. A moment later there was a violent crashing in a nearby patch of jungle. A water buffalo, frightened by the blast, was making off.

While the Malays were cutting up the deer, I went up to the summit alone. Looking down at the ocean on all sides was like being at the masthead of a giant ship. The waters flashed in the sunlight, the wind was sweet and cool, the colors of sea and sky magnificent. Close beneath my feet were open, parklike stretches alternating with dark jungle that plunged steeply downwards.

All the time I was on the lookout for a giant lizard. Soon a large dark object moving in the distant grass caught my eye. I lifted my field glasses. Sure enough, it was a varanid — a giant lizard, and a big one, too. There was something almost unbelievable about it. He was a long way off, at least a half a mile, but he looked enormous, striding down a grassy slope. The sun slanted down the hill so that a black shadow preceded the black beast as he came. Then he stood up on his hind legs, balancing against his tail, like a small dinosaur. He swung his grim head this way and that, obviously hunting, his sharp eyes searching for anything that moved. A primeval monster in a primeval setting. I wondered if I were the first white man to set eyes on this ancient survivor from the past.

I watched until he disappeared in a heavy patch of jungle, then I went down and rejoined the natives. They had started a fire and were cooking some venison. It was a simple matter to impale strips of it on sticks of green bamboo and hold them over the blaze.

At last we started back. While passing through rolling parkland, I was attracted by some fat blue pigeons booming in a patch of thick jungle to my left. We stepped through the barrier wall of leaves; just inside was a lava pool of water. From this pool two ducks burst upwards; before the ripples subsided there was a sudden violent crashing behind me. It sounded as though a bamboo forest was being broken into splinters. The Malays shouted *"carabao."* Immediately I jumped back into the open and saw a great solitary water buffalo coming full speed straight towards me. His nose was in the air, his sweeping horns laid back against his flanks. Judging from the ferocity of his appearance he seemed to be charging, but I believe it more likely he had scented us in some whirling current of wind and was seeking escape. So I jumped back into the jungle and clambered up a steep rock and stood there waiting. Suddenly I remembered that a water buffalo will not charge into thick jungle. They are creatures of the open plains and want to fight only in the open. My men had vanished; there was not a sound. The bull stood at the edge of the jungle only a few feet away. Finally I heard him lumber off at a gallop, his hoofs pounding on the hard ground. Warily I emerged and looked around. My two Malays crept out of hiding. They looked quite unhappy, as if my running away had let them down. Without a word we headed home.

On the way, I was reminded of Mogul Emperor Akbar's wonderful saying, "Allah does not count the days that are spent in the chase." This certainly had been a great day — one that would not be counted, that would live forever in memory.

On arrival, I learned that Defosse and Dunn had found many lizard tracks and due to the abundance and variety of game had had an altogether delightful time. The first day's reconnoitering had been crowned with success and we had every reason to be elated. After lengthy consultation, it was decided to tackle the low country first. It was much easier to reach and there were no buffalo tracks, thus a safer area for everybody. Unquestionably, Komodo was a magnificent island. With its dramatic beauty and abundance of game and the presence of large numbers of the great lizards, it more than fulfilled my dreams.

The Hunting

THE NEXT DAY we camped at the head of Telok Sawa. It was an enchanting spot. We appropriated several old huts built by prisoners placed on the island by the Rajah of Sumbawa. They were completely open and the light monsoon breeze, cool and pleasant off the water, blew through them. The roofs of woven palm leaves were mellow and bearded with age and rattled dryly in the wind. Tangled things dangled from them and swayed to and fro; and they concealed a rich assortment of crawling life — spiders, scorpions, centipedes, lizards, and snakes. The first morning we found a green pit-viper. A most interesting collection could have been made from our shelter alone.

Inside, it was very comfortable. We built some chairs and a table large enough to hold a lamp, ammunition, notebooks, flashlights, and boxes of every variety. Behind us was a raised bamboo platform on which we slept.

Our plan was to put out baits to attract the lizards, so the next day while Dr. Dunn started his general collecting, Babs and I with two natives went in one direction and Defosse with two natives in another. After shooting a deer for the Malays, we ran onto a large boar. He was on the edge of a sandy ravine that offered nice cover for approaching lizards. I shot him and secured him with a strong rope to prevent the lizards from dragging him off. That

[177]

done, we built a "boma" about thirty feet away. It was high enough to stand up in, with a door at the back that could be closed from inside. Two apertures were left facing the bait — one to look or shoot through; the other for a camera lens. The interior was so dark no animal outside could see any motion within.

After that we went exploring up the sandy draw. In a little while we came to a spot at the foot of the pinnacle country that combined beauty with the most striking physiographic features of Komodo, the volcanic plugs jutting into the sky. It was a perfect setting, we thought, for the scenic background of a habitat group in the American Museum, so I took many pictures.

Soon afterwards, one of our barefoot Malays, about to jump down into a ravine, saw a deadly poisonous viper beneath him in the very spot where he would have landed. We caught it alive — it was a *Vipera russellii* — and removed its fangs so as to take it back to Dr. Dunn.

Then in a shaded ravine we came upon a large cave beneath a tangle of overhanging roots. It was the den, or *"rumah"* as the natives called it, of the great lizard. On Komodo, the great lizard is king of the carnivores, so the excavations could not have been made for purposes of safety. It is far more likely these cold-blooded reptilians require burrows as protection against a too-great temperature change. Since earth retains heat, a burrow at the right depth beneath the sun-beaten surface tends to equalize temperature throughout the twenty-four hours. Furthermore, during the extreme heat of midday, this dark retreat would provide protection against desiccation.

In order to get a closer look into the den, I parted some branches at the entrance, when suddenly my forearm became red hot. I looked down and saw that my whole arm was covered with fire ants. So dauntless and predatory are these remarkable insects, they will even bite into the flame of a match until consumed by it.

I jumped aside, dropped my gun, and for a few awful minutes experienced the ferocity and pain of attack. Babs agreed that although scorpions and centipedes were plentiful, the ants were the
worst of it.

Late that afternoon, she and I went to get some pigeons for supper. We could hear a hundred different calls but could see nothing.
Then, as the sun went down, they began flying everywhere
through the golden light, but none within killing distance. As we
walked up the beach toward home, I shot two ducks, practically
by moonlight. We could hear the wild pigs grunting around us,
and our campfires shone ahead on the circle of huts and the naked
bodies of the natives. Then came a supper of soup, toast, roast pig,
fried potatoes, carrots, rice cakes with syrup, and coffee. After
this, the guns were cleaned, plans laid for the morrow, and bed
felt very good.

The next day, small lizards already were arriving at the baits.
Defosse and Dr. Dunn watched from one boma, Babs and I from
another. Voracious as they were, it was interesting to see what a
careful lookout the lizards kept, especially the smaller ones, who
seemed terrified every time a larger animal appeared. When a small
lizard suddenly dashed away, it was almost certain that a larger one
was approaching For several minutes we might see nothing and
then suddenly, from behind a tree, a big black head would appear
and remain motionless while his dark beady eyes, sunken beneath
their projecting supraorbital bones, would survey every inch of
ground. When the beast was assured that all was well, he would
lower his head, flash a long yellow bifurcated tongue to pick up
the scent, and move rapidly toward the bait as if ready to bolt the
whole carcass with one greedy gulp.* The impression he gave as

* According to Dr. C. M. Bogert, curator of Herpetology at the American
Museum of Natural History, "all lizards with protrusible forked tongues thus far
tested employ the tongue to pick up odorous particles that are carried to the
organs of Jacobson."

he came ponderously forward was one of great weight and strength. Indeed, although the small ones look rather slim and agile, the adults are thick-set, muscular creatures with a very heavy body.* After a length of seven feet is attained, the weight increases so that at between seven and eight feet it is, I believe, doubled.

In the process of gorging, the long sharp claws are used indiscriminately to scrape and tear while the thin, recurved teeth with serrated edges rip off great chunks of the foul meat. The beast maneuvers this by seesawing back and forth on braced legs, wrenching at the bait with every backward move. Sometimes, in this position with jaws buried deep in the meat and neck curved forward and down, he resembles Tyrannosaurus, the tyrant dinosaur of Cretaceous time. When a piece of flesh has been detached, he lifts his head and gulps down the whole slab, regardless of size. As the food goes down, the skin of the neck becomes distended like that of a snake. Then he licks his chops, rubs both sides of his face on the ground as if to clean it, and lifts his head to look around. On one occasion, a lizard swallowed the whole hindquarters of a boar at one gulp — hoofs, legs, hams, vertebrae, and all. If he is surprised when so engaged, the results are apt to be disastrous, for the beast is easily excited and immediately disgorges.

One of the most characteristic positions of *Varanus komodoensis* is taken when he is scanning the surroundings with head aloft. Hindquarters and tail are on the ground, forelegs braced, head reaching into the air. In this position he will remain motionless for many minutes and, occasionally, if desiring a still better view, he will sit up on his haunches with forefeet dangling like those of a rabbit. This attitude though rarely assumed is most impressive.

In the boma, no precaution need be taken about noise, for these

* Their maximum weight was judged to be not far from three hundred pounds.

diurnal creatures ignore sounds. Many times we shouted without the slightest effect.

For many days we took moving pictures and made notes while larger and larger varanids made their appearance. In the meantime, Defosse had prepared a snare and had captured seven alive — two quite large. Since the other five were not big enough to bring back to the Bronx Zoo in New York, we released them on the beach to test their swimming ability. Also we wanted to know whether they would take to the sea of their own free will — an important question with regard to their restricted distribution. Of five lizards let loose, one large and one small one fled to the sea without the slightest hesitation. Two others headed for the jungle, while a fifth ran down the beach for a hundred and fifty yards, went into the grass, then deliberately turned and walked down to the water's edge, and swam far out into the bay. The largest one which had taken to the water immediately remained submerged for a full two minutes and then reappeared a hundred yards away, swam down the beach for half a mile, walked ashore and ambled slowly off into the jungle. When swimming at the surface with head well above water and long undulating tail, the Komodo dragon gives every appearance of a sea serpent. Yet on the whole, these lizards cannot be said to be first-class swimmers—their movements being somewhat clumsy and ineffective. Despite this, their swimming ability should have enabled them to extend their range through the Lesser Sunda Island group unless certain unknown factors established severe limitations. Dr. Bogert speculates whether the abundance of herbivorous mammals on Komodo and Rinja might not have created a niche in the environment and that *Varanus komodoensis* was the only predator available to fill it.

By this time we had found cobras, pit-vipers, true vipers, and back-fanged snakes, all abundant. Komodo, like India, southern

China, and Formosa, is cursed with all four classes of poisonous snakes.

The true viper was Russell's viper, native to India; as they were then unknown in eastern Malaysia, the finding of one on Komodo was of unusual significance. Moreover, as the Komodo viper is the identical species that appears in India, it would seem certain that at one time it must have extended over the entire intervening area and that its range was subsequently reduced.* Here again we came up against an interesting problem. What conditions favored its survival on Komodo? What has caused its extermination through most of Malaysia?

Several species of poisonous snakes that give so much trouble in India, where between 20,000 and 25,000 deaths occur annually due to ophidic accidents, were well represented on Komodo. It was necessary, therefore, to be extremely careful, especially as we had nothing but a general serum which was more than likely to prove inadequate.†

One day as we watched an eight-foot lizard from the boma, he suddenly stopped feeding, reared up, looked intently into the jungle for a few seconds, then turned and dashed away. I felt something exciting was going to happen but for a long time there was nothing to be seen. Then about fifty yards up the sandy draw a very large lizard strode ponderously into view. He was a heavy, powerful animal well over nine feet long and much the biggest we had seen so far. This was a real dragon. He would do perfectly, I

---

* Russell's viper has since been recorded from the island of Java.

† The demand for snake serum is constantly increasing, and for that reason the effect of different venoms has been observed very accurately. Amaral points out that the composition of the poisons of different species of snakes is variable. That is, the venom of the water-moccasin, which is a fish eater, is very active towards fish; that of *Micrurus elaps*, which is a snake eater, is very active toward other snakes; while that of *Bothrops insularis*, a tree-living avivorous species, has an instantaneous effect on birds. Those poisons, therefore, whose toxic effect is particularly adapted to cause immediate death to certain animals, have a variable effect on man.

thought, for the Museum group. I started the movie camera and obtained some wonderful footage as he advanced cautiously step by step, the great bulk of his body held clear of the ground. A ragged customer, black as dead lava, every aspect spoke of infinite existence. As he drew closer and raised himself on muscular forelegs, I could see the blistered scars and indentations of his bony armor. But once at the bait, he did not seem content with ripping chunks from a newly killed boar that had been tied there the day before. Instead, he took the whole boar in his jaws and started rocking back and forth with all his power, trying to wrench it free. It was a seesaw motion so violently performed I felt the rope might break any moment and I would lose the animal. Though I wanted a lot more movie footage, I did not dare risk it. So I picked up my rifle and shot him. He was a heavy load to carry back to camp and we estimated his weight at well over 250 pounds. That animal is one of the two in the Reptile Hall of the American Museum today.

Having completed our studies of the lizards from our camp on the beach, we decided to move up to the spot I had found high on the mountain ridge, in the center of the island. Our main purpose was to capture a giant monitor for the Zoo, for the two we already had were disappointing as to size. Defosse went ahead with the natives to get the camp ready.

Before leaving the beach, we transferred our two captured lizards to a new and stronger cage, and we had quite an exciting time doing it. With the cages set end to end, and the doors open in between, we first attempted to make the animals move by prodding them, but this was of no avail. Finally, we tied some dried grass to the end of a long stick, set fire to it, and inserted it at one end. This at last had the desired effect and, one after the other, their red mouths open, their jaws drooling slime, they rattled into their new cage, hissing horribly, lashing their tails, and scratching so violently that their claws came off.

[1 8 3]

The Capture of the Giant

THE NEXT DAY we had a severe climb. However, on finally topping the last rise of ground, the sight that greeted us was pleasing beyond words. A large basin of rolling parklike country was dotted here and there with patches of jungle. On the floor of the basin, Defosse had prepared a circle of palm huts, open at both ends to the cooling breeze. The natives were hanging a dead buck in the shade of a mimosa tree. Wind rippled the fields of grass, and a few white clouds drifted over the summit.

Shortly after our arrival, Chu served a delicious meal in his usual surprising fashion. It began with strong nourishing soup, the origin of which I suspected was deer horns in velvet — one of his favorites. The main dish was more delectable and much more potent than the soup and even Defosse could not pinpoint the ingredients. After we had all guessed wildly, I complimented Chu in the highest terms and asked him for an explanation. Whereupon he grinned joyously from ear to ear and said, "Pleasy, Masta, no ask." We never did find out.

After supper, while Babs took a bath in one of our rocky pools, Defosse and I went off exploring. There were fresh buffalo tracks everywhere, which made us quite uncomfortable. We headed up to the divide and on the way saw innumerable deer and wild boar and pigeons of every variety whose booming voices resounded through the jungle. On the open hillside was a great hole under a massive boulder in front of which was a level spot. Here, obviously, Varanus basked in the sunshine and absorbed the necessary body heat before he began his day's hunting.

As we reached the backbone of the island, a big buck sprang out in front and coughed at us; a strange sound from so beautiful a creature.

[1 8 4]

Once on the divide, we just sat there looking for a long time. Then, when the mist crept up the thickly wooded gulches and the moon swam up above the palm trees, we started talking. "One might take many walks in many countries of the world," Defosse said, "and not have one half as interesting as this has been. I would like to bring my whole family and settle here and be the king of Komodo."

When we returned to camp, everyone else had gone to sleep save two natives who were playing their bamboo flutes by the campfire. A white moon glistened on wet grass. There was the gentle movement of a sleepy forest — small voices murmuring from its leafy darkness. Motion and silence and sound were interwoven. When the night wind brushed the ancient hills it was as if the spirit of Komodo were sadly sighing.

Beyond the rolling open country surrounding our camp was a big black wood that swept up the steep mountain slopes and merged with the cloud forest above. On entering it, Dr. Dunn saw in the space of a few yards a black cobra, a centipede of enormous proportions, a scorpion, bats, and other creatures fascinating to a zoologist. Defosse disliked the place and called it the "Prehistoric Wood"; he cared little about venturing into its depths. Dunn, however, a tall and angular herpetologist, prowled around in it for hours on end — lost himself, had a wonderful time, and finally emerged with a smile of glee and a various assortment of venomous creatures that were exhibited in turn to all before being immersed in formalin.

As for Babs and myself, we were inquisitive but our curiosity was quickly satisfied, and when we emerged from the wood it was with a feeling of shaking off something unpleasant in which we had been entangled. One day we penetrated to the very womb of this forest — a place where great blocks of porous lava were strewn in every direction. Everywhere were coiling vines and contorted creepers that dangled through midair from the green canopy above. Giant hawsers, twisted, gnarled, and knotted, ugly in shape, hung suspended overhead. Lianas encircled trees in a viselike embrace. Epiphytic plants sprouted from every limb. In all the aisles of the jungle grew superb specimens of the banyan, from the sweeping branches of which cables plunged to the ground, taking root, feeding and supporting the branch so that in turn it could drop new stems to earth and raise new branches in the air. On all sides were inextricable tangles of knotted, musty, and undulating roots which crawled over the earth until they united and rose in the form of a flying buttress to support some tremendous tree.

Babs and I plunged through this place of gloom and at last, following a buffalo trail, emerged at one step from a dismal solitude into the light of day. It was a relief to get out of that stifling forest and stand in the open sunlight once more with the wind in our faces and the waving grass about our feet. Below us was the bay and in the hazy distance a magnificent view of volcanic mountains rising one above the other.

We had been standing there only a few minutes enjoying the scene when suddenly a big black Varanus emerged from the Prehistoric Wood to our left. At the same moment a wild boar trotted out in his direction from an isolated clump of bamboo in front of us. Now at last, I thought, we may see whether a dragon lizard will attack a full-grown boar. We sank quietly into the grass and I took out my field glasses. The lizard was motionless on the edge of the jungle, watching the boar who trotted unsuspectingly toward him. The lizard, evidently fearing discovery, flattened himself in the grass. At this moment the boar caught the lizard's scent and headed off toward the small patch of jungle at right angles to his former course. Presently the lizard reared up and, seeing no boar, wandered leisurely into the open, stopping at frequent in-

[186]

tervals to have a good look. About this time the pig emerged again, saw the lizard headed in the wrong direction, and, satisfied that his route was clear, ambled along in his original course, stopping now and then to root. At this moment, the lizard suddenly turned, ducked, and headed back after the pig. However, the pig saw him coming and ran away and so the affair ended. No verdict could be reached on such meager evidence, but I find it hard to believe that enough animals die a natural death on Komodo to supply the thousands of Varanus with food. In view of the fact that few small mammals exist on the island, they must kill deer and small pig for a living.

Moreover, my conclusion was supported by the Assistant Resident at Bima, who stated that a large specimen of *Varanus komodoensis* had been taken alive on Komodo by Chinese poachers. This animal was brought to Bima and temporarily chained to a tree. While chained, a small horse strolled too close, whereupon the lizard jumped at the horse and took a great piece out of his side. When I asked to see this horse, the Assistant Resident assured me the unfortunate beast had been so severely injured it had to be shot. This story, for whatever it may be worth, was corroborated by the rajah.

As Babs and I were about to continue on our way, we were startled by Yiakut, our porter, who at frequent intervals was emitting loud grunts, and hunting gingerly under his sarong as a monkey might for a flea. Suddenly he made a grab and with a series of gleeful noises pulled a green tree-viper out along his bare skin from a fold in his garment and held the venomous creature in the air.

On returning to camp, the natives reported having seen a particularly ugly monster at the edge of the Prehistoric Wood which they excitedly described as the largest *boeja darat* (land crocodile) yet seen. He was a very wary fellow so we decided the best way to get him alive would be to build a trap at the edge of the forest, bait it with deer or pig, and then hide close by in a boma, ready to run out and lash him to a pole as soon as he was caught in the noose. Accordingly, Defosse killed an old tusker for bait, and the Malays set to work on the trap. Heavy stakes were pounded into the ground all around the bait except for a large opening at one end. The stakes were lashed together with rattan and the whole contraption carefully camouflaged with branches and leaves. A live tree was selected as the spring pole. The branches were cut, the rope tied to the top and then, with the combined strength of some fifteen natives, the tree was bent over and the noose set at the opening in front of the trap.

There was, however, to be one difference between this set and all the others we had built hitherto. We did not want the trap to spring when small fellows came to feed. It might spoil the whole show, for the wary old lizard would probably be watchfully lurking in the immediate vicinity. The release was therefore attached to a string that ran along the ground to the boma. The trap could not be sprung until the string was pulled. In this way we could watch everything that went on and release the spring pole at just the right second to send Mr. Dragon whirling aloft. Then we could rush out with our natives and make him fast. The string leading to the boma was well covered with leaves and the boma itself most carefully camouflaged. I tested it several times. Already I visualized the great reptile dangling in midair. The whole contraption was Defosse's handiwork and it was thoroughly pleasing to operate.

The next day we were on the job early in the morning, for the bait had already begun to smell. For a long time we waited in the boma, chatting together in leisurely fashion until a huge reddish centipede crawled into our dark hiding place. For a moment the excitement within the four walls was intense. However, one of the

Malays succeeded in deftly severing the beast with his machete and order was restored. After that, we did not feel much like stretching out and making ourselves comfortable, and it was just as well — for two more scorpions presently made their appearance. These were dealt with after the fashion of the Malays who either hold them over a hot ember till they pop or else cut off the stinger and then play with them as one would with a toy.

By this time we were uncomfortable in our cramped quarters, but as the sun was well up it was time for the dragon lizards to be abroad. Presently a small Varanus appeared and maneuvered around and around the trap. He was followed very soon by a much larger beast (about the size of those that eventually reached the Bronx Zoo) who immediately entered the trap and tried to drag the whole boar out. But the boar had been carefully lashed in place and could not be budged. Presently I saw him look up and then turn and flee into the jungle as if the devil was after him. Obviously the big one must be coming. However, we waited without seeing or hearing a thing for about half an hour. Suddenly one of the Malays who had been peeping through the back of the boma made a strange sound; he seemed to be unduly excited. Looking through myself, I saw the reason why. Here at last was a real monster that properly deserved the name of dragon.

He was motionless, one black eye fixed on the boma. I did not dare move. Now he started forward again. He was headed right for the boma. One of the natives who could see what was happening shrank back. I could see the beast well. He looked black as ink, his bony armor was scarred and blistered. His eyes, deep-set in their sockets, looked out on the world from beneath overhanging brows. Defosse, old hunter that he was, waited patiently without saying a word. Now the lizard's footsteps were plainly audible, and as he approached I wondered why he did not scent us. He passed right by on one side of the boma. I could have reached out and touched him with my hand. The natives were restless and Defosse spent his time keeping them still.

After the beast passed by, there ensued half an hour of suspense. He seemed to be very wary of the trap. He would walk up to the opening and almost put his head into the noose but never quite far enough. Then he would inspect everything very closely, snaky tongue in constant motion and always, just as we expected him to take the final step, he would turn abruptly to walk away and sit motionless, looking into the surrounding jungle for five or ten minutes on end. This happened over and over again. We all became jittery.

Just at this moment I heard a vague hum in the distance. It grew louder and louder and then, in a great roar, something seemed to be descending on our heads — as if an airplane were diving down upon us with the engine full on. The sound of millions of wings filled the air: a great swarm of bees moving over the boma. Very rapidly the sound died away again into a mysterious hum barely audible, and after that I was conscious of a deathly silence save for a slight rustling of leaves. The big lizard still remained immovable. Then suddenly he became decisive.

He walked quickly up to the opening, stepped through the noose, and seized the bait. I jerked the release and it went off. Immediately the dragon found himself sailing into the air. A moment later there was a terrible cracking, for, as the beast fell again, the rope tightened and under his weight the spring pole broke and bent far down so that our prize, instead of being suspended in midair, was on the ground, tugging at the tether which held him about the middle. Then as the natives ran out to surround him, the ugly brute began vomiting. The Malays did not dare to go within yards of our captive, so it was time for Defosse to get into action. He had been practicing with the lasso for weeks past. A strange pair they made, the old hunter and his grim antagonist — who by this time

The Komodo dragon can move very fast. This animal was close to ten feet in length.

Photo by Dr. A. Hoogerwerf

was lashing himself into a frightful rage, the foam dripping from his jaws. But Defosse was wise. He was taking no unnecessary chances. The first throw missed and he coiled his rope again as methodically as if he were practicing on a tent peg in camp. The lizard was clawing frantically to get away. Defosse saw an opening and stepped up quite close behind him; this time the rope landed neatly around his neck. It was beautifully done. Quickly the rope was made fast to a tree, and another rope was thrown around the tail to prevent that weapon from doing damage. There being no more danger, the Malays stepped bravely forward with a long stout pole. With many more ropes they finally succeeded in lashing the still fighting animal to the pole. After that we jubilantly started back. Once in camp, we thrust him into a twelve-foot cage which had been especially built for him. As he was slowly introduced at one end of the oblong box, the thongs that held him were cut one by one. When he felt free to move again, he lashed himself into another magnificent fury, then began vomiting with a smell so appalling we left him at some distance from camp.

That was another beautiful tropical night. The camp slept silently under the jungle moon, but not the dragon. He was getting to work. In the morning, we found to our dismay our prize catch had made good his escape. This loss was the greatest disappointment of the entire expedition. We had felt so sure of him we hadn't even taken photographs. The steel mesh that covered a large square airhole at the top of his cage (the strongest, incidentally, that could be obtained in Batavia) had been ripped open, the gaping hole evidence of a strength we had not suspected.

It had been another delightfully cold night, but it was our last in the mountains, for the next day we had to leave that earthly paradise and return to our ship. Our camp was situated at nearly two-thousand-foot altitude and as the temperature falls at the rate of about one degree fahrenheit per three hundred feet altitude, it should have given us a difference of about seven degrees between there and sea level. This fact, however, does not account for the night temperatures that we actually had there, which ranged between 50° and 60°F. The mountainous terrain must have sucked down much cooler air from above.

Our collections were now complete, and we were ready to move on. Of the Varanus, we took two live adult specimens and twelve dead; fourteen in all — one less than the allowance of fifteen given us by the Governor General. All in all, we were well satisfied as we made our way back to Telok Sawa where the *Dog* lay waiting at anchor.

Babs and I were very hot on arrival so we decided to take a swim off a coral island nearby. The beaches of red sand slipped off into green water where live coral grew. Beyond that, it dropped away into the deep blue of many fathoms. Thousands of fish swam in and out among the polyps. Now and then a large black fin sailed by over the still water. Then there was a commotion — small fish jumped in every direction and the black fin disappeared. As we threw off our clothes and eased gently into the sea, a reddish light slanted across the bay and struck the beach of red sand. Our little island was like a spot of fire in an ocean of greens and blues. We kept close to shore, diving among the beautiful growths of coral of which the island was made. It was delightfully cool and refreshing. Clouds of smoke issued from the stack of the *Dog*. Our ship was getting under steam.

In a short time we were sailing away from one of the most charming and romantic islands in the world. As it receded into the hazy distance — a fascinating sculptured form, weird and indefinite — I found myself conjuring up a vivid image of a long dark shadow slithering through the deep recesses and marly mountains of his fabulous volcanic home, with long yellow tongue constantly flicking, literally tasting the air as he stalks abroad in ever-lasting search for something dead or something to kill — a grue-some ponderous predator with a brain no bigger than a nut, clothed in an armor of bony plates with black all-seeing eyes and needle-sharp serrated teeth to slice the thickest hide.

In my mind's eye, his every aspect gave a sense of the great age of reptiles from which he is derived and which dominated the earth some hundred and fifty million years — a time so vast that man's coming is by comparison no more than a fleeting second.

The dragon was there. We had found him. He was valid. He fulfilled what we had come so far to see — an unforgettable picture of the primordial past of this extraordinary world.

Meanwhile, as night hurried out of the east and the flying fish darted here and there over the water like so many streaks of silver, the *Dog* stood out to sea, briskly punching the waves on her way to the little-known island of Wetar, which lies at the extreme eastern end of the Lesser Sunda Island chain.

In due course, the captured dragons reached the Bronx Zoo, and I was told that while they were there the average attendance in-creased by some thirty thousand people a day.* But the animals did not survive long. The actual cause of death was never defi-nitely established, though a friend had an interesting thought when he wrote:

> "But the lizards, I'm sorry to say,
> Became gaunt and just faded away;
> For they only could thrive
> Eating chickens alive,
> Which was banned by the S. P. C. A."

* As is true of so many wild animals, a dragon lizard when seen in a zoo — a lethargic, deflated captive — scarcely gives any impression of his aggressive, alert appearance in his wild home.

PART FOUR

11

An Outlandish Land

"Man is the hunter still,
    though his quarry be a hope, a mystery, a dream."

Trouble on the Mosquito Coast

MY FATHER for many years was president of the Port Henry Iron Mines in Port Henry, New York. When I was sixteen, he took me through the mines and I became so fascinated by the vast stopes and underground workings that I developed a permanent interest in mining.* The result was that in the summer of 1921 I was employed as assistant to the well-known mining engineer, Jack Baragwanath. We spent several months in the mountains of Brazil exploring the potential of the Serhenia Diamond Mine. It produced excellent diamonds but the venture was dropped for lack of a suitable agreement with government authorities.

In the spring of 1924, not long after returning from the Orient, I ran into Baragwanath one evening and over the dinner table he told me a most intriguing story of a lost silver mine on the Mosquito Coast of Nicaragua. The eastern shore of Nicaragua, bordering the Gulf of Mexico, was then a great wilderness of rain forest

* I studied mining engineering at Harvard, and took an M.A. in geology at Columbia.

[197]

stretching from the small town of Bluefields southward past the still smaller town of San Juan del Norte (Greytown). To the west it reached the divide where the more abrupt slopes break down toward Lake Nicaragua. According to Jack, this was a primitive, savage land, well named the Mosquito Coast. From one of its rivers, he said, a Jamaica Negro by the name of George Simpson had emerged in 1917 with a fabulous find of silver ore.

Simpson and his partner had made several expeditions to tap wild rubber trees. One of these was up the Rio Maiz to a point opposite a large sugar-loaf mountain. As they meandered southward looking for rubber, it was impossible to keep track of just where they were. On the third day they came upon a long outcropping of rock on the backbone of a ridge. Simpson rested his pack against this ledge. Sitting there, he picked up an extremely heavy piece of rock. With this he began breaking additional pieces off the ledge. They all contained a mineral of a dull lead-gray color. Simpson decided to take two pieces with him, each weighing about six pounds. Before leaving, he traced the outcrop for some two hundred yards. All of it appeared to be ore.

Returning to Bluefields, he took a sample to the local blacksmith and asked him whether it contained gold. The blacksmith pulverized a piece on his anvil and after mixing borax with it, melted it down in his forge. This he did three times, each time obtaining a button of what he said was lead. They were the size of an American silver dollar but much thicker.

Not satisfied with the diagnosis, Simpson broke his ore into small pieces and placed it together with the buttons in his luggage. After that he drifted down to Costa Rica, where he worked as a mucker in the Aguacate Mine; in charge was a highly reputable American engineer named Rynerson. Rynerson was friendly to Simpson and the latter finally developed sufficient confidence to tell his story. He gave Rynerson one of the treasured buttons and a few small samples of ore, which Rynerson promptly had assayed. The ore was a black sulphide called argentite — a rare but very rich form of silver. It ran 16,000 ounces of pure silver to the ton. Rynerson was so impressed he applied for leave of absence; a month later he and Simpson set off for the Rio Maiz. It would be impossible, Rynerson said, to describe the troubles they had in reaching the Maiz. They lost most of their provisions and their dory-canoe was destroyed in the surf.

At the mouth of the Maiz, Rynerson purchased a small dugout and supplies from some Negroes, two of whom agreed to help him up the river. But they hit bad rapids, their canoe was smashed, and they lost nearly everything. That bad water became known as "The Big Americano Rapids." Rynerson and Simpson proceeded along on foot. Simpson found the remains of his camp but he soon lost his old trail and could not find it again.

After roaming about in the area of the outcrop, they ran out of provisions; they were forced to head back to the mouth of the Maiz. They had a hell of a trip, nearly starved to death, and were lucky to get out alive. The journey had taken them something over six weeks.

When Rynerson told this story to Jack Baragwanath, the latter believed it, for he knew Rynerson well.

Silver is rare in Central America and there was no other mine from which Simpson could have obtained the samples of argentite. Moreover, it was inconceivable that he would have returned into such hostile country without an honest incentive. But even though I gradually became convinced that somewhere in the jungle bordering the Maiz River there must be an outcrop of very rich silver ore, I debated a long time whether to go after it, for pursuit of a lost mine on a hazardous coast did seem somewhat foolhardy.

On the other hand, I had been on pavements too long and was ready again for adventure. So I told Jack Baragwanath I would undertake the search.

Since Simpson had disappeared, I tried to get Rynerson to accompany me but his wife was ill in South America and he could not leave her. However, he gave me a lot of detailed information concerning the country and the exact spot on the river from which to head southward into the jungle.

Rynerson advised exploring each ridge and cutting trails from place to place to prevent getting lost. He said I would need six to eight men and a boss for them. He warned of the dangers of malaria and dysentery. Rynerson sent me his map and his description of landmarks and waterways and bearings on volcanic peaks. His final injunction was "Don't go alone," but since he himself was unavailable I had no choice. I went alone.

Roughly a month after Jack Baragwanath first told me about the lost mine, I found myself in a thirty-foot boat, beating up the coast of Central America toward the town of Bluefields. Bluefields was the take-off place for the jungle. As my destination on the Rio Maiz began to come within reach, the idea of locating one little outcrop of weathered rock in that stark wilderness seemed incongruous and impossible. Some fifty miles south of Bluefields was the Punta Gorda River. Thirty miles south of that lay the Rio Maiz. With no natural harbor on the whole coast, it would be tough going, but I had sent word ahead to have dugout canoes and the best eight bushmen of the area available at the mouth of the Maiz by April 24th. It was now the 21st. No confirmation of arrangements was possible in such a land so I was forced to trust to luck.

Bluefields did not turn out to be reassuring. It was so lowly, so utterly without pride that vultures roamed its only street unmolested or sat waiting in ugly silence on the gable peaks. Pigs rooting in the long uncut grass competed with them. Main Street ran out at both ends into the jungle. Its buildings gave the sense of imminent collapse. Shutters were drawn against the sun for most of the day. When it rained, the drops resounded in a drumming tattoo on the rusty corrugated roofs. The whole place was dead with heat, humidity, and depression.

Though drained and cleansed twice a year by the rainy seasons, Bluefields is riddled with disease — a fetid and unhealthy sore upon the land.* Dust or mud and the smells of cooking and sewage predominate. Two policemen in dirty white cotton uniforms lounged about during the day and occasionally fired at a vulture. Those on night duty were supposed to prove they were awake by blowing on an empty rifle cartridge every three minutes.

There was one good-looking woman in the town, the wife of a mahogany man, and every time she went up or down the street, everybody watched. It was her rear view that attracted their close attention. Eyes followed her all the way up the street and all the way back again.

In Bluefields nothing happened — nothing, that is, but an occasional murder or rape, and such was the inherent lassitude of the populace that few things less than murder or rape were sufficient to cause comment.

Managua, the capital of Nicaragua, was a hundred and seventy-five miles away across a virtually impassable barrier of mountainous jungle through which no road existed. This dense, trackless forest, endlessly dripping, was so remote, so unimportant, so inaccessible, Managua ignored its existence. The Mosquito Coast was left to its own devices, an area in those days as lawless as our old

---

* In his book *The Mosquito Coast*, written in 1855, E. G. Squier says: ". . . in no instance did these establishments survive a second year, nor in a single instance did a tenth of the poor colonists escape the grave. The Prussians at Bluefields suffered fearfully. At one time within four months after their arrival out of more than a hundred there were not enough retaining their health to bury the dead, much less to attend to the sick."

West. But I did not know this in advance. The true nature of the country crept up on me by slow degrees.

I had come well equipped with anti-venom and a long list of tropical medicines including emetine and quantities of quinine which I was already consuming. Food supplies were easily obtained, and three days later I set off in a deeply laden launch, headed for the open sea. The launch was so narrow I could reach across it. It was badly overloaded, sluggish to handle, and behaved as if waterlogged. No paint had touched it for many moons and I pictured a hull well eaten by the *torredo* borers. In the stern was a one-cylinder heavy-duty engine with an enormous flywheel to keep it going between explosions. Over this ancient piece of rust hovered two Negro engineers. They looked thoroughly dejected and down at the heel.

There was, however, one redeeming feature, namely Willie, the owner, a half-breed Indian — a rugged fellow with courage in his eyes and an honest smile. Last but not least was Robert, my unpromising black cook of some two hundred pounds. He sat scrunched up on the duffel amidship.

At about 2 A.M. we chugged out through the lagoon and across the bar. We were already well down the coast when dawn broke over a calm sea. It looked old and gray and the big oily swells swept gracefully in to be destroyed on the shore in a welter of foam. A wall of jungle came down to the beach. There was not a sign of life anywhere — just a solid wilderness of dark green jungle and gray sea with a narrow strip of seething foam between. We cruised along about a quarter of a mile offshore, headed for the Rio Maiz.

At Monkey Point the shoreline indented so we were much farther from the beach. For a long time I looked westward at the dark green ridges and volcanic peaks where the mist hung heavily in patches, giving the effect of steaming jungles. The air was damp, sticky, and oppressive, everything was wet to the touch. Willie stood silently at the wheel. Robert lazed on the provisions. Astern, the engineers were invisible behind the duffel amidship. Standing erect, my head almost touched the canvas canopy that stretched over the entire well. We were five human beings risking our lives on the high seas in a twenty-foot unseaworthy craft. So long as it stayed calm and the rusty old engine kept going, things would not be too bad. But what if the engine stopped or the wind came up? South of Bluefields there was not a harbor on the whole coast — nothing but lagoons at the mouths of rivers with protective, ever-changing bars off shore.

But the distant jungle was fascinating with the wisps of mist trailing among the peaks. Sitting there absorbed by my first view of a true rain forest and wondering about the early Spanish explorers who had passed this coast in search of a passage to the Western Ocean, I suddenly heard above the chugging of the engine and the swish of the boat an angry, shattering sound so colossal in volume my mind was completely at a loss for an explanation. I looked at Willie and he, seeing my astonishment, repeated several times *"el congo, el congo"* — a statement that did not help me at all. I asked Willie to stop the engine so I could hear better. From deep in the jungle came an endless series of mighty reverberating roars that rolled like thunder out across the water, roars so enormous they sounded even mightier than the elephants I had heard in Indo-China. Later I came to know the source at first hand, but for the moment language difficulties left me suspended.

Soon after continuing our journey, a school of common dolphins began to jump past our boat. I lay on the bow and looked down on them. Even at our slow pace, they seemed to be riding the bow wave, the almost imperceptible up-down of the flukes propelling them with rhythmic power. Again and again they broke surface for a snorting gulp of air. Willie was watching them too. "D'ya see de way dey's a'whackin' dere tails agin de water? Dat mean she's gonna blow."

"Well, I guess we have time to make the Rio Maiz, Willie, haven't we?"

"Yeah," he said, looking up thoughtfully into the sky. "I guess we make it."

Another native superstition, I thought. What have porpoise tails to do with the weather? Yet the thought made me uneasy so I decided to relax on the provisions and forget it for the present.

When I came to, we had covered the remaining ten miles to the Maiz. The sea was still smooth and oily. There was the river and the bar, but as my eyes wandered along an endless line of breaking seas I said to Willie, "Where is the channel?"

"I don't see none," he replied.

"Wait a minute, let's have a good look." I climbed out onto the bow and stood up. Willie made a series of circles, coming as close to the breaking waves as he dared. After a good ten minutes of the closest scrutiny, I heard Willie's voice: "I don't see no channel. She musta closed up."

"No, I don't either," I replied. "The seas are breaking clear across — but I see a lot of shark fins."

"Yeah, plenty dem fellers 'round. Dis no place for swim."

This was a dismal setback. Here we were within one hundred yards of the river, a safe lagoon within reach, and we could not break the barrier. For a few minutes I thought hard.

"Willie, where's the nearest place we can make a landing?"

"Punta Gorda, sar, dere ain't no other."

"Is there anyone that lives along this coast that has a dugout?"

"Yes, sar, dere's Felix Henry, lives 'bout tree mile from here."

I had heard of Felix Henry, a Negro, and I knew he was a good bushman, one of the men I had counted on taking me up the Rio Maiz. By the time we drew abreast of his thatched hut, a torrential

downpour had struck us. The whole ocean was dancing with tremendous drops. I saw a man leave his hut at the edge of the jungle
and make his way to the beach where he shoved a little dugout into
the water and came rocking out through the surf toward us. Several times he stopped to bail and when he finally drew up alongside, I saw a terrible-looking "sambo" — mixed Indian and Negro.
He was badly scarred and had a hideous, malign expression. On his
hips he wore a brace of six-shooters.

After greetings, I told him that I was going up the Rio Maiz and
wanted him to come with me, and that since the bar was closed I
would make it worth his while if he would bring a large dugout so
that in a series of trips we could land our provisions.

"Ya can't go up de Rio Maiz," was his reply. "Dat murderer
gone up dere an' won't let nobody pass."

"Who is 'that murderer,' " I asked, "and who has he killed?"

From Felix's replies I gathered he had had a long-standing feud
with one Alberto Calero and that a vengeful Calero had recently
come down the coast to kill him. But Felix was away when he arrived. After a long wait Calero, smoldering with rage and exasper-
ation, started up the beach only to run into Felix's father-in-law.
So he shot the father-in-law to relieve his feelings.

"Dat happen just dere tree day ago," said Felix, pointing to the
beach. Calero then went up the Maiz and entrenched himself. He
was well armed. Before leaving, he announced that he was coming
back to get Felix and several others whose names he mentioned,
adding that he would kill anybody who came up the river. Felix
said Alberto Calero had recently shot six men for various trivial
reasons. Everybody near the mouth of the Maiz had been thoroughly intimidated. In fact, all the men I had planned to take with
me into the jungle had fled. Felix was the last one to leave and he
intended to set sail in his dory that day.

This was a bad moment. All my plans were blocked and I was

bitterly disappointed. I thanked Felix for his information and he left, riding the rollers toward the beach amid a blasting downpour of rain.

During our talk, we had been rocking around in the swelling seas with a dead engine. Now our engineers, on a signal from Willie, cranked up the single cylinder and away we went again, wallowing through a heaving ocean. It was then for the first time that I noticed a change in the feel of the boat, and something ominous in the look of the sea. The waves were still flattened by the deluge, but there was a subtle difference in the way we met the swells. Some hidden force in the distance was driving them in harder. We began to heave up and down more abruptly. Then, out to sea, I saw a lot of whitecaps and I remembered the porpoise tails and Willie's prophecy.

Very soon the wind creeping in off the ocean hit us and we began to cut deeply into the waves that struck our starboard bow. Our whole world was slanted with wind-driven rain. It struck so hard the surface of the water became a sheet of dancing silver.

The Punta Gorda lagoon became our only hope. To reach it, we had to head out northeastward right into the blast. We hardly made any progress at all. I glanced at Robert and the fear in his face was most disquieting. A small boat in a heavy sea tautens the nerves, and we were deeply laden in a cranky craft that could easily be swamped.

The northeaster was freshening every minute. Very soon the rain let up and waves began breaking over the bow and smashing down inside. Robert was sick. The two engineers sat in the stern and bailed steadily. Willie and I were using our bodies in the bow as a breastwork against the waves. It was surprising in that narrow launch how much water we could keep out. My eyes stung from the salt and my nose was full of it.

The steering gear was loose and I noticed that Willie did not know how to ease his boat on the steepest seas, so we simply slammed into them. For five hours we thrust our way northward. Then there began to be a sense of darkness in the sky; night was not far away. Off our starboard bow I saw a waterspout. The long purple snakelike funnel curled off the water and headed up into a black cloud. It did not seem to be drifting our way but I kept watching it, knowing well enough what it could do to us. Then the engine stopped. Willie jumped astern as we flopped about in the beam seas. I looked for life preservers. There were none. I glanced at Robert, my mountain of a cook. He was praying. Our lives depended on a single cylinder. In a moment, Willie got it going again but the next half hour was desperate. Every big wave that thundered down on us brought with it the menace of destruction. Every little while the engine stumbled and missed a beat. A cormorant came close, flying low over the water, his snaky neck twisting this way and that.

We had to keep well off shore on account of the Punta Gorda shoals which were a seething mass of foam. Our progress was barely perceptible. At last we found ourselves abreast of the Punta Gorda bar. Beyond lay the lagoon and safety. But when I looked at the seas boiling over the bar in reckless confusion, I didn't see how we could possibly get through without swamping.

We had been working up the coast against the wind. Now we would have to turn and run before it. Willie watched the waves carefully, and made his turn between the big ones. It was well done and I saw that he knew how to run before the sea better than against it. But every overtaking wave swung our stern around. The bow plowed deep, the engine raced, and I was fearful of broaching. Willie watched over his shoulder, trying to anticipate the waves with his rudder.

With the wind and seas behind us, we were making good time and before I knew it we were in the narrow channel with a roaring turmoil on either side of us. The fury of the wild Caribbean seemed to have let itself loose on that bar. The river current sweeping out against the incoming waves caused them to curl up twice their normal size. Willie was doing well until a large bank of black water came running down on us, picked up our stern and twisted it half around so that we were headed straight for the shoals.

Before we had time to straighten out completely, the next wave caught us. It was mast-high and carried us at least sixty yards. Just before the breaker crumpled on the bar with the noise of a waterfall, our bow caught in the solid flat water ahead and we broached, coming within an ace of rolling over. It left us broadside with a dead engine. If the next wave caught us in that position, it was all over. In the channel itself there were four or five feet of water but the current from the river was so strong a swimmer would be carried out. And on the shoals on either side it looked as though a man would not last long. Willie had told me that less than a month before a good seaworthy decked-over boat had foundered on that bar and all hands had been drowned.

The moment Willie became aware that the engine was dead he jumped back over the provisions to start it himself. At the same time I grabbed a long pole and shoved hard against the bottom, turning the bow. The engine caught at the first twist. The wheel was already hard over so we were very nearly straight again in the channel when the next wave caught us. Even so it broke over the stern before it lifted us and sailed us ahead with engine screaming.

"Stay where you are and keep that engine going!" I shouted to Willie.

"All right!" he screamed back. "Follow de dark water."

As we ran the crest of another wave, I saw that the worst was over. The current was racing out to meet the incoming seas, but the rollers were half broken before they reached us. A moment later we had left it all behind and were chugging quietly through the smooth waters of the lagoon. I noticed then that the inhabitants of Punta Gorda had lined the shore to watch us. Willie came back to the helm; I dug into my packsack for some cigarettes. So great was the relief from strain I began to feel light inside.

Robert crawled out from his retreat, blinking. We cruised across the lagoon and made fast to a rickety dock at the edge of the village. Suddenly I realized we had had nothing to eat all day. I felt very tired and half starved.

The village was a series of primitive huts along the sandy bank of the lagoon; behind was swampy malarial ground. The people were mostly "sambos." They looked sickly and dirty and dull and hopeless. It was a terrible place. Light was fading fast but I still had time to take a walk with my little rifle, and shot half a dozen turtledoves in the head as they sat in the trees. They would go a lot better than baked beans. After that I drank a bottle of beer and smoked cigarettes and had supper in the empty ramshackle hut that had been assigned to me. Long after dark I retired under my mosquito netting. Tired as I was, I lay awake thinking about what to do next.

I went over in detail the whole story of the lost mine. There was still no doubt in my mind that a vein of very rich silver ore did outcrop somewhere on top of a ridge south of the Rio Maiz. But were the instructions detailed enough to be sure of making the search in the right area? Was the map good enough?

Obviously the only remaining hope of finding the lost mine was to strike for the Maiz above Calero's stronghold. That would mean a long tough trip through rain forest filled with obstructing ridges. It meant also that if I succeeded in reaching the Maiz, I would have no idea how far I was from the sea. The sugar-loaf peak would thus be my only means of determining the starting point. And whom could I get to accompany me and transport all the supplies for a two-month expedition?

Even though the odds were now very poor, I could not bring myself to abandon the project without at least one more effort. The mosquitos were swarming outside my netting and I made up my mind, no matter what else happened, to leave at the earliest moment that unhealthy and dreadful village whose total human disintegration induced extreme depression.

Up the Punta Gorda

AT DAYBREAK I awoke. The broad sweeping lagoon was a dead calm with a wall of jungle coming down to its sandy edge. There was not a single aperture — not one black hole — in the solid green face of it. Birds were calling from its high canopy, and I thought I recognized the screech of a macaw.

The green jungle and the gray sky were reflected in the still water. In the bow of a small dugout, a boy stood with long spear raised ready to strike. He was poised motionless and beautiful. Another youth in the stern moved his paddle with skillful caution. I saw the boy in the bow point with his left arm and the canoe turned slightly. A moment later he threw his three-pronged spear and impaled a large fish which he lifted into the canoe. Then he speared another and another. I realized that these two boys were probably obtaining the day's food supply for the entire village. I watched them for a long time when I suddenly saw a tremendous splash and knew they had hit something big. The boy in the bow dropped to his knees and held onto his spear so that the canoe was pulled over the surface by the battling fish. After a while, he brought the fish alongside and paddled back to the village where they beached their catch. It was a six-foot sand-bar shark that had come up into the brackish water of the lagoon, a female, and as they pulled her up the beach she gave birth to half a dozen pups that flopped about in lively style. Everybody gathered around to see, and I wondered whether they would eat the shark or let it lie and rot with other fish carcasses that littered the beach and already were emitting a putrefying odor and attracting swarms of flies.

After breakfasting on my turtledoves, Willie announced he would make an attempt to leave whenever the sea dropped. At floodtide, he said the bar would not be too bad. Captain Rankin and the *Vanguardia*, he told me, were due at Punta Gorda in a couple of weeks, but he added that Rankin would only attempt to cross the bar if the weather was good the day he arrived. The prospect of being indefinitely marooned on the Mosquito Coast was not inviting, but I decided to stay.

There was one intelligent and energetic man in the decaying village of Punta Gorda, Pesario — half-Spanish, half-Indian. With Willie as interpreter, I learned from Pesario that the greatest bushman in the country was an Indian called Juan who lived about five miles up the river. If anybody could travel the bush to the Rio Maiz, he could. So I made arrangements for Pesario to take me to Juan.

We got the largest dugout in the village — it had to be large to accommodate Robert — and started paddling upstream. The sun was blistering and with the combination of heat and humidity it was a relief to get away from that dreadful village. Soon the river narrowed to a hundred yards and the dark current increased. Pesario took advantage of all the eddies and some of these brought us close to shore.

As we approached a steep bank, something big hurtled out of the sky, landed with a tremendous splash in the river and promptly disappeared. A moment later there was another startling crash through the underbrush followed by a resounding thump. A big green iguana rushed headlong to the edge of the bank and sprang just in front of our canoe with a sprawling splash into the river and dove out of sight. When threatened, nothing can prevent these lizards from seeking safety in the water — not even a drop of fifty feet onto solid ground. I wondered how they could withstand such an impact, for they seemed to land any old way with the full smashing thud of their soft bodies against hard limbs and harder earth. In time, I became used to these sudden crashing descents from the higher levels of the forest, but I never got over the surprise of it. No sensible creature should behave in such a seemingly disastrous way. Each time it happened, Robert twitched with a spasmodic frightened jerk that nearly upset the canoe, followed by a burst of shaking laughter.

As we progressed up the river, large crocodiles shot from the bank and hurtled into the stream. On rounding one bend, I saw a festoon of ropelike lianas drooping from a high overhanging limb. It hung in giant folds to the very surface and swayed in the current. A group of monkeys had climbed down for a drink of water and hung just above the river, scooping water in their little hands — a juicy morsel for a hungry croc. But higher up were other members of the tribe on the alert and, seeing us emerge into full view, they chattered their warning and those below swarmed up the great ropes and disappeared into the jungle amid many excited calls and a great shaking of green branches.

For a while I saw only kingfishers. With many bright colors and alarming strident voices, they dropped from some high perch toward the water, shot across it with fast beats and rose again ahead of us to alight at some new watching post. This was full afternoon on a tropical river. The sun beat down and saturated us with equatorial heat. Pesario kept on quietly paddling, when suddenly a slender green lizard not more than eighteen inches long darted from the bank in a catapulting leap and raced across the water on its hind legs. It moved with incredible speed on the surface. The soles of its feet must have had corrugations to provide friction against the water to sustain such a pace for so long. Finally, when well out toward the middle of the river, the twinkling feet — much speedier than those of a sandpiper — slowed and gradually sank deeper and deeper until the entire animal was engulfed and had to swim. Called locally the *kakamuk*, this was a creature known to the Spaniards as the Jesu' Cristo lizard because of its ability to walk on the water.

Half an hour later, on rounding a bend I saw a clearing on the right bank. In the middle of the clearing was a hill reaching at least one hundred feet above the water and on top of the hill — so located to catch every breeze — was a large shack with verandas on two sides. As a dwelling it was so much finer than anything I had seen on the Mosquito Coast I could hardly believe my eyes.

Pesario shouted and in a moment Juan appeared on the veranda and held up his arm in Indian salute. My immediate impression was that here at last was a fine man. He descended the hill with easy strides and met us as we pulled up at his dock. He was barefoot with tight-fitting trousers and naked from the waist up. His hair was black and long and judging from the smooth skin and well-muscled, erect body I judged him to be not more than twenty-eight or thirty years old. He greeted Pesario in Spanish and shook hands with me. He helped us with our duffel, and we climbed the hill to his veranda. Inside was a clean earthen floor, well swept. His diminutive Indian wife was tending a handmade adobe oven while naked children between the ages of two and ten hovered about peeping at us.

I told Robert to sling my hammock between two of the upright posts that supported the veranda. While swaying there in colossal comfort and looking down at the dark river, I noticed an enormous tree in the clearing. On the tree were hundreds of suspended nests, much larger than those of our Baltimore orioles but similar in design, and many hundreds of black birds with yellow tails. They were a colony of *oropéndolas,* and their raucous, rasping, strident calls were invariably accompanied with a falling forward off the perch like an acrobat from his bar, followed immediately by a gymnastic return to the original position. It was a fascinating performance executed speedily and with precision. The tree was called the *hibo* and since these striking birds had yellow tails, I thought of them ever afterwards as the Yellow Tails of the Hibo Tree.

That evening we sat for a while on the veranda looking down at the beautiful river and listening to bird calls from the forest. With Robert as interpreter, we held a conference on how best to proceed. Juan said there was a tributary of the Punta Gorda that drained the area toward the Maiz. Since it was navigable, I was hopeful it might lead us a long way southward. Juan agreed to come with us for some very reasonable pay.

My night in the hammock on Juan's veranda was perfect. Several times I woke up and listened to strange cries in the jungle. They were fascinating sounds and the fact that I had no idea what made them only increased my desire to get into the jungle and find out at first hand.

The Rain Forest

IN THE MORNING we started, four of us plus supplies in one big dugout. After several hours of paddling we came to a tributary. It was unexpectedly small and I could see at once that it would not take us far. Juan and Pesario talked in rapid Spanish and I was never more disappointed not to know the language. Iguanas continued to tumble out of the sky and Jesu' Cristo lizards made the dash across without sinking.

For a while we made good progress. Then the banks narrowed

and the stream twisted and turned in ever sharper angles. By late afternoon, we had to get out repeatedly to haul the canoe over submerged logs and debris. Long before dark, we reached the navigable end of the river and decided to camp.

Climbing the steep bank to the level ground above, I found myself for the first time in a real rain forest. Up to now, the exterior wall of the jungle, presenting a solid blanket of green, had seemed to conceal a mysterious, unreachable interior. Now I was inside. It was exciting and while Juan and Pesario made camp and Robert prepared supper, I ventured off into this new strange world.

The first thing that struck me was the brownness of the floor of a rain forest. So little sunlight seeps through the green canopy high above that the floor itself is nothing but moldering leaves and fungus and lichens and rotting logs and toadstools and cobwebs, everything that gives the sense of death and disintegration and decay. It is a dark brown world perpetually dim and the smell of it is the smell of mold and damp rot and the rich accumulation of thousands of years of deep dark organic matter. It held within itself the combination of supersaturation and heat and putrefaction. I kicked a toadstool. The inside was dry and it crumbled into dust. Here there were no seasons — no winter, no summer, no autumn for the leaves to fall in, so they drifted down constantly, silently tumbling and fluttering here and there to join the big rot on the forest floor.

Immediately above this brown bottom was a dense youthful vegetation that impeded passage. At eye level it was thick and heavy but it was easy to slice through and wilted under the strokes of a machete. Widely spaced between this young succulent growth were the forest giants that rose a hundred feet to the sun, the successful ones in the great battle for survival. They towered like the pillars of a giant temple into the vault above, and as I looked between their elephantine trunks the deep green eerie light of late evening made me feel as if I were in a canyon of the sea.

Somewhat fearful and not wishing to get lost, I moved cautiously with eye on compass and very soon came upon a spring bubbling strongly out of the ground. Around it was green moss — the first green I had seen on the forest floor. It was inviting to a thirsty man and the flow was so strong I felt sure there could be no contamination, so I knelt down and put my hands on either side of the spring and lowered my head to drink. As I was about to sip, my eye caught the slightest movement and I raised my head to look right into the face of a large black hairy tarantula. Though I like most forms of the animal kingdom, tarantulas have always given me a spasm of revulsion right down the backbone. There is something quite terrifying about them. The sight of this hairy, venomous beast struck a chill right through me. I pushed back hard with my arms and rose to my feet all in one motion. As I did so, the tarantula made a small jump and darted away.* I thereupon beat a retreat to camp.

On arrival, I told what had happened. Juan understood immediately and laughed with delight and called it the *picacaballo* — the horse-biter — so now I knew the native name for tarantula.

Juan and Pesario had already erected a shelter of palm fronds and a fire was burning in front of it. Robert had tied my hammock between two trees nearby and was preparing supper. He was clumsy around the campfire and we did not have much of a meal.

Afterwards, I crawled into my hammock and lay back to watch the night descend rapidly upon the forest. Mountain lion and jaguar were here and I hoped to hear their calls. Tree crickets were filling the jungle with a rasping that was shrill and ear-piercing. Tree frogs with adhesive disks on their little feet climbed anywhere they wished and called mightily, their voices booming through the growing gloom. Stretched out in the hammock and

---

* This tarantula was probably the long-legged arboreal form that is capable of small jumps.

looking up, I got a wonderful sense of the forest trees zooming skyward, their tops blanketing off the outside world so completely that down below the air was still and suffocating. It was sticky and sometimes the scent of blossoms wafted downward was thick enough to cut. From every side came the droning sounds of countless myriads of *bugules* but fortunately mosquitoes were temporarily absent.

As darkness settled deeper into the forest, I kept thinking of the mine and puzzling about how to reach it. Already the problem looked very tough but even if I never found it, I was beginning to feel there would be some compensation in the sheer fascination of the jungle.

Just before the blackness was absolute, there was a shaking of branches and a troop of night monkeys arrived. They are strange little creatures with round saucer eyes, the only ones of the monkey tribes that are out after dark. They spotted us and came down to investigate as close as they dared. After they left there was a moment of silence and I thought I felt something brush by and wondered if it could have been a vampire. Then I sensed that scores of tiny eyes were looking at me from everywhere in the darkness. I had no flashlight to catch their reflected beams but I knew they were there and I felt naked and exposed. The hypnotic feel of the jungle was beginning to take a grip on me and I called to Robert for my mosquito netting. Even that much protection, flimsy as it was, gave a sense of security.

In the middle of the night I woke up. The moon had risen and here and there tiny shafts of silvery light cut through the darkness as through the windows of a gloomy cathedral. I could see the tree trunks now. They were black and immense and they soared endlessly upward to another world. The whole feel of it was eerie and threatening. Once again it seemed as if I were at the very bottom of the sea and it was hard to breathe.

At this late hour the jungle was silent. Then from far away came a strange wailing cry, so deeply mournful it seemed to epitomize the very essence of sadness. It was repeated again and again — a wavering and spooky sound, as of a savage spirit lost. I longed to know what it was that made such a heart-rending appeal to the night. It could have been the goatsucker — a nocturnal bird which the natives of Trinidad call the "Poor-Me-One" — "poor me" meaning "me all alone." Of all wilderness voices, it was the loneliest I ever heard, but whatever it was, I was happy for the moment that he was far away.

After breakfast the next morning, I told Juan to take me as far as possible southward in a single day and yet return to camp that night. Increasingly I had the sense that we were inadequately manned to cope with the difficulties that could already be foreseen. Had I had five or six reliable bushmen, the outlook for overland transportation would have been very different, but I had only two. Moreover, Robert's sheer bulk and softness was certain to be a handicap. Nevertheless, I was determined to carry my plan to a definite conclusion.

Immediately after breakfast we started. Juan was barefoot and carried nothing but a machete. I wore knee-high "*bottes sauvages*" from the Gaspé as a protection against snake-bite, and field-gray coolie cloth trousers and shirt from Indo-China. A hunting knife and rifle and a little leather bag over my shoulder with sandwiches and a canteen of tea completed the outfit. A compass with a leather thong was in my breast pocket.

Juan led the way, slashing with his powerful machete, and the underbrush sagged and tumbled in his path. This was to be a day of endless surprises.

Hardly had we left camp than Juan leaped to one side, striking down with his machete. The action was so fast I had no idea what it was all about until directly in front of me I saw the writhing severed form of a large snake. "Fer-de-lance," said Juan, and I knew now this was one of the pit vipers of the tropics, just as deadly as our Florida rattlers and almost as large. Now that he was harmless, I looked at him closely and could see between the eye and the nostril the facial pit that enables all his kind to strike just as accurately in the dark as in the daytime. For Juan, with his bare feet and unprotected legs, it was a close shave, and I could not conceive how any man intent upon cutting brush that engulfed him at head height could at the same time have noticed on the ground a coiled reptile whose concealing coloration was almost perfect.

We proceeded on our way and soon came into a swampy area with a strong smell, and the tracks of many beasts. "*Wari*," said Juan. I looked at the cleft-footed prints and knew that we had run on the trail of the fearful white-lipped peccaries, sometimes called the *chancho de monte*, or forest pig. Their stench is strong and their courage fabulous. Though not much over three feet long, a sharp downward pointing tusk makes one a savage antagonist. Running sometimes in herds of two and three hundred, it is said that the *wari* never turn aside. Even a jaguar is not safe from attack. They root and chomp and are quick to anger and wherever they move they spell death to the snakes — even poisonous ones which they easily destroy.

Before long the vegetation became less thick. Juan was pleased and we sallied along at a great rate, scarcely looking at the ground, so secure did we feel in the wake of the *wari*. I was hoping to catch up with them but we didn't, and after a while we left their trail and got into heavy going again. Juan's machete was sharp as a razor and it flew back and forth unceasingly. A man must have a powerful arm to make speed through rain forest.

Presently we came to a muddy opening where we saw large three-toed tracks which I recognized as tapir, the favorite food of jaguar. "*El danto*," Juan called it, and we followed the tracks, for he had only just passed by. The tapir's nose is elongated to half a trunk. He is wedge-shaped with narrow forequarters and a powerful rear to help him, perhaps, in driving through the forest in headlong escape. A moment later we heard him doing just that. He had waited until we came quite close, then broke and bolted off noisily as an elephant.

No sooner had we proceeded on our way than once again Juan jumped to the side and slashed downward. This time it was a *tamagás* that he sliced in two, another venomous snake. I began to realize how numerous are the poisonous reptiles of the Mosquito Coast. During months of travel in Indo-China, I had not seen one cobra. Here, in the course of a few hours, we already had met two pit vipers and it happened once more during the afternoon. The price of survival for the barefoot wanderer of these forests is an almost unimaginable degree of alertness. No wonder many "rubber men" get bitten. Only then did it hit me that I should not have left my snake serum in camp.

The fer-de-lance and the *tamagás* were well worth seeing, but there were two other snakes that excited my curiosity far more. One was the boa constrictor, whose relative the anaconda reaches such a prodigious size in the Amazon basin. The other was the bushmaster, the most terrifying poisonous snake of the New World — terrifying not just because of its great size but because, like the king cobra of India, it has been known to attack man unmolested.* The bushmaster was reported in Costa Rica, and on this dark leafy floor his red-brown mottling would make him almost impossible to see. While looking at the now dead *tamagás* and wondering about the bushmaster, I had casually placed my hand on a large tree and was leaning against it. As soon as I did so, Juan very gently reached forward, took my hand and pulled it away. His

* The bushmaster reaches a length of twelve feet.

thoughtful gesture was a reminder of the importance of keeping your hands to yourself in the rain forest.

At noon, we sat on a log for lunch. Juan inspected it first very closely and then cut away the moss and damp wood so that we had a dry seat. I wanted to get some idea how far we were from the Maiz so I set one twig on the log to indicate the Punta Gorda and another to indicate the Rio Maiz. Then I tried to get Juan to show in relation to the distance between the rivers how far we had come. He was quick to catch on but his answer was very disappointing, for according to his estimate we had only come a small fraction of the way. Moreover, he made up-down motions with his hands indicating there were many ridges between us and the Maiz. This was another blow. More and more the sheer weight of circumstance was driving home the discouraging thought that I would not be able to reach the Maiz. My morning's walk through this terrific jungle persuaded me that we did not have the manpower to get there with the necessary supplies. External conditions were forcing a decision. It was a hard one to accept but I felt it creeping up, bit by bit. At first, eagerness keeps you forging ahead. Your eye is set only on the distant goal. Then, one by one, the obstacles gnaw at you and loom larger and larger until at last you begin to see the possibility of defeat, vaguely at first, but with increasing recognition. The farther I went that day with Juan, the more it sank in that I was butting my head against a stone wall, and that to persist in driving on could easily end in disaster.

While brooding thus about my plans, I was suddenly diverted by a file of soldier ants passing near the log. Of all the small creatures of the jungle, they are the ones for whom one quickly develops the greatest respect. A butterfly happened to land nearby and a group of the soldiers must have sensed its arrival with their fast-moving antennae for the next moment they were all over it. The butterfly never had a chance and, as I watched, they severed the legs and wings and carried off the dismembered body. It was fascinating to see what blind, brainless creatures, animated by instinct alone, could do. I learned later that the Mosquito Coast has a species of ant called the *bala* which is very black and about an inch long. Unlike most ants, it is solitary and said to be very dangerous, for its bite is supposed to make you temporarily blind. Here there were mites to burn you and *garrapatas* to burrow deep and fester and give you *garrapata* fever, and chiggers whose parasitic larvae infest your hide, and of course, an ample supply of fleas. Just about every form of biting, stinging, and burrowing creature seemed to be well represented in this forest.

Sitting on the log, I scuffed my feet in the leafy ground and noticed a large beetle. I got down on my haunches for a closer inspection and started scratching the ground with a stick. The moldering forest floor was full of life — creatures that oozed and wriggled and lashed and crawled and sprang and burrowed and all, including the snails, wearing the somber colors of their dark, dank environment. These too, like the ants, were fumbling forms controlled by instinct, all battling for survival. The richness of life in these few inches of moldering matter was beyond imagining. Many of its denizens would have been horrifying to look at through a magnifying glass. A brooding toad sat nearby with pigeon-toed forefeet tucked well in and one yellow eye occasionally blinking. In marked contrast to this lowly community, a group of parrots and macaws screamed overhead. Theirs was a world of sunlight and gaudy colors, wind and storm and flashing movement. The roof of the forest was in every respect the opposite from that which gave it sustenance, and I longed to be up there to see it closely too.

During lunch, I had more than ever the sense that the forest hemmed us tightly in on every side. Silent, implacable, and mysterious, it stood there in its thick green leafiness with a strong tinge of lurking death. It seemed to be watching us and I had the feeling too that it was listening. In a thousand different ways it could strike at our defenseless flesh. A man could spend a lifetime studying this forest and still be ignorant of a large percentage of the teeming animation that was in it.

It was now one o'clock and time to be homeward bound, but I was amazed to discover that Juan, instead of heading back on a trail that had already been opened, chose to circle through new country. Sometime after lunch we came on an opening with hot springs bubbling in it and some wonderfully colored crystalline formations on the edge of the spring. In country so recently volcanic, it was not strange to find hot springs. We saw the tracks of a mountain lion. Then a big fat bird burst noisily up ahead of us. It looked much like our partridge and I thought it must be a tinamou, an ostrich-like bird that has retained the power of flight and is famous as good eating. Juan called it the "*gongalola*," and he pointed to six o'clock on my watch and made a mimicking call indicating that the bird always called at six in the evening.

In this rain forest, nature has explored and inhabited every niche in the environment. No tiniest space remained unutilized by competing forms highly adapted to a specialized circumstance.

Even in the world of mammals, the magnificent process of evolution had concocted incredible creatures. What human brain could conjure up a sloth or an armadillo or an anteater — ultimates in the bizarre? Yet by adaptation, nature — ever sifting and sorting and experimenting — has created them through the amazing mechanism of mutant genes. I longed to see one of these weird animals before the day was over but failed to do so. Nothing happened — nothing but a quick flash and another severed snake until suddenly, directly ahead, the whole jungle was shattered with the same volcanic rumbling that I had first heard out on the water. It was an earth-shaking sound. Juan turned and grinned at me and murmured "*el congo*" and as we advanced I became aware that it came from high up. The closer we got the more thunderous it grew. Giant overwhelming roars, one after another, then many together, and I thought again of the elephants in Indo-China. At last we saw branches moving, so we stood still and waited. Not until then did it suddenly dawn on me that "*el congo*" could be nothing less than the howler monkey, whose enormous resonating chambers in the throat enable it to emit such a prodigious and awe-inspiring sound.

From the very term "howler" I had always imagined a rather high-pitched scream, but the howler's voice is a sonorous thunder, like the deep long-sustained booming of a volcano.

In a little while, we began to see these large monkeys with brick-red hair. After they had finished bombarding the jungle with sound, one of them spotted us and gave an alarm. The others became very excited, there was a great shaking of branches and heads here and there peeking down. I was anxious to see a howler close to, so when one large animal came into full view, I fired. In a moment his hands loosened and he seemed about to fall but his prehensile tail was curled around a limb and he remained hanging there after death, while the other howlers raced away through the tree-tops. I thought surely the tail muscles would finally let go, but Juan shook his head and after about fifteen minutes, I reluctantly agreed to leave. Later I learned that the natives had a trick to make the tail release, but I never learned what it was and certainly Juan showed no inclination to use it that afternoon.

All day we had been moving through the dim twilight of the jungle floor. Now it was rapidly getting darker and I began to wonder if Juan knew where he was. How he could know was beyond understanding, for sense of direction depends a great deal on how far you can see. And all day the range of visibility had been not much more than zero. To make a whole day's circle under such conditions and to come out where you wished required, it seemed to me, nothing less than a compass in your head. Even the great Archie Miller, I felt certain, would have gotten lost here, for there were no shadows, no moving clouds, no wind to steer by, nothing but perpetual, almost ghostly, dimness blanketing off the outer world. And yet in this dimness Juan pinpointed his return with unbelievable exactness. When no more than a few hundred yards from camp, he struck our outgoing trail and followed it home.

This had been a day of days, and no sooner did we reach camp than I stretched out in my hammock and made notes in my diary while the whole of it was fresh in my mind. Just before dark Juan called to me and said "*gongalola*" and pointed. I listened and heard a lovely birdcall repeated several times. Again Juan said "*gongalola*" and smiled as I nodded understanding. By my watch it was a few minutes before six. The bird might have been more accurate than my timepiece.

Though filled with fascination, this had also been a day of deep discouragement. That night my sleep was troubled with the torment of indecision. Pride was involved. I hated to give up the search, yet deep down was a small voice urging me to abandon hope. Could these disturbing thoughts have been due to the inner stirrings of illness?

Impending physical ill-being may well mold the cast of our mind. Sleep was fitful and in the early morning I had cramps in my insides. At breakfast I could not eat and I told my men we would head back to Punta Gorda. Decision had been thrust upon me. My search for the lost silver mine had come to an end.

As we prepared to leave, there came a sound as of surf breaking on the shore. A subdued hush fell upon the forest. The sound grew louder and finally in one great roar it broke over our heads as the whole jungle vibrated with enormous raindrops. Heavy as this tropical deluge was, it took a long time for the water to leak through our screening canopy to flood the floor below. When the rain stopped, the entire jungle was as if in a cloud, steaming and still, more then ever like the undersea.

We headed back downriver to Juan's house. All day I got weaker as my illness progressed. Though I did not know it then, I had contracted amebic dysentery — which stayed with me for eighteen years. No doubt it had been passed on by some cook in Bluefields with contaminated hands. So my trip was at an end and I was forced to rest content with an all too brief experience in the rain forest of the Mosquito Coast with that never-to-be-forgotten Juan, who made it possible.

There followed many painful and anxious days of waiting in Punta Gorda. The depression of illness, added to the frustration of failure and the uncertainty of departure from that miasmatic town, were hard to live with.

But it was not the end of the search for the silver mine, for eventually the *Vanguardia* did arrive and I got safely home where I told my story to my brother-in-law Blake Lawrence, with the result that he, too, felt the challenge of the Mosquito Coast and determined to battle its hazards in pursuit of the elusive mine.

Since Blake not only ascended the Maiz and met the murderer but found an outcrop of ore on the backbone of a ridge, his story is the logical continuation of mine and an essential supplement.

12

Blake's Story

"You shall see storms arise, and, drenched and deafened, shall exult in them."

THIS IS Blake's story just as he told it to me on his return. It is impossible to recall all he saw on his expedition to find the lost silver lode or his feelings as the menacing obstacles that he encountered grew worse, but I shall do my best. If I have left out some things it is only the fault of memory and too sketchy a diary made of our conversations.

Blake was fortunate in obtaining a really wonderful man as his head Indian, Sam Hudson. He was tireless, resourceful, proud and competent, and he knew the jungle like a book. As cook, he had a Negro by the name of Lockwood who constantly complicated matters by being desperately afraid of being left alone.

These two men joined him as he was leaving Bluefields on a twenty-five-foot auxiliary sloop commanded by Captain Eric Rivers. Before reaching the bar the mainsail was furled and heavy canvas dropped from the roof and lashed tight to the deck on three sides of the cockpit. Thus nobody inside, including the captain, could see in any direction except front. In front of the cockpit was a small mast to which two Negro boys lashed themselves. Amidship were two engineers. The captain shouted at them, "For Christ's sake keep that engine going — it's rough," and they disappeared, pulling the hatch tight behind them.

Slowly Captain Rivers felt his way out of the lagoon past the recent wreck of the S. S. *California*. There was a clear view of the bar. The incoming waves mounted higher and higher until finally they curled over and smashed down in a yellow band of seething foam.

Then came two bells calling for full speed ahead and down came the forward canvas, leaving the captain and his six passengers and heaving turtles and screeching parrots walled in on four sides with one black hand stuck through a hole in the canvas to indicate which way to go. Captain Rivers whirled his wheel according to the motions of the hand. In a moment the boat began to pitch and plunge. It staggered and reeled under each smashing wave — the engine beat dropping to a slow chug, gaining again between blows. Water seeped in under the canvas and rushed around their feet. After a while, the motion eased and lengthened, the shudders when she met the seas lessened until finally came the cry "All clear of the outer bar."

About noon the next day they arrived at San Juan del Norte. It was like a half-deserted Bluefields. There were rows of unpainted houses with the usual assortment of vultures squatting on the tin roofs. There was tall grass in the wide streets and a sparse, despondent population that seemed to be doing nothing and wanting nothing.

Fortunately, the house Blake was in was well protected. An alert tame young peccary lived underneath it to kill snakes and tarantulas, while a bittern ran around his room cleaning up ants, flies, spiders, and other small house game. However, even the bittern could not handle the "grass bugs" which tortured him all

Top:
The Mosquito Coast, along which Blake made his journey to and from the Rio Maiz.

Bottom:
Sam Hudson near mouth of the Rio Maiz.

night. A flock of green parrots in the next room loudly acclaimed the dawn so he was up and off at a good hour.

The sand beach of the Mosquito Coast did not have the usual friendly feeling of a beach. And yet, between snake-ridden swampy forest and a shark-infested harborless sea, it presented a long narrow ribbon of safety. But the sand was soft and difficult to walk on.

Blake found two kinds of peccary tracks all along the beach — the collared and the white-lipped. Sam Hudson always referred to the latter as "*wari*." Guan and curassow were common and both were good eating. Sam's dog, Pregunta-le (Ask Him), had the good sense to keep clear of the jungle. Instead, he gaily pursued hundreds of little fiddler crabs running across the sand.

Shortly after noon, the Indian River thwarted their advance. It was a broad belt of yellow current whose banks so swarmed with crocodiles of all sizes they reminded Blake of a Coney Island beach. In midstream there were many black fins. The men quickly built a raft but the bull, which they had brought to tow their cart, had to swim. Blake wanted no "blood frenzy" so he was careful to miss the many targets in stream and ashore, but while crossing with the bull in tow, he kept firing into the water while the men beat on the raft with heavy sticks. Amid the commotion, the bull crossed safely.

North of the Indian River they came to a great coconut plantation extending along the edge of the Caribbean for many miles. Jack Golder, the Arizona-born manager, was a garrulous fellow with two prominent gold teeth and tattooing from neck to toe. He even proudly displayed on his private parts the delicate artistry which he admitted had been most painfully applied. Golder was quite a man. In spite of syphilis, he was enterprising and courageous and survived well the dreadful heat and humidity and utter debilitation of the Mosquito Coast. He was a typical frontier character whose love of the raw wilderness made him proud of the snake bites he had survived, of the three hundred and eighty odd-sized crocs he had shot in the swampy jungles behind his house, of his dangerous encounters with the *wari*, not to mention the so-called jumping *tamagás* and the bushmaster, "that dread snake" which he claimed "will not give ground before a man but rises up and pursues him through the jungle."

The men spent the night there and Golder's Indian wife gave them a fine breakfast. The Spanish River lay ahead and once again they built a raft. The bull became very weak and started to stagger so everybody turned to and did most of the pulling.

On and off during the day there were heavy showers and by the time they arrived at the Maiz everybody was dead tired — that is, everybody but small, wiry Sam Hudson. Sam was pure Indian. All his life had been spent in the jungle and he was quite accustomed to carrying a hundred pounds in a rubber sack with tumpline and shoulder straps. He did the work of three.

Already Blake had gotten farther than I ever did, for he had now arrived at the mouth of the Rio Maiz. His first milestone had been successfully achieved. The target — the lost silver mine — was beginning to come in range.

There was a little shack there and they promptly moved in. Pregunta-le was bitten by a tarantula that raced across the floor. Almost immediately the dog seemed to become paralyzed and lay with eyes tight shut, but a few days later he had fully recovered.

Two Indian boys, Pancho and Marciano, were due from Punta Gorda with a boat to go up the river but there was no sign of them, so the men cleaned the hut and waited.

It began to rain again and the wind was high. The bar of the Rio Maiz looked rough and dangerous. They cooked a meal of beans and rice and crawled into their hammocks. For a long time Blake listened to the noises of the jungle and the pounding surf. It was June 23rd and he feared the rainy season had begun in earnest. He was very discouraged.

The next morning was beautiful and clear, but since there was still no sign of Pancho and Marciano, there was nothing to do but wait. Crocs were numberless along the edge of the river. They were watching for something to pass within range of their slashing tails.

After a frustrating, wasted day, a Negro came around the bend above their camp. He offered them pork and plantains. Blake was quick to present tobacco and coffee in return. But it was the Negro's boat that really interested him: a fine eighteen-foot dugout with a good beam.

When the sun plunked down over the horizon an hour later, the Negro lit a torch and holding it high walked along at the very edge of the river, occasionally slashing down with his machete. Schools of mullet driven inshore by the ravenous predatory fish in deep water succumbed to this assault from the beach. It was the easy fishing season, so they had no difficulty in making a deal for the boat. That night after midnight, Sam Hudson headed northward along the shore on foot to Punta Gorda to collect Pancho and Marciano. He simply announced his departure and went. Blake had not asked him to go.

The next day there was a high wind and the shallow bar of the Maiz was sensational. Nothing could have lived on it. An endless series of steep combers twenty feet high seemed to detach themselves from the sea and rush across the bar into the river's mouth, subsiding there under boiling caps of yellow foam.

About 11 P.M. Sam arrived with Pancho and Marciano. All three were very cheerful. In less than twenty-four hours, Sam had traveled close to sixty miles on the heavy beach without food or rest. In addition, he had built rafts to cross two small rivers — all this in the terrible heat and humidity of the Mosquito Coast.

Pancho and Marciano, it appeared, had made repeated attempts to launch their dugout but, though able seamen, they were swamped each time. When their boat was badly damaged and a helping friend injured in the heavy surf, they gave up and waited to see what would happen. The dugout that Blake had obtained had indeed been a piece of good fortune. Without it, the whole expedition would have foundered there and then.

The next morning they started up the river at seven o'clock. It was broad and smooth and they moved along swiftly through the mystery and splendor of an undisturbed jungle. There were brightly colored herons, white with blue markings; kingfishers, macaws, bright green parrots with green heads, and colonies of yellow-tails with their long pendulant nests.

Iguanas plunged from overhanging limbs. Crocodiles slithered off the banks. The swampy areas along the lower river looked green and forbidding. The heat of midday gradually descended on them and there was a monotonous hum which seemed as heavy as silence. Ahead was Calero, well fortified and well entrenched. He had an evil reputation in Bluefields, for after I was there he became the principal in a killing while resisting arrest. After escaping, he made his way through the jungle all the way to the Rio Maiz where he established himself at his former base about twenty-five miles from the border of Costa Rica. What a trip that must have been for one man alone! Unquestionably Calero was a superb bushman.

A posse of three men was sent to get him, expecting him to run for the border. Instead, he came down the river to meet them — killed two and wounded the third. Sam Hudson said he had wiped the posse out in an open fight in the jungle. In any case, no other posses were sent after him, and he became the undisputed king of the river.

Rumor had it that Calero's blood had cooled; otherwise Blake's Indians would never have dared pass his camp. By late afternoon the river was running swiftly through low hilly country. They passed Black Water Creek and saw Calero's house on a sharp hill on the left. It commanded a long straight stretch of river. They halted a quarter of a mile below the house and Sam Hudson went on alone and unarmed through the bush to see him. Calero was off in the jungle but his Indian wife told Sam it would be all right to pass. Three guns were loaded as a precaution and they slipped quietly by, making camp about a mile above Calero's house. That seemed to be a safe distance without being a scared distance. There was no point in losing face with Calero.

To the delight of the Indians, they had now moved into hunting country and were exposed to the indescribable volume and variety of jungle sounds.

Blake thought it wise to set a watch that first night near Calero and took the first stretch himself. With feet and legs in a heavy canvas, his body under a frame covered with mosquito netting, and a kerosene lamp hanging in a corner of the hut, he was attempting to write a few words in his diary, when just before 11 P.M. without the slightest warning Calero and his boy walked in out of the darkness. There had been no sound of his little dugout on the river or of his approach, but Blake knew at once it could be none other than he. His wife had obviously told him they were not unfriendly, but he had come to investigate. Swarthy and powerful with hot-tempered eyes and a drooping black mustache, he looked every inch the confident brigand and adventurer he was. Dressed in the usual rolled-up white cotton pants, loose cotton shirt and soft leather shoes of Central America, he was predominantly Spanish in appearance — cruel, arrogant and competent — perhaps the violent seed of Cortes's men. Blake made friends with his boy by giving him a pocketknife and cemented relations with Calero by turning out Lockwood to cook up some beans and rice and coffee and by giving him two tin plates, two spoons and one table knife. For someone in Calero's entirely isolated position, these were treasures indeed. The conversation was voluminous and ran well on into the second watch.

Calero's real pride was his boy. He said, "Ever since he could walk he has walked behind me barefoot through the jungle and he has never been touched by a snake." Blake did not at the time realize what a boast that was. Finally Calero picked up his machete and his rifle, which he had laid down when he first arrived, and left.

The next day the river got much swifter and they came within hearing distance of the rapids. Soon their poles and paddles were useless and all except Lockwood were in the water up to their necks, guiding the boat into eddies, making fast on one side of the river and letting it slide through white water to the other. They narrowly missed capsizing several times. The swimmers were roped together like mountaineers. Fortunately, they were now in waters above crocodile country. It took them three hours to get up the Great Americano Rapids, and two hours to surmount the Little Americano Rapids. While they were in the water, they saw a jaguar. He was a magnificent, fearless, proud animal, and when he stepped out of the wet jungle into the sunlight his beautifully spotted coat was golden. But the sun did not last long. In the afternoon the heavens really opened and the rain poured down. The river turned reddish in color and started to rise. They selected the highest bank they could find and went ashore.

Making camp in the rain forest deluge was an altogether miserable experience. The rain swept in and poured off the broad leaves in heavy streams of water. They were suddenly cold as well as wet. The three Indian boys worked quickly as a team. One would cut and clean softwood poles for supports and crosspieces for the roof. A second would gather "wife-beater" vines to bind them together. The third would cut the low palms and collect leaves for thatching. Meantime, Lockwood and Blake would be clearing the ground around the house site.

The heavy storm settled down into the higher trees in a steaming cloud and the jungle darkened. Sam warned everybody: "Don't touch trees with the hands. Don't take a step without clearing all the low grass with a machete." They killed two *tamagás* while making camp. The hostility of the jungle was creeping up on them. The danger of moving hand or foot onto a snake or near a coiled one was very great.

The following day was clear but the river was running red and high and they decided to stay where they were. A strong wind swept over them, blowing the mist and clouds away and they could hear trees, loosened by the heavy rain, crashing to the ground.

It was a comfortable day. Blake took his first real bath in rainwater in the boat and watched some "water dogs" (otter) sliding down the muddy banks and playing in the rapids. That evening Sam came down with a bout of malaria. Blake dosed him heavily with quinine and knocked his fever.

The next day was June 30th. They were off again early. Simpson's map was a simple affair. Without compass headings, it showed the coastline; the river going back into space in a fairly straight line with the sugar-loaf mountain drawn in to the right of the river; and just opposite on the left of the river was the area where the mine should be. The river was quite a twister, so that a spot "opposite" a mountain was, as a practical matter, impossible to determine. However, there was a prominent peak to the north and since it was much the highest anywhere in the area, it must have been the one referred to by Simpson. The river was getting smaller and smaller. As they paddled and pushed along with their poles, sharp Indian eyes picked out some signs of an old camp on the left. Blake could see nothing until he went ashore, but then he was shown the cuts and other indications of a "rubber man's" camp. While clearing the campsite, he was suddenly frightened by finding the air alive with large "bees." Hundreds of them came pouring out of holes in the mud under his feet and went whizzing about at high speed in all directions, often flying into his face. There was not a sting among them and the boys paid no attention to them, saying they would soon go away, which they did.

That night Blake began to feel sure they had located Simpson's campsite. The second milestone on his journey had been reached. The search was not yet hot but at least it was getting warm.

The next day Sam and Blake climbed the sugar-loaf mountain, which they called La Palmerosa. They judged it to be at least two thousand feet high. It was long after noon when they reached the top of the mountain, and heavy clouds had settled down so that they could see very little. They had to hack through mango trees and then they came to high river-grass and tall umbrella palms and in one place the floor of the jungle was covered with wild garde- nias with thick waxy petals and without scent. They had to hurry dangerously to get back to camp before dark and were glad to find that all was well. Their total score for the day was seven snakes killed and they were certainly not hunting for them.

The following day they packed into the new camp. The three Indian boys carried eighty to one hundred pounds apiece and Lockwood did his best. They traveled over sharp ridges all the way. Thunder showers hit them throughout the day. They could see no lightning through the trees but the thunder produced a strange rolling hollow sound — as if they were inside a drum with someone beating a slow tattoo just over their heads. And though they did not sense much wind, they often heard the sickening crash of falling trees. Because it was extremely humid, everybody felt tired. When the rain poured down their backs during a heavy storm, they became cold and shivery. But usually they were soaked with sweat anyway. Blake had noticed that morning as he shaved that all color had washed out of his face and he was turning a dead sweaty white. They arrived soaked through. As they were wringing out their wet clothes, they heard strange grunts followed by several roars. There, moving easily through the lower trees and peering down, was a large band of the great howler monkeys. Sam excitedly called "great monkeys, great monkeys" and rushed to get Blake's rifle. They were carrying their young clinging to their backs and more curious than fearful of the men. Sam wanted Blake to shoot, but he would not. Fifteen minutes later they heard their frightful roars far away.

Pancho was bitten by a *bala* ant while collecting wood for the fire. He was in agony. Blake opened the skin and applied permanganate, which gave local relief, but Pancho's arm was paralyzed from his shoulder down and he said he could not see. They had to help him to his hammock. Sam immediately went collecting and dropped two live *bala* ants into formaldehyde. They were just under an inch long.

They were now about eight miles from the river and according to Simpson this was approximately the distance he had wandered when he sat on the outcrop of rock and took the ore samples that started all the trouble. This camp was therefore, Blake felt, close to the designated area.

The search was progressing nicely with increasing excitement, but when the torrential rains came down, enthusiasm washed out. The Mosquito Coast in the rainy seasons has a rainfall of over sixty inches a month — as compared, say, with an *annual* rainfall of a little over thirty inches in New England. Every day there seemed to be more rain. Every day it got darker. Every day the danger of snake-bite increased.

Blake ran east-west lines through the forest. It was very dark and raining and for the first time the boys showed hesitation about traveling. Darkness and snakes were a bad combination. Sam, knowing something of the story, was looking for wild rubber trees and it was not long before he found scars made by a "rubber man." Sam had suddenly become the alert Indian on a trail. He moved along very carefully, picking up a series of scarred trees. Following these clues they crossed a ridge and came to a long outcropping of rock. Blake scrambled up onto it, broke off a large piece and examined it carefully. It was very heavy and it was black with sparkling particles exactly as Rynerson had described. Then it suddenly hit him. This was the mine. The argentite was right in his hand. It must be the mother lode. Feverishly he broke off more and more samples all along the ledge to be sure. It was all black and heavy and sparkling, surely a silver sulphide ore. Forgotten were the snakes and the rain and the horrors of coming through the jungle. Now it was all worth while. There was a fortune in that ledge. All he had to do was mark it well so they could return.

In high spirits they returned to camp. On the way, Sam stopped and pointing to the right with his machete said "Pig pen." There was an area perhaps forty yards in diameter in the dense jungle where all the low brush and even small trees were flattened into the yellow mud by a large band of *wari*. They had rooted and trampled everything to pieces, almost as if in rage.

All returned safely to camp and Blake was thankful, for it had been so very dark all day the danger of snakes was worse than ever. In fact, travel conditions were deteriorating so fast it became obvious it would be too hazardous to attempt to go any farther. This fact together with the conviction they had already located

Simpson's prospect decided Blake to stop the search and retreat to the river.

July 6th opened up with heavy rain. It was so dark they did not dare go out and risk stepping on snakes. Pancho chose that moment to announce that he had lost two brothers by snake-bites and had never seen anyone completely cured after being bitten. In the afternoon, they returned to the prospect. To Blake's untutored eye the rock outcrop looked very intriguing. He continued to feel as elated as one can feel under a deluge of rain. All of them had some degree of dysentery. Sam had some continuing fever, but the quinine was beginning to run out. That day they killed three *tamagás*. One of them was very aggressive — he coiled back, raised his head, showed the pink inside of his mouth wide open and took no evasive action. They had become very conscious of snakes, and Lockwood could be seen walking around inside camp with his machete in hand — which seemed an exaggerated precaution.

The next day they cut a complete rectangle around the outcropping. It rained hard and again it was dark. They killed two fer-de-lance under the roots of trees, one of them just under seven feet long. Blake cut off his head for the formaldehyde bottle. Clearing was very hard work, as they had to cut trees as well as brush to establish the claim, and then they had to try to make a vista so that they could take a compass shot at La Palmerosa. They were covered with mud and very dejected when they returned to camp. That evening they heard the *petroel* sing "the most beautiful song in the jungle." They had a violent thunderstorm in the night — they could see nothing but a dull glow when the lightning came crashing down, but the volume of sound was so startling they had the sensation of being enclosed in a hollow cave with the thunder rolling around inside.

The following morning it seemed to be clearing. Pancho volunteered to climb a tree at the claim and take a compass reading on La

Palmerosa. He went up seventy feet like a monkey. Blake was worried lest a snake or a *bala* ant or a scorpion bite him, and expected to see him come hurtling down. But he got his readings. In the evening a large band of spider monkeys came by and Sam shot a female carrying a young one on its back, which they picked up. "Mica" was soon tame and affectionate and enjoyed traveling with her long tail wrapped closely around Blake's neck while she peered around the brim of his hat. That evening Pancho was again bitten by a *bala* ant and again suffered pain and paralysis of his lower arm.

While Blake was making a final inspection of the claim, Sam wandered off to look for more "rubber man" signs, but soon hurried back and excitedly beckoned him to follow. A quarter mile away was a steep eroded bank of yellow clay pitted with holes. Lying or slowly crawling about were more than a hundred fer-de-lance. They had run into a nesting place and there were all sizes of snakes in evidence, some of them very long and thicker than his arm. As he watched, he became conscious of man's innate fear and dislike of snakes — he was shocked and disgusted by the scene.

On July 9th they packed out to Camp No. 1. They were all tired, and Blake remembered that his knees trembled and that to his dismay he slipped and fell once or twice. They again killed four snakes during the day. The boys had turned the dugout right side up, so Blake had a very welcome rainwater bath in it when he arrived. The river was a red torrent and perhaps ten feet higher than when they had left.

The very thought of leaving the rain forest raised everybody's morale. On July 11th, in high spirits, they started down the river, going like fury over the top of everything. Only at Great Americano Rapids, which then looked and sounded like Niagara, did Blake get scared and require that the boat be lightened. Where they had toiled up, they now raced down on red water. Within five hours they were back at camp above Calero's house, and Sam went off alone to see him. Calero sent plantains and tobacco in anticipation of a present of more kitchen utensils. Then he came to supper. As there were three guns to Calero's one, Sam thought the odds were fairly even. Calero invited Blake to join him on a puma hunt the next morning. That was something he could not miss. However, he again set a night watch.

Calero and his boy arrived right after breakfast and led the way downriver in his little dugout. At Calero's house they picked up two yellow curs, scarred from head to foot and vicious-looking. They passed through his little sugar and tobacco plantations and then went out into jungle entirely different from what they had been traveling through up the river. The trees were predominantly palm about thirty feet high and the jungle beneath was much more open. They waded through mud and stinking yellow water up to their knees. Calero walked ahead with a yellow cur splashing on a leash. Right behind him was his boy, barefoot. Flanking him and moving parallel was Sam with the second dog on a leash, followed by Blake with the young monkey riding on his neck. Behind came Pancho with Pregunta-le on a leash. They found puma tracks but none very fresh and the dogs were not unleashed. Blake slipped and fell against a tree, getting a nasty thorn deep in his arm just above his wrist. He did his best to get it entirely out, but a few days later a serious infection set in. They found no puma. Back at camp that night everybody took turns at watch. No one grumbled.

In the morning, Lockwood was ill. There was no alternative but to stay over. Calero wondered why they had not passed and came to see. Having nothing to do, they arranged to set off again on a puma hunt. This time they ran onto fresh tracks, unleashed the dogs and then had to chase after them as they went off, barking and yelping, through the jungle. Running through mud and swamps was both unpleasant and frightening. But there was no choice because a puma, given time, could so easily kill the dogs. The puma was up a tree when they arrived. There was no pleasure in bringing him down.

Calero then took them through his stand of corn to his still. They instinctively felt this was dangerous and were careful to avoid touching his corn whiskey. Only once had Blake seen Calero turn ugly. Blake had asked if he could take a picture of him. Whereupon Calero immediately backed away with a dreadful look in his eyes and it could be seen that he was thinking of picking up his rifle. So Blake just put the camera back in a packsack.

By this time they had seen enough of Calero and decided it would be wiser to spend the night downriver at the bar. So they packed up hurriedly, leaving the brigand some beans and rice and further kitchen utensils. Blake suspected he would have committed murder for them. They had a fine fast ride to the mouth of the river. Now that they were back at the beach, it was as if safety had been regained and everybody was happy.

The next morning a serious error in judgment was made. In spite of torrential rain, Pancho and Marciano thought they could take the boat out over the bar and make their way down the coast while the rest walked, carrying bare essentials. Blake did not risk the ore samples, the monkey, his diary, medicine kit, guns, and a few personal things. The bar looked fairly calm. However, Pancho and Marciano barely got out into the surf before an oversized breaker caught them and swamped the boat. The next wave turned them over and dumped everything into the water. The boys were left clinging to the bottom of the boat and had great difficulty getting back to shore, as the swollen river kept pushing them out.

Now they had no transportation problem and walked down the beach to San Juan del Norte. It took two days. The beach was heavy and covered with driftwood, seaweed, and trash from the storms. On the way, an Indian couple came running out to say that a man had been bitten by a snake. He had been hit on the back of the hand when up a tree and had fallen twenty feet to the ground. He looked young and strong but was very ill and his breath came in terrible gasps. The poison was obviously affecting his breathing. The Indians had cut open his hand, which was badly swollen. It was impossible to know whether there were any serious injuries from the fall, but in the eyes of the Indians, medicine was the only hope and Blake had to administer it. He had never given an injection before. He rubbed off the man's stomach with iodine and taking a fistful of his stomach muscles, jabbed in the needle and gave him the full dose of anti-venom as slowly and carefully as he could. Then he applied permanganate to the ugly wound on his hand. The man was hardly conscious and there was nothing more to be done. It was learned later that he recovered.

Captain Rivers's boat was at San Juan del Norte when they arrived and after another dreadful trip they finally reached Bluefields, thoroughly exhausted. Blake had a red streak of infection running up to his armpit.

On July 19th Blake sent Pancho with a sample of the ore to be analyzed. For two days he waited and lived in hope. It must be the ore: it had the same color, the same feel, and it seemed to fit perfectly the picture Jack Baragwanath gave that brief afternoon in New York. Those two days seemed endless.

While waiting, Blake went to see Dr. Marshall, a man so outstanding and so well educated one knew instinctively that only some desperate circumstance could have brought him to this outer fringe of civilization.

Dr. Marshall treated Blake's arm and told him how very ill I had looked when I got back to Bluefields. He said he had found positive indications of intestinal parasites, and believed I had amebic dysentery. (American doctors did not discover the amebas for eighteen years.)

[243]

After that Blake just walked around — nervous and sick and high-strung — waiting for the reply. He went down to the waterfront and back again. He paced the horrible main street of Bluefields, watching the vultures. At night he lay tossing. So much seemed to hang on that report. A whole new world might well lie in the answer.

On the second afternoon Pancho returned with it in hand. Blake took the envelope and walked down to the waterfront and sat on the dock, alone. Finally he ripped it open. There was only one short paragraph.

"We are sorry to report the samples assayed showed no more than a trace of silver."

He crumpled the sheet in his palm and threw it into the ocean. Then he walked back to his boardinghouse and sent a cable in code to Jack Baragwanath as prearranged.

The gloomy tidings made his parting with Sam Hudson all the sadder. He gave him what possessions he had left. Hating Bluefields, Sam immediately went off with a lumbering crew. Pancho and Marciano bought a small boat. Cheerful as ever, they took off in it. They seemed to embody the spirit of adventure.

So Blake concluded his story. He, too, had emerged from the jungle with a bad infection. All three of us, Rynerson and Blake and I, left the Mosquito Coast with the same feelings — we were lucky to get out alive.

But this was still not the end of the search for the mine. Several years later, Jack Baragwanath organized a strong, well-financed expedition. It was headed by an experienced, Spanish-speaking mining engineer by the name of G. A. Joslin. With his assistant, McIsaacs, and twelve machete men, they combed the area and found nothing.

So the silver mine is still there — well hidden by the deep forest of the Mosquito Coast and well guarded by ever-changing shallow bars and fer-de-lance and *tamagás* and rapids and heat and rain and *bala* ants and every conceivable variety of biting and stinging and venomous creature that nature has devised.

Add all these together and they present a formidable barrier to any would-be explorer uninitiated to the lurking hazards of this outlandish land.

Afterword

Look to the Wilderness

"Thus too with man. . . .
Threatening with his multitude all life."

THE United States Forest Service has established a definition
of a wilderness as any area not less than five thousand acres
with no road through it — an area, in other words, that a jeep cannot rattle through.

By this definition, only 2 per cent of the land of the forty-eight
States (excluding Alaska and Hawaii) can still be designated as
wilderness. And even in these dwindling remnants there is tourist
pressure for yet more paved roads.

Already the fight to preserve wilderness is all but lost to those
who, like a recent arrival in Yellowstone Park, cried out, "Ranger,
this is my third National Park today — what is there to see?"
These people photograph a mountain peak, their wives, their children, the bears, and pass on with scarcely a glimmering of understanding or appreciation of what they have seen. By the millions
they buzz past blurred landscapes. They view the wilderness from
highways reeking with gas fumes. Two hundred yards from the
highway, the tourist is no more, yet his presence alters the whole
sense of wilderness.

If every town had a town forest, a section of wild land without a road, where shrub, swamp, pond, trees and all wildlife, including predators, were left undisturbed — a place where those in need could revive their spirits by contact with the sources of life — it would be a boon to our race, for many people need the woods far more than they realize. Wild country is a sustaining force to spirits worn down by the wracking turmoil of too many people. Just the knowledge that it is there close at hand to escape to can be a balm to frayed nerves. Between man and nature there is a deep affinity. Though mysterious in quality, nobody can deny its existence. A return to wilderness is tranquillity regained, love of the wilderness brings exultation.

But it is not just the affinity between man and nature that is important, for man craves challenge. Some of the greatest experiences of life involve struggle with the elements. It is good to get soaked through and frozen and half-starved and exhausted and even lost, for these are the common experiences of man's past. They are infinitely more important than protection and security, for we are battling animals. Our spirit needs primitive contention against wind and cold and storm and tide. Above all, we need it when young.

My farm land had been badly mutilated by destruction of timber, erosion of the topsoil, and drying up of springs. It will be a long time before nature and proper handling can restore the good earth to full health and productivity. But it is on its way back.

How fine it was the other day to see a coyote stalk across one of my fields, and to watch a fox circling some Canada geese that were prepared to give him battle, and how much better still one night when in a blizzard I came up close to a bobcat that had killed three of my sheep. The farm seemed suddenly so wonderfully wild. Thank God for our predators — those that still have the wit to survive against every machination of man. The balance of nature needs them. Man needs them. They add something that nothing else can provide — they make a place *feel* wild. Let us not seek their destruction.

Why does man wish to trap every last otter and mink and lynx and wolf and mountain lion and wolverine? What a pity that so many should fail to see the necessity of their existence. Usually it is due to a failure to appreciate the full round orderliness of our natural world. What would a jungle be without a jaguar or leopard!

In the last analysis, wilderness is disappearing through the sheer pressure of too many people.

In the beginning man was born and lived in the wilderness. The wilderness cradled all the races of the world. Man's need for it goes back to the deepest core of his being. Any youngster sensitive to the beauty of nature and sufficiently exposed to it is certain to become deeply affected. To such a one an hour's walk alone in the forest is as inspiring as the finest church service is to others. He becomes a lover of the natural world as distinguished from the world that is made by man. His strongest spiritual emotions may concern the forests and the animals that live there. In wilderness is wonderment, fulfillment, a sense of freedom and elevation of the spirit. Unhappiness drains away, the troubles of childhood vanish. Inner peace and calm replace injury, turmoil, strife and discontent. The healing woods heal both body and mind.

As this feeling grows, there comes an awareness that we are part of a great continuum, for within the vast panoply of divergent life lies fundamental unity: the similarity of protoplasm, of structure, of sensation and reproduction. The living substance is basically similar throughout all species. Thus man has kinship with all of life.

[249]

And this goes further still. Our relatedness does not end with other animate forms. We have kinship also with the trees and all growing things which directly or indirectly support our lives. And beyond these, we are deeply related to the entire inanimate world that sustains life, both animal and vegetable. For the whole of it, all living cells, reflect that which gives it sustenance.

If we sit alone in the wilderness and look and listen and brood, after a while we merge with it. The ego and its surroundings become as one. The desire to be "in tune with the universe" springs from our innermost being. The sense of belonging adds to our peace of mind. To acquire the wisdom to live in harmony with nature: this is our greatest goal. It transcends all other values.

When the spirit reaches out in recognition of the simple fact that our substance has been put together for but a brief span, that we have risen from the dust and to dust return, there comes a unifying emotion that in the deepest sense we are a part of all that is about us.

How can we maintain these values when wilderness is such a rapidly dwindling commodity? What right have a few generations to destroy what God has brought forth from the very dawn of time?

Fortunate are those who have discovered the infinite riches of the wilderness. Days in the open go on and on. They are measureless and filled with time. There is hardly a beginning or an ending. The greatest of all gardens are the gardens of the wild. They cost not a penny to maintain and they are the most beautiful.

Wilderness is a temple that cannot be rebuilt like a bombed-out cathedral. It is infinitely complex. Every part is interwoven on another. From the prowling predator to the enzymes in the soil, the ecological relationships are subtle and deep yet so carefully balanced it is unlikely the same ones will ever be restored.

To top a rise of ground and find vast stretches of inimitable prairie inhabited only by the wild animals that belong to it — this is treasure unsurpassed. But it is treasure that we squander, for man rarely values what he has. It is only when it is gone that he begins to sense the depth of his loss.

We need a million million voices — not crying *in* the wilderness but crying to preserve it. Let us save every swamp and bog and forest and desert and canyon and mountain fastness that we can. It is the great garden of inspiration for our total future. It is the elemental heritage of the human race. Let us save wilderness everywhere. It is our birthright.

"How lightly might this earth bear Man forever!"

DATE DUE